BTEC
FIRST

HOSPITALITY

endorsed for
BTEC

ALWAYS LEARNING

PEARSON

Published by Pearson Education Limited, Edinburgh Gate, Harlow, Essex, CM20 2JE.
www.pearsonschoolsandfecolleges.co.uk
Text © Pearson Education Limited 2013
Typeset by Phoenix Photosetting, Chatham, Kent, UK
Original illustrations © Pearson Education Limited 2013
Illustrated by Phoenix Photosetting and Vicky Woodgate
Cover design by Pearson Education Limited and Andrew Magee Design
Cover photo: SuperStock: Image 100
Picture research by Caitlin Swain
Indexing by Sophia Clapham

First published 2013

16 15 14 13
10 9 8 7 6 5 4 3 2 1

British Library Cataloguing in Publication Data
A catalogue record for this book is available from the British Library

ISBN 978 1 446 90606 4

Printed in Slovakia by Neografia

Websites
There are links to relevant websites in this book. In order to ensure that the links are up to date, that the links work, and that the sites are not inadvertently links to sites that could be considered offensive, we have made the links available on our website at www.pearsonhotlinks.co.uk. Search for the title, 'BTEC First Hospitality Student Book' or ISBN 978 1 446 90606 4.

Copies of official specifications for all Pearson qualifications may be found on the website: www.edexcel.com

A note from the publisher
In order to ensure that this resource offers high-quality support for the associated BTEC qualification, it has been through a review process by the awarding organisation to confirm that it fully covers the teaching and learning content of the specification or part of a specification at which it is aimed, and demonstrates an appropriate balance between the development of subject skills, knowledge and understanding, in addition to preparation for assessment.

While the publishers have made every attempt to ensure that advice on the qualification and its assessment is accurate, the official specification and associated assessment guidance materials are the only authoritative source of information and should always be referred to for definitive guidance.

BTEC examiners have not contributed to any sections in this resource relevant to examination papers for which they have responsibility.

No material from an endorsed book will be used verbatim in any assessment set by BTEC.

Endorsement of a book does not mean that the book is required to achieve this BTEC qualification, nor does it mean that it is the only suitable material available to support the qualification, and any resource lists produced by the awarding organisation shall include this and other appropriate resources.

Contents

Acknowledgements

The publisher would like to thank the following for their kind permission to reproduce their photographs:

(Key: b-bottom; c-centre; l-left; r-right; t-top)

Alamy Images: allesalltag 23, Andrew Wood 113, Anthony Hatley 27, Bailey-Cooper Photography 2 217r, Carlo Bollo 141b, Convery flowers 110, Directphoto.org 121, incamerastock 141t, 275, Jas Gibson 287, Joe Hawkins Photography 172b, John McKenna 151, Juice Images 83, keith morris 16, Kpzfoto 244, LAMB 251, Londonstills.com 138b, Loop Images Ltd 154, M4OS Photos 250t, Mar Photographics 11, Marc Macdonald 18, MARKA 144b, Martin Shields 144t, Mouse in the House 195b, Nick Lylak 293, Peter Noyce 214b, Petro Feketa 25b, Radius Images 57, RubberBall 166, Science Photo Library 61, Tetra Images 247, VIEW Pictures Ltd 215; **artwork@fairtrade.org.uk:** 28; **Bananastock:** 38, 132; **Brand X Pictures:** Burke Triolo Productions 187tr; **Comstock Images:** 184tl; **Corbis:** 108, Zero Creatives / cultura 55; **Courtesy of the NHS / National Patient Safety Agency:** 83br; **Crown Copyright:** Public Health England in association with the Welsh Government, the Scottish Government and the Food Standards Agency in Northern Ireland. 265b; **DK Images:** Andy Crawford 192, Clive Streeter 181l, David Munns 178tc, Ian O'Leary 181r, Peter Bull 97tc, Will Heap 80b; **Fotolia.com:** Andres Rodriguez 260, @ Frog 974 184tr, Günter Menzl 233, Lester120 31, Nomad_Soul 184br, Photobank kiev 24, xy 184bl; **Getty Images:** Andersen Ross 48, Image Source 15b, Ivan Hunter 3, Javier Larrea 214bl, Jetta Productions 37, Purestock 66, Ryan McVay 246, Steve Debenport 58, Tetra Images 133, 137t; **Imagestate Media:** John Foxx Collection 119; **Pearson Education Ltd:** Studio 8 202, Jon Barlow 79, 115, Gareth Boden 102, 104, 158, 168, 262, Cheuk-king Lo 80t, Debbie Rowe 15t, Handan Erek 72, Jörg Carstensen 134, Rob Judges 178b, 178bc, 281, Naki Kouyioumtzis 22, David Sanderson 95t, 95b, 97cl, 97br, David Sanderson 95t, 95b, 97cl, 97br, Jules Selmes 19, Image Source 204, Stuart Cox 211; **PhotoDisc:** D. Falconer. Photolink. 25t, Dennis Gray. Cole Publishing Group. 176b, Marshall Gordon. Cole Publishing Group. 178t; **Plainpicture Ltd:** Cultura 263, Fancy Images 71; **Public Health England:** 268; **Reproduced with the kind permission of Lincat:** 195t, 195c; **Shutterstock.com:** Bikeworldtravel 214tl, David Burrows 118, Emily Taner 7, Pressmaster 161, senkaya 217l, Songquan Deng 288, Thomas J. Sebourn 103; **SuperStock:** Blend Images 123; **Veer/Corbis:** Aleksandrs Jemeljanovs 78b, Andresr 264, Asb 232, Brebca 172t, Brian Jackson 265t, CandyBoxImages 42, 60, 105, CandyBoxImages 42, 60, 105, Carpeira 187cr, Corepics 205, David Stuart 73, dgilder 253, Dmitry Bairachnyi 6, Dmitry Kalinovsky 39, eugeneel 167, Faraways 238t, giuseppeparisi 291, goldenKB 174, Henri Ensio 228, hunt 70, Inga Nielsen 176t, Iofoto 261, irkaejc 187br, ivelin 78t, Jabiru 176c, Joerg Beuge 189, krsmanovic 214t, Kzenon 169, leaf 201, Leungchopan 9, lovleah 69, mangostock 210, Monkey Business Images 187bl, 269, 276, monticello 187cl, naumoid 267r, Norman Chan 250b, Olly 4, pixart 2, pixinity 36, Robert Kneschke 257, .shock 4t, shock 235, Take A Pix Media 101, Tomas Skopal 238b, travismanley 234, Xalanx 267l, Yuri Arcurs 197; **www.imagesource.com:** 203

Cover image: *Front:* **SuperStock:** image100

All other images © Pearson Education

The author and publisher would like to thank the following individuals and organisations for permission to reproduce their materials:

pp. 4, 9, 140 Adapted from The British Hospitality Association (2013) 'The Agenda for 300,000 New Jobs'.

p. 4 Adapted from Valuation Office Agency (2013), 'Rating Manual Volume 5'. © Crown copyright 2013.

p. 5 Adapted from Business Employment Survey (BRES), Labour Force Survey (LFS), Oxford Economics (2013) 'The Agenda for 300,000 New Jobs'.

pp. 5, 11, 12, 40, 42, 137, 138, 144 Adapted from People 1st (2013) 'State of the Nation Report 2013'. People 1st is the sector skills council for the hospitality, passenger transport, travel and tourism industries focusing on transforming skills in the sector through the development of world class qualifications in management and leadership, customer service and craft skills. For more information, visit www.people1st.co.uk.

p. 26 Adapted from '2011 Census – Population and Household Estimates for England and Wales, March 2011'; Office for National Statistics licensed under the Open Government Licence v.1.0.

p. 28 Adapted from The Carbon Trust (2012) 'Hospitality: Saving energy without compromising service'.

p. 28 Adapted from Keep Britain Tidy (2011) 'Branded Litter Study 2010/2011'.

p. 83 Clean your hands campaign poster. Reproduced, with permission, from the NHS/National Patient Safety Agency.

p. 84 Time/Temperature ratios. Adapted from Foods Standards Agency. © Crown copyright 2013.

p. 100 Risk assessment form. Contains public sector information published by the Health and Safety Executive and licensed under the Open Government Licence v 1.0.

p. 143 Adapted from '2011 Census, Population and Household Estimates for the United Kingdom', Office for National Statistics licensed under the Open Government Licence v 1.0.

p. 173 Adapted from Love Food Hate Waste (2013) 'The facts about food waste', http://england.lovefoodhatewaste.com/content/facts-about-food-waste-1.

p. 175 Adapted from Health and Social Care Information Centre (2013) 'Statistics on Obesity, Physical Activity and Diet: England, 2013'. Copyright © 2013, re-used with the permission of the Health and Social Care Information Centre. All rights reserved.

p. 265 Eatwell plate. © Crown copyright. Department of Health in association with the Welsh Assembly Government, the Scottish Government and the Food Standards Agency in Northern Ireland.

p. 267 Adapted from Department of Health (2011) 'Physical activity guidelines: Fact sheets 1–5'. © Crown copyright 2011.

p. 267 Adapted from Department of Health (2004) 'At least five a week: Evidence of the impact of physical activity and its relationship to health. A report from the Chief Medical Officer'. © Crown copyright 2004.

p. 277 Adapted from The British Hospitality Association (2011) 'Health Works: a look inside eating-out: A Report by the British Hospitality Association'.

p. 283 Adapted from Department of Health (2011) 'Healthy Lives, Healthy People: A Call to Action on Obesity in England'. © Crown copyright 2011.

Every effort has been made to trace the copyright holders and we apologise in advance for any unintentional omissions. We would be pleased to insert the appropriate acknowledgement in any subsequent edition of this publication.

About this book

This book is designed to help you through your BTEC First Hospitality qualification and covers nine units from the qualification.

▶ About your BTEC First in Hospitality

Choosing to study for a BTEC First Hospitality qualification is a great decision to make for lots of reasons. The Hospitality industry is very diverse and offers a wide variety of exciting careers here in the United Kingdom (UK) and on an international scale. So, whether you want to be a sous chef at a Michelin-starred restaurant, an events coordinator running big-name corporate events or a front office manager for a large international hotel chain, a BTEC First Hospitality qualification can help you achieve your dream job. Your BTEC will sharpen your skills for employment or further study, and help you to take that first step in progressing your career.

▶ About the authors

Sue Holmes is the Hospitality and Travel Coordinator at a large further education (FE) college. She has taught for over 18 years on a range of programmes from Entry Level to BA (Hons). She has extensive experience of writing units and teacher support material.

Elaine Jackson has worked in education for over 24 years. She worked at a large FE college in Yorkshire and was responsible for the planning, delivery, assessment and internal quality assurance of several hospitality programmes. Elaine is a member of the British Institute of Innkeeping (BII) and the Institute for Learning (IfL). During her teaching career, Elaine has produced numerous teaching and learning resources.

Tracay Mead was head of department for more than ten years and has taught a range of subjects and levels, including hospitality, in further education for more than 17 years. She is an experienced Internal Verifier and External Moderator, and has been writing units for qualifications for over a decade.

Kathryn Morgan has worked in the FE sector for over ten years, delivering BTEC Levels 1 to 3 in Hospitality and Travel and Tourism. In 2013, Kathryn was awarded a Certificate of Distinction in the Welsh region by the Pearson Teaching Awards in the FE Teacher/Lecturer of the Year category. She also runs a restaurant with her husband and has provided contract catering services for prestigious events such as the Ryder Cup.

How to use this book

This book contains many features that will help you use your skills and knowledge in work-related situations, and assist you in getting the most from your course.

These introductions give you a snapshot of what to expect from each unit – and what you should be aiming for by the time you finish it.

How this unit is assessed.

Learning aims describe what you will be doing in the unit.

A learner shares how working through the unit has helped them.

▶ Features of this book

There are lots of features in this book to help you learn about the topics in each unit, and to have fun while learning! These pages show some of the features that you will come across when using the book.

Topic references and learning aim labels show which parts of the BTEC you are covering.

You will find an introduction at the start of each topic with a short activity to help you get started.

Key terms appear in blue, bold text and are defined in a key term box on the page. Also, see the glossary for definitions of important words and phrases.

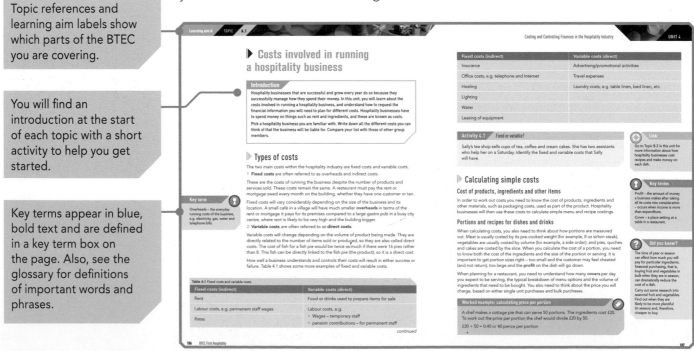

Activity 4.1   Fixed or variable?

Sally's tea shop sells cups of tea, coffee and cream cakes. She has two assistants who help on Saturdays. Identify Sally's fixed and variable costs.

Activities will help you learn about the topic. These can be completed in pairs or groups, or sometimes on your own.

Discussion

You have been working at the Bear Hotel for three years. Last night was the staff Christmas party and as a result four of the housekeeping team have phoned in sick. The hotel was full last night and all 50 rooms need cleaning. There were 35 departures and 15 stayovers. Of the 35 departures, 25 of the rooms are booked by new customers arriving this evening. You have just two housekeeping staff to complete the tasks required.

Discuss how the remaining staff can work together to clean the rooms and ensure customer satisfaction.

Then, think about times when you have worked as a team. What went well? How could you have improved the efficiency of the team?

Discussion point, with a short activity or discussion about the topic.

Assessment practice 9.7

1 Which **two** of these problems are linked to a diet high in sugar, salt and fat? [2]

    A Obesity ☐   C Hair loss ☐   E Irritability ☐

    B Poor memory ☐   D Weight gain ☐

2 State three problems associated with drinking too much alcohol on a regular basis. [3]

A chance to practise answering the types of test questions that you may come across in your exam. (For Units 1 and 9.)

Assessment activity 4.3   *English, Maths*   2C.P6 | 2C.M3 | 2C.D3

Your department's open evening looms and your teacher/tutor has asked you to prepare a presentation that focuses on the income statement for the end-of-year student prom event. You have the following information.

- The total revenue as a result of ticket and photo sales was £6,500.
- The cost of sales was calculated at £2,022.
- Expenses included utilities at £15.00 and wages at £80.00.

1 Prepare an income statement for the end-of-year student prom.

2 Analyse the impact of expenses incurred on the success of the hospitality event and how these expenses affect the net profit figure.

3 Identify and justify recommendations for improving net profit.

Activities that relate to the unit's assessment criteria. These activities will help you prepare for your assignments and contain tips to help you achieve your potential. (For all units except Units 1 and 9.)

Tips

- You could use photographs of the event to make your presentation more interesting, and also to show how some of the income was generated.
- Make sure your presentation is clear and that any figures for sales and expenses are accurate.
- Ask someone else to check your calculations to make sure there are no errors. You should also check that there are no spelling or punctuation errors if you are using slides or display boards for your presentation.

Someone who works in the Hospitality industry explains how this unit of the BTEC First applies to the day-to-day work they do as part of their job.

WorkSpace

Harry Tuma

Trainee chef, Cornwall

My parents have always grown organic vegetables, so they never used chemicals on the soil or plants. I've not inherited my parents' love of gardening, but I do think it's important to know where our food comes from and how it is reared or grown.

When I was looking for a part-time job I got a job in our local pub. They use locally produced food and have a seasonal menu.

After two years at college studying for my A levels while working part time at the pub, I decided that I wanted to be a chef. I was lucky as the manager of the pub offered me an apprenticeship doing a Level 2 NVQ Diploma in Professional Cookery. I'm close to completing my apprenticeship and I'm confident that I made the right decision in training to be a chef.

I love going to work. I get to decide what the specials will be, based on what is in season and what our local suppliers have available. I've been to see where and how the fruit and vegetables are grown at the local farms and market gardens, so I know where the food comes from. Our fish is from sustainable sources and our meat is from a local farm. The food is fresh and of the best quality – we know and trust our suppliers and I know that we're using the best ingredients. The menu prices are not expensive and our customers get really good value for money.

About six months ago, I suggested that we add a section to the menu introducing our suppliers, so that our customers could also see where their food is coming from. The manager thought it was a great idea. Now our customers are always commenting on how important they feel it is to have confidence in what is in the food they eat. We're also seeing an increase in customers coming to the restaurant because they've heard about our food ethos.

12

Think about it!

1 Are there any other ways in which Harry could improve his skills?

2 How else could Harry and the team promote the seasonal and local nature of the produce they use?

3 Would a job like Harry's appeal to you? Why?

This section gives you the chance to think more about the role that this person does, and whether you would want to follow in their footsteps once you've completed your BTEC.

▶ BTEC Assessment Zone

You will be assessed in two different ways for your BTEC First in Hospitality. For most units, your teacher/tutor will set assignments for you to complete. These assignments may take the form of projects where you research, plan, prepare and evaluate a piece of work or activity. The table in the BTEC Assessment Zone explains what you must do to achieve each of the assessment criteria. Each unit (except Units 1 and 9) in this book contains a number of assessment activities to help you with these assessment criteria.

Assessment criteria		
Level 1	**Level 2 Pass**	**Level 2 Merit**
Learning aim A: Understand effective working skills in the hospitality industry		
1A.1	**2A.P1**	**2A.M1**
Identify working skills needed to work effectively in the hospitality industry, using examples from two different businesses.	Describe, using examples from two different hospitality businesses, the importance to the businesses, customers and staff of having effective working skills in the hospitality industry. **See Assessment activity 2.1, page 62**	Explain, using examples from two contrasting hospitality businesses, the benefits for the business, its customers and staff of having appropriate working skills. **See Assessment activity 2.1, page 62**

The table in this BTEC Assessment Zone explains what you must do to achieve each of the assessment criteria, and signposts assessment activities in this book to help you prepare for your assignments.

Activities in this book will show you the kinds of task you might be asked to do to meet these criteria when your teacher/tutor sets an assignment.

For Units 1 and 9 of your BTEC, you will be assessed by a paper-based examination. The BTEC Assessment Zones for these units give useful information about what the exam may consist of and some general advice about how to approach the types of questions you may need to answer.

A Questions where the answers are available and you have to choose the correct answer(s) that fit. *Tip: Always make sure that you read the instructions carefully. Sometimes you may need to identify more than one correct answer.*

Examples:

The AA assess and rate hotel and guest accommodation providers using a star-system. Identify one of these that is not an AA star-rating? [1]

A 1 star

B 3 stars

C 4 stars

D 5 stars

E 6 stars

Answer: E

Identify two of these that would not use the services of a Contract Food Service Provider? [2]

A School

B Hospital

C Cruise liner

D Armed services

E Fine dining restaurant

Answers: C and E

You will find examples of the different types of questions you may need to answer, as well as sample answers and tips on how to prepare for the examination.

Study skills

Take it further

If you become distracted by social networking sites or texts when you're working, set yourself a time limit of 10 minutes or so to indulge yourself. You could even use this as a reward for completing a certain amount of work.

▶ Planning and getting organised

The first step in managing your time is to plan ahead and be well organised. Some people are naturally good at this. They think ahead, write down commitments in a diary or planner and store their notes and handouts neatly and carefully so they can find them quickly.

How good are your working habits?

Improving your planning and organisational skills

1 Use a diary to schedule working times into your weekdays and weekends.
2 Also use the diary to write down exactly what work you have to do. You could use this as a 'to do' list and tick off each task as you go.
3 Divide up long or complex tasks into manageable chunks and put each 'chunk' in your diary with a deadline of its own.
4 Always allow more time than you think you need for a task.

▶ Sources of information

You will need to use research to complete your BTEC First assignments, so it's important to know what sources of information are available to you. These are likely to include the following.

Key term

Bias – people often have strong opinions about certain topics. This is called 'bias'. Newspaper or magazine articles, or information found on the internet, may be biased to present a specific point of view.

Remember!

Store relevant information when you find it – keep a folder on your computer specifically for research – so you don't have to worry about finding it again at a later date.

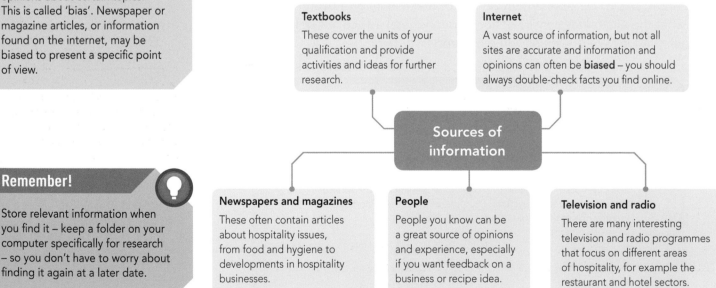

Textbooks
These cover the units of your qualification and provide activities and ideas for further research.

Internet
A vast source of information, but not all sites are accurate and information and opinions can often be **biased** – you should always double-check facts you find online.

Sources of information

Newspapers and magazines
These often contain articles about hospitality issues, from food and hygiene to developments in hospitality businesses.

People
People you know can be a great source of opinions and experience, especially if you want feedback on a business or recipe idea.

Television and radio
There are many interesting television and radio programmes that focus on different areas of hospitality, for example the restaurant and hotel sectors.

▶ Organising and selecting information

Organising your information

Once you have used a range of sources of information for research, you will need to organise the information so it's easy to use.

- Make sure your written notes are neat and have a clear heading – it's often useful to date them, too.
- Always keep a note of where the information came from (the title of a book, the title and date of a newspaper or magazine and the web address of a website) and, if relevant, which pages.
- Work out the results of any questionnaires you've used.

Selecting your information

Once you have completed your research, reread the assignment brief or instructions you were given to remind yourself of the exact wording of the question(s) and divide your information into three groups.

1 Information that is totally relevant.
2 Information that is not as good, but which could come in useful.
3 Information that doesn't match the questions or assignment brief very much, but that you kept because you couldn't find anything better!

Check that there are no obvious gaps in your information against the questions or assignment brief. If there are, make a note of them so that you know exactly what you still have to find.

▶ Presenting your work

Before handing in any assignments, make sure:

- you have addressed each part of the question and that your work is as complete as possible
- all spelling and grammar is correct
- you've referenced all sources of information you used for your research
- that all work is your own – otherwise you could be committing **plagiarism**
- you've saved a copy of your work.

▶ Find out more

A range of activity sheets to help you develop the study skills you will use on your BTEC course is available at www.edexcel.com/quals/firsts2012/hospitality/.

Ask your teacher/tutor for more details.

Key term

Plagiarism – If you are including other people's views, comments or opinions, or copying a diagram or table from another publication, you must state the source by including the name of the author or publication, or the web address. Failure to do this (so you are really pretending other people's work is your own) is known as plagiarism. Check your school's policy on plagiarism and copying.

Introduction

Hospitality and catering is a service industry that is made up of lots of different types of businesses. Almost everyone will have experienced some aspect of the industry. It offers employment to millions of people in the United Kingdom (UK) alone and is one of the UK's biggest industries. In this unit, you will investigate the structure, size and different areas of the hospitality industry, as well as the products and services it offers.

Hospitality and catering businesses rely on other industries to successfully deliver their products and services, and you will look at the importance of these relationships in this unit.

Finally, you will investigate the trends that affect hospitality businesses and the impact of these trends. You will also be able to see how hospitality businesses respond to market and customer demands.

Assessment: You will be assessed using a paper-based exam lasting 1 hour and 15 minutes.

Learning aims

In this unit you will:

A understand the structure and service provision in the hospitality industry

B understand hospitality operations

C understand how current issues and trends impact on businesses within the hospitality industry.

> I have always enjoyed meeting new people and thought that a career in hospitality would give me the chance to travel as well. When I started the Level 2 qualification, I realised there were a lot of different types of jobs I could do – and wanted to do! This unit helped me to understand the different hospitality operations and ownership types, and to realise how everyday matters in the world impact on hospitality businesses.
>
> Molly, *BTEC Level 2 First in Hospitality student*

Introducing the Hospitality Industry

▶ The structure and services of the hospitality industry

Introduction

The hospitality industry can be divided into different areas. You will need to know the main areas and types of businesses that operate in each one, as well as the products and services they offer.

In pairs, list as many different examples of hospitality businesses that you can think of. Then, think about how you would group the businesses. To help you get started, a five-star hotel and a guest house are two examples that come under the area of 'hotels'.

When you have finished, compare your list with lists created by other pairs. As a class, use your examples to produce a master list.

Did you know?

A report by the British Hospitality Association (BHA) showed that in March 2013 the hospitality industry was the UK's fourth largest employer – directly employing over 2.68 million people.

Source: 'The Agenda for 300,000 New Jobs' (2013), a report by the British Hospitality Association.

The hospitality industry in the UK is made up of thousands of different types of businesses, ranging from hotels and hostels to cafés, mobile catering units and beverage providers.

- **Hospitality businesses** provide accommodation, food and beverages, entertainment and other services for guests, visitors, travellers and tourists.
- **Catering businesses** belong to a branch of the hospitality industry which provides customers with food and beverages.

Hospitality businesses fall broadly into seven areas: hotels, restaurants, public houses (pubs, bars and nightclubs), membership clubs, hospitality services, events and contract food service providers.

Let's look at how the industry is structured and the range of products and services that are provided by hospitality businesses.

▶ Hotels

The hotel area is one of the largest employers within the hospitality industry. In 2008, there were about 47,000 hotels, Bed & Breakfasts (B&Bs) and guest houses in the UK (Source: Valuation Office Agency, 2013, 'Rating Manual Volume 5').

Hotels can be divided into the following three categories.

1. **One- to five-star hotels** – some high-end luxury hotels claim to be six- and seven-star hotels but the star-rating officially only goes up to five stars. Ratings are awarded according to what is offered by the hotel in terms of the range and quality of the facilities.
2. **Budget hotels** – Premier Inn and Travelodge are examples of budget hotel chains.
3. **Bed and breakfast** accommodation.

All three categories of hotel offer rooms to their guests in exchange for payment.

The amount you will pay to stay in a hotel will vary depending on the type of hotel and if it is star-rated. You could expect to pay from £20 per person per night to stay in a guest

What star-rating do you imagine a hotel like this might receive?

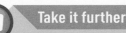

house to hundreds, or even thousands of pounds, for a night at a world-class luxury hotel. The prices of hotel rooms usually reflect the standard of the accommodation, the products and services offered by the hotel and the facilities that are available.

Universities offer accommodation to non-students, usually outside term times, in halls of residence, and hostels are also a popular form of accommodation for travellers who want to meet people. Both types of accommodation provision provide rooms for a fee, and bathroom facilities are normally shared.

| Activity 1.1 | The Quality Assessment Scheme |

Within the hospitality industry, different accommodation rating systems are used. In small groups, research the Quality Assessment Scheme that is used by businesses such as VisitEngland, VisitScotland and the AA to rate types of accommodation. Prepare a short presentation of your findings.

Restaurants

The restaurant area is the largest employer in the hospitality industry. In 2012, it employed 53 per cent of the total number of people in hospitality employment (Source: Oxford Economics, 2013). There were 3,800 more restaurant businesses in 2012 than in 2011 (Source: People 1st, 2013, 'State of the Nation Report 2013'). It is a very dynamic area and responsive to customer needs.

The restaurant industry can be categorised into several groups.

1 Fast food businesses – for example, chain restaurants such as Pizza Hut and McDonald's, as well as kebab shops and fish and chip shops.

2 Cafés and coffee shops – these can be part of a chain such as Caffè Nero and Costa Coffee or they can be independent local cafés and shops.

3 Mainstream restaurants – these can be chain restaurants, such as Nando's and Frankie & Benny's, but can also be **owner-managed**, local restaurants.

4 Fine dining restaurants – these restaurants offer high-quality food at a more expensive price than other restaurants. Heston Blumenthal's three-Michelin-star restaurant, The Fat Duck, is an example. Being awarded a Michelin star is the dream for many chefs.

Many restaurants are classified by the type of cuisine. Examples of cuisines include Chinese, Indian, Vietnamese, French and Italian.

| Activity 1.2 | Restaurants in your area |

Write a list of the restaurants in your local area which fall under the following headings.

- Fast food
- Fine dining
- Chain
- Restaurants classified by cuisine

Do you think that visitors to your area have a good choice of different types of restaurants?

Take it further

Using the internet, carry out some research into different star-rated hotels in your local area. Find three hotels in each star-rated category and compare their facilities.

As a group, discuss the differences between the hotels in different star categories.

Key term

Owner-managed – when the owner of a business is the same person who runs it.

Did you know?

There are many rating systems that rank the quality of restaurants. One of the most widely recognised and respected systems is the Michelin series, which awards one to three stars. Each year the Michelin Guide to Restaurants and Hotels is published, providing information about selected restaurants and hotels that have been highly rated by anonymous inspectors.

Link

For more information on the management and ownership of pubs go to Unit 2: Working in the Hospitality Industry, Learning aim A, Topic A.1.

Key terms

Brewery – a place where beer is made on a commercial scale so that it can be sold to pubs, bars and restaurants.

Licensee – someone who holds a special licence to sell something, in this case alcoholic beverages.

Outsourced – when a business decides to ask a contract food service provider to meet their catering needs.

Did you know that top DJs can be paid hundreds of thousands of pounds for one gig?

Take it further

Jamie Oliver started a campaign to improve school dinners in 2004. Carry out some research on the internet to see what you can find out about the campaign.

- Do you think the campaign has been successful?
- How has the government responded to it?
- What do you think are the problems of providing nutritious school meals?

Discuss your findings with your class.

Pubs, bars and nightclubs

Traditionally, pubs and bars have sold and served beverages. However, many businesses in these areas also offer food and dining options in order to attract more customers and generate more income.

Management and ownership

Pubs can be categorised by their type of ownership.

1 **Managed pubs and bars** are owned by a **brewery**. The manager and staff are employed by the brewery.
2 **Tenanted or leased pubs and bars** are owned by a brewery but leased to a **licensee**, who holds the licence for the pub. The manager runs the pub or bar independently. The pub sells the brewery's beer and ales.
3 **Free houses** are owned and managed by a licensee who is able to offer beverages from any supplier.

Many sports and social clubs also contain bars and restaurants which provide them with additional income. Many clubs will hire out their facilities for parties and wedding receptions, again to generate additional income.

Nightclubs

Nightclubs play music, have dance areas and serve food and beverages – and the majority of nightclubs charge an entrance fee. At many clubs, the DJs are the main attraction – top DJs can command a large fee for one gig. Some nightclubs are very exclusive and attract a lot of celebrities. Exclusive clubs operate a strict entry policy and you are only allowed in if your name is on the guest list. Some nightclubs play a certain music type or genre. Larger hotels may have their own nightclubs and some clubs have live music.

Contract food service providers (outsourcing)

Many businesses will provide on-site catering options for their staff, such as a canteen providing breakfast and lunch. Sometimes this operation is **outsourced** to a contract food service provider who is paid to run these services. Contract food service providers often run the catering services in schools, universities, hospitals, prisons, care homes, large private businesses, airlines, oil rigs and the armed services.

Other types of businesses that use contract food service providers are television and media companies, who need to feed their staff on set. Event companies also use the services of contract caterers who provide services for festivals, sporting events and corporate hospitality events.

Activity 1.3 Contract food service providers

Carry out some research to find out the services offered by four well-known contract food service providers. Choose one of the providers and make a poster.

Hospitality services (in-house)

The same businesses that use contract food service providers may choose instead to provide food and beverages for their staff, clients or visitors themselves – even though it is not the main focus of their business. This is known as in-house catering.

The catering operations are run like any other department of the business – the department will be given a budget for staffing and resourcing. In-house catering operations can be very big; for example, cruise ships will have several different operations on a ship that will cater for different customer needs, from fine dining restaurants to bar snacks and buffets. Some cruise ships need to cater for the needs of around 3,000 passengers. That is a lot of people to feed daily for breakfast, lunch, dinner and snacking!

Assessment practice 1.1

A hospital is considering using a contract food service provider to supply all the catering in the prison. State one advantage and one disadvantage to the hospital of doing this. [2]

Membership clubs

There are two main types of membership club.

1 **Non-profit members' clubs** – these are owned and managed by club members. Members pay subscriptions to the club on a yearly basis for their membership. Examples of non-profit-making clubs include:

- working mens' clubs
- masonic lodges
- politically affiliated clubs
- British Legion clubs
- sports clubs such as rugby clubs, cricket clubs, gyms and snooker halls.

2 **Private members' clubs** – these are profit-making clubs and often have a strict application process for membership (some only accept members if they have been nominated by other members). There is often a joining fee and then subsequent yearly membership fees. An example would be The Groucho Club in London.

Events

The events area is diverse as it covers several different types of event, many of which take place at specific times of the year. For example, Cheltenham Cricket Festival is an annual sporting event held over 12 days in July, the Isle of Wight Garlic Festival is held every year over a weekend in August and the Glastonbury music festival is run over five days in July.

Some events attract specialist catering services: medieval-themed food at a medieval re-enactment festival or locally grown foods at a farmers' market. Other events offer corporate hospitality packages, which range from fine dining to simple hand foods such as sandwiches, or even fish and chip vans.

Many hotels offer conference and meeting facilities, as well as being a venue for weddings and parties. These events will offer a food and beverage service, for example, teas, coffees and pastries may be provided at the start of a business meeting, or a sit-down three-course meal at a wedding for over 100 people.

Discussion

Which membership clubs are available in your local area? Which one(s) would you like to be a member of, and why?

If possible, look at the clubs' websites, pictures and 'About' information to get an idea of what they can offer their members.

What do you think are the logistics of providing catering services at an event like Glastonbury Festival?

▶ Scope and range of the hospitality industry

Hospitality businesses operate on both a local and national scale.

Local

There are many independent local hospitality businesses which have a single outlet or a few outlets in a small area. These businesses provide products and services that meet the needs of the local market and so they are often more specialised and unique. They are not part of a national chain and are instead owned by individuals.

National and international

There are many national and international businesses within the hospitality industry. These businesses have chains of outlets which offer the same products and services in all of their outlets across the world. Examples of large chains include:

- KFC
- Costa Coffee
- Ramada Hotels
- Pizza Express
- Frankie & Benny's
- Premier Inn.

Customers know what they will get when they visit a national or international chain. The interior of the chains look similar and the quality of the products and services should be consistent.

Location

The location of a hospitality business is crucial to its success. It influences the types of products and services on offer, the types of customer who visit and the price at which the products and services are sold. A hotel in the Scottish Highlands, for example, will not attract customers looking for a city break; and a hotel in London will not advertise to attract customers who want a quiet weekend walking in the countryside.

Size of the business

Many hospitality businesses are very small, for example, an independent café may only employ two or three people. It may have a relatively small **turnover** and only generate enough profit to provide its owner with a modest income. In contrast, the hospitality businesses that run the well-known national chains are multi-million-pound operations and employ thousands of people.

Discussion

What are the benefits for the customer when buying from national or international chains?

Remember

The growth of the internet has meant that hospitality businesses of all sizes and in all locations can promote themselves on an international scale by creating and maintaining a website or online presence.

Key term

Turnover – the amount of money taken by a business in a specific period.

| Activity 1.4 | Local and national hospitality businesses |

Create a table containing two columns with the following headings: local and national. List at least 20 businesses which can be found in your nearest town or suburb that would fall under each heading. Then, think about the following questions.

- What is the main focus of each business?
- Can you identify any patterns in the types of businesses that you have found?
- Are there larger numbers of a certain type of business and fewer of others?

Scale and size of the industry

The hospitality industry is the UK's fourth largest employer, employing over 2.68 million people. The industry accounted for 27.7 per cent of jobs growth in the UK between 2010 and 2012. It generated £52.7 billion in profits and wages spent by hospitality staff, contributed £39.6 billion in tax **revenue** paid to the Treasury and £9.8 billion in earnings from foreign exports. (Source: British Hospitality Association, 2013).

Changing environments

The hospitality industry is resilient and has been resistant to the challenging economic environment. It continues to adapt, develop and expand. The industry news is regularly focused on the planned openings of new restaurants, pubs and hotels.

A good example of the industry's ability to adapt is illustrated by the popularity of pop-up restaurants and food businesses around the country. These types of business literally 'pop up' in a location for a short and set period of time and often respond to current trends in food.

Purchasing power

Purchasing power is the amount of goods or services that a unit of money can buy. Purchasing power is linked to **inflation**. In general terms, if inflation is high then this increases the cost of buying the same amount of goods and services for a business. The higher cost of the goods and services is passed on to the customers and prices go up. This can mean that fewer customers use or buy a business's goods or services – a particular problem for smaller businesses, which rely on being able to price competitively. If inflation is low, then a business can buy more goods and services with its money so, in theory, the saving is passed on to the customers by charging them lower prices.

Products

The hospitality industry produces a wide range of products and services: accommodation, food and beverage service provision, facilities management, event management, vending and information on products, for example restaurant menus and room tariffs.

Food

Food is an important product for pubs, bars, coffee shops and hotels. When a customer buys a cup of coffee they can often buy cakes, biscuits, scones, sandwiches and snacks too. The food on offer will be selected to meet the needs of the customers in order to maximise sales and minimise waste.

Chain restaurants will change their menus according to the season, but many popular dishes will be kept because they appeal to customers all year round; for example, fish and chips. Smaller and fine dining restaurants will change their menus more often, maybe even daily, as the chef has the opportunity to use locally grown or produced food that is in season.

Key terms

Revenue – the income of an organisation, especially a large amount.

Inflation – the rise or fall in the general level of prices of goods and services in an economy over a period of time.

Take it further

In pairs, make a list of all the things you would need to think about when setting up a pop-up restaurant. You may need to do some research.

What type of business might provide the product shown in this photograph?

Beverages

There are three main categories of beverages:

- soft beverages, for example, fruit juice, fizzy beverages
- alcoholic beverages, for example, cider, ale, beer, wine, spirits
- hot beverages, for example, coffee, tea, hot chocolate.

Activity 1.5	Coffee shops – chain or independent?

Make a list of all the coffee shops and cafés in your local town. How many are part of a chain and how many are independently owned?

Make a list of the products that one chain coffee shop/café and one independently-owned coffee shop/café sell. Are the products very different? Why do you think they are similar or different?

Accommodation

The average room in a hotel, bed and breakfast or guest house will have similar items such as a bed(s), a TV, a wardrobe and tea and coffee making facilities. Many bed and breakfasts and guest houses offer a lounge with a TV, seating area and maybe a games area that residents can use. Many accommodation providers offer Wi-Fi as customers expect internet access as standard, even if there is a charge for it. Larger three-star to five-star hotels have public areas that are open to non-residents, and they will also offer food and beverage services to non-residents.

Information on products

People who work in hospitality businesses must provide customers with information on products and services as part of their job. Customers will ask questions about anything from the price of a room, to the ingredients in a certain dish, to what wine goes with their meal. The following list shows a number of ways in which information can be provided for customers.

- Menus will contain a description of each dish and some may recommend wines to accompany each dish.
- Brochures and leaflets allow businesses to provide customers with information in written form, for example, opening days and times.
- Tariffs will be displayed in a hotel foyer or outside the hotel to let customers know the price of rooms.

Discussion

Traditionally, brochures and leaflets have been paper-based and sent to customers in the post. As a group, discuss other methods that hospitality businesses can use to contact and inform their customers about products and services.

▶ Services

In addition to offering products, the hospitality industry also offers services to meet the individual needs of its varied customers. Many other industries use hospitality providers' food and beverage services when they do business. This business ranges from major events such as exhibitions, trade shows and conferences to meetings and **seminars**. Many hotels have business facilities and offer accommodation packages for those attending events. These packages include the use of the business facilities as well as cheaper room rates for any delegates staying over.

Key term

Seminar – a meeting where people can get together to discuss business or to receive training.

Facilities management

Larger venues, for example, hotels, can provide facilities for conferences and large functions. A dedicated team will be responsible for looking after the management of the facilities (for example, the rooms, chairs and tables and equipment) and making sure that clients' needs and requirements are met.

Event management

It is quite common to hold events at venues, whether a corporate event or a personal one (for example, a wedding, anniversary or birthday celebration). An events manager, or a member of the team who has the responsibility for coordinating events, will be employed by the hospitality provider to help customers plan and organise a successful wedding, party or event.

Vending

Vending machines are a way of providing food and beverages to people 24/7 without having to employ anyone to serve them. There may be vending machines around your school or college. A vending machine company will be in charge of topping up items in the machines and for maintaining and collecting money from the machines.

Discussion

As a group discuss the following.
- Why do you think businesses would use a meeting room at a hotel?
- Why do you think a hotel is a good place to hold a seminar?
- What is the benefit to the hospitality business of offering business services?

TOPIC   A.2

▶ Business ownership within the hospitality industry

Introduction

Hospitality businesses can take many forms, from a market trader with a takeaway business to a large contract caterer supplying goods and services to several firms. Whatever the size, a business will have a structure. It might be one person trading on their own (a sole trader) or a large corporate business with many shareholders. We are going to look at some of these structures in this section.

Try to think about some of the benefits and drawbacks of running different types of businesses.

▶ Different business ownership types

Hospitality businesses are owned in a variety of ways. There are a number of different types of ownership.

Sole traders

A sole trader is a business that is owned and run by one person, although they may employ staff. In 2012, there were 181,500 individual business sites operating across the hospitality and tourism sector. One in five of these were sole traders (Source: People 1st, 2013). This means that a lot of people run their own businesses within the hospitality area. In the eyes of the law, the business and owner are the same, making the owner responsible for paying off business debt and losses.

A sole trader business could be anything from a food van to a large hotel or an events management business.

Table 1.1 outlines the advantages and disadvantages of being a sole trader.

Table 1.1 The advantages and disadvantages for sole traders

Advantages	Disadvantages
Own boss – can make own decisions and be flexible	No one to share **risks** and make decisions with
Business is easy to set up (and close if necessary) with few start-up costs	The costs and time commitment can be high, e.g. it can be difficult to take time off
Owner can keep all the profits	**Unlimited liability** – if the business gets into debt, the sole trader must pay off the debt (this may mean selling own possessions, e.g. house, car)
May not need to employ staff/pay wages	Harder to raise money if the business is to expand/survive

Partnerships

A partnership is a business that has two or more owners and can have any number of employees. In 2012, 15 per cent of businesses in the hospitality and tourism sector were partnerships (Source: People 1st, 2013). Responsibility for running the business is shared between the partners. Partnerships can be a small business, for example, two people who run a public house or a very large business. John Lewis is a very well-known and large partnership.

The pros and cons of a partnership are shown in Table 1.2

Table 1.2 The advantages and disadvantages of working in a partnership

Advantages	Disadvantages
Responsibility for running the business and making decisions is shared	Business partners might not always see eye to eye and might argue
More capital (money) can be raised to run and expand the business	Unlimited liability – if the business fails, the partners will have to pay the business's debts, even if this means using their own money
Access to a wider range of skills, talents and ideas – benefits of shared expertise	The business can be harder to close down
The time and costs commitments are shared	The profits have to be shared

Limited companies

The ownership of a limited company is divided up into equal parts called shares. Whoever owns one or more of these is called a shareholder. If the company is successful the shareholders will receive dividends (money paid out at the end of a successful financial year). There are two types of limited company.

Private limited company (Ltd)

Private limited companies are often small businesses and family-run affairs. However, Hilton International Hotels (UK) is an example of a larger private limited company.

The pros and cons of a private limited company are set out in Table 1.3.

Table 1.3 The pros and cons of a private limited (ltd) company

Advantages	Disadvantages
The shareholders have limited responsibility for the debts of the business – they are not personally responsible for the debt	This type of business is more complicated to set up with more legal formalities involved
The shareholders receive a share of the **profits**	Control of the company becomes more spread as the structure grows
Easier to raise funds to help the business survive/grow	Employees who are not shareholders might not be so committed to the business

Public limited company (PLC)

PLCs are often large businesses. Shares are usually traded on the stock exchange and can be bought by members of the public. The directors are paid a salary to run the company and may, or may not, own shares. Whitbread is a public limited company.

The benefits and drawbacks of public limited companies are outlined in Table 1.4.

Key term

Profit – the amount of money a business makes after taking all its costs into consideration – occurs when income is more than expenditure.

Table 1.4 The benefits and drawbacks of public limited companies (PLCs)

Advantages	Disadvantages
The shareholders have limited responsibility for the debts of the business – they are not personally responsible for the debt	This type of business is more complicated to set up with more legal formalities involved
More access to finance, e.g. more shares in the company can be sold to the public to raise money	Loss of individual control
The value of shares can go up	The value of shares can go down
	Annual reports have to be published by law and this can give away information to competitors
	There is a threat of being taken over by competitor companies

Franchises

A franchise is where a business (the franchiser) allows another business (the franchisee) to trade under its name and copy its business idea in a particular location. It is a joint venture between the two. The amount of money you would have to pay to run a franchise will depend on its size. Examples of franchises are Pizza Hut and McDonald's.

The pros and cons of this type of business are shown in Table 1.5.

Table 1.5 The advantages and disadvantages of running a franchise for both parties

Advantages for franchiser	Disadvantages for franchiser
They earn more money from people who pay to use their name and business idea	If a franchisee runs their business badly, this will reflect badly on the company name and damage its reputation and brand
The business can grow quickly	

Advantages for franchisee	Disadvantages for franchisee
They have the support of the franchiser who has lots of experience and can supply training and financial advice	They do not have full control of their business – they have to follow many rules set by the franchiser
They gain an established business name and brand, which customers will recognise as having a good reputation	Franchises can be expensive to buy
The franchiser usually provides advertising, packaging and equipment	If the franchiser's business fails, so will that of the franchisee

Link

Go to Topic A.1 in this unit for more information on in-house catering and outsourcing.

In-house and outsourced catering

In-house catering is when a business decides to manage its own catering, even though providing food and beverages is not part of its normal business. For example, this could be a business in retail, travel or corporate hospitality – it could also be a school, prison, hospital or local authority. The advantage of this ownership style is that it allows the business to control and oversee what is produced. However, if the business is not experienced in catering, then it may have difficulties in managing and controlling costs, waste management and quality of food and service.

Outsourced catering is when a business brings in an external supplier to provide catering. Many businesses tend to outsource to a contract food service provider. The advantage of this is that a contract food provider has experience of providing this kind of service. The disadvantage is that the business may have limited say in the delivery of the catering.

Assessment practice 1.2

Simon would like to open up his own pizza restaurant. He is undecided whether he should go it alone, and set up as a sole trader, or if he should apply for a franchise. State one advantage and one disadvantage of each option for Simon. [2]

▶ Type of support given by other industries to the hospitality industry

Introduction

There are many ways in which other industries support businesses within the hospitality industry and this section is going to look at some of them.

Think of a hospitality business in your local area – it could be a small, family-run café or a large company catering for large-scale events. Which other industries does the business need help from to keep trading?

▶ Industry support for hospitality businesses

The hospitality industry does not operate in isolation. It has to work with, and rely on, other industries in order to provide products, goods and services to its customers. Some of these industries are listed in Activity 1.6.

Activity 1.6   No one operates alone!

In pairs, create a table to show examples of how the following industries support the hospitality industry: banks; food, beverage and equipment suppliers; the entertainment and beauty industries; employment agencies; telephone, TV and broadband providers and transport companies. An example for the travel agent and tour operator industry has been completed to get you started.

Other industry	Support
Travel agents/tour operators	Tour operators buy hotel rooms as part of package holidays and travel agents sell the package holidays.

What support do the industries shown in these photographs provide to the hospitality industry?

Travel agents/tour operators

Tour operators arrange and book holidays and excursions for people. They advertise and promote locations, providers and services offered by hospitality businesses. They need to know what products and services a hospitality business provides (for example, range of rooms, hotel services, food and beverage choices, ease of location, availability and **accessibility** of excursions and so on).

Tour operators commit to buy a number of rooms for the whole season so they can guarantee availability for their customers. Hotels may have contracts with a number of tour operators so they can maximise their **occupancy**. Tour operators will also pay a lot less than the **rack rate** as they bulk-buy large numbers of hotel rooms.

Transport businesses

The hospitality industry relies on transport to bring customers to their door, so they need to stay fully informed about what transport is available. Customers may ask

Discussion

As a group, discuss the advantages for the accommodation provider in offering an all-inclusive option.

Key terms

Accessibility – the extent to which a customer or user can obtain a product or service at the time it is needed.

Occupancy – the number of rooms being used.

Rack rate – the standard price for a hotel room before any discounts or offers have been deducted. The rack rate can vary depending on factors such as the day of the week or the season.

restaurant staff to recommend a taxi company; hotels could be asked about local buses, car hire or transfer to the nearest airport.

Banks

In order to start any business you need finance. It is also important to know about how to manage finance and the different charges you will need to pay as a business owner.

Most banks have a business team who will be able to provide financial advice and explain what financial services and support is available for new businesses. They would be able to help you with a business plan, a loan, upfront investment capital, loan repayment schemes, banking schemes with the best rates of interest, business and employee insurance, and much more.

Suppliers

Suppliers provide the hospitality industry with the products they need to provide their goods and services. These products range from **perishable** goods such as fruit and vegetables, to toilet paper and cleaning materials. Products can be delivered on a daily basis, for example, fruit and vegetables and clean bed linen. Some are delivered weekly, such as beverage stock for the bar, and some can be delivered monthly such as cleaning products and stationery.

All of these goods need to be delivered, which requires transportation – another way that the transport industry supports hospitality businesses.

Personal services

A lot of hotels and cruise ships offer their customers additional services to improve their stay. Cruise ships need to entertain their customers during the days when they are at sea so a big programme of sports and leisure events, stage shows, beauty therapies, hairdressing services and shops are provided on board. Hotels also like to keep business in-house, so they offer their customers these services as an incentive to stay at the hotel rather than venture out and spend money in other local businesses.

Telecommunication and technology businesses

Access to Wi-Fi and fast broadband speeds are now an expected service in hotels and restaurants because so many hospitality customers use smartphones, tablets and computers.

Hospitality providers also need good internal communication systems so they can respond quickly to customer enquiries and requests. These systems include walkie-talkies, internal phones and emails.

Businesses also need suitable hardware and software to run effectively. Many bars and cafés have computerised till systems with buttons that identify the name of the product being sold rather than simply the price. Each time a sale is made the stock is reduced by the amount sold. A system like this gives a business several advantages.

- It accurately monitors stock levels.
- It allows a business to identify when stock is missing.
- It allows a business to monitor what products are selling well and not so well.
- It allows a business to identify when stock needs to be ordered.

Have you seen a till like this used in a hospitality business?

Recruitment/staffing agencies

It can be difficult, expensive and very time-consuming to find the right person for a job vacancy and all hospitality businesses want to employ the best person for the job.

For a fee, recruitment agencies will advertise the post, choose the most suitable applicants and supply the hospitality business with a shortlist of candidates for interview. The agency will attract suitable people in a variety of ways, for example, by encouraging people to sign up for job alerts via email, by posting job specifications on external job-search websites to reach a bigger audience and by placing adverts for the job in national and trade magazines.

| **Activity 1.7** | Finding the right person for the job |

In pairs, make a copy of the following table and list the places you could advertise each job post. The first one has been completed for you.

Post	Place
General manager of an independent 260 room, 4* hotel in the Scottish Borders	National newspapers, Scottish newspapers, trade magazines (such as *Caterer*) and recruitment agency websites
Head of housekeeping for a luxury boutique hotel	
Saturday waiting staff for local town centre café	
Receptionist in Dubai for a large international hotel chain	

Waste removal and recycling services

All hospitality businesses have to look carefully at the waste they generate, how they can minimise it and how to dispose of it.

Wasted food and products represent wasted money. If too much food is being thrown away then a business needs to establish why. Is it that the food is not very good or that the portions are too big?

All waste and rubbish needs to be collected and disposed of correctly to prevent a health and safety **hazard** and avoid pests that will be attracted to rotting food. For example, food waste bins must be used for food, plastic bins for plastic items, glass bins for glass items – so that items can be effectively picked up by recycling services and properly sorted.

Utilities businesses

All hospitality businesses need utilities to operate. These include gas, electricity and water. Like telephone and broadband providers, the utilities market is fiercely competitive and businesses need to shop around for the best deals.

It is important that utility operators provide a good and consistent service to hospitality providers. If a hotel suddenly has no water supply, due to a burst pipe, then guests will be affected because they won't be able to take a shower, flush the toilet or eat in the hotel's restaurant.

Discussion

As a group, discuss why a hospitality business needs to monitor its food waste. Make a list of possible reasons.

Key term

Hazard – something that could be dangerous.

Assessment practice 1.3

1   State three ways in which a bank could support a new café. [3]

3   State two advantages to a busy city centre bar of using a computerised sales system. [2]

▶ Operational processes

Introduction

By looking at how a hospitality business purchases goods and materials, how costs are managed and how quality standards are achieved, you will gain an understanding about how a business operates. In this section, we will go through the different stages of a business's operations.

Think about how staffing levels and skills could bring about either the success or the downfall of a busy café and takeaway business.

▶ Purchasing materials, goods and services

How do hospitality businesses purchase the materials and goods they need to carry out their business? There are two main types of supplier that hospitality businesses buy from and they are:

- **wholesalers**
- **retailers**.

Wholesalers buy stock in large quantities from the source (for example, 400 bags of potatoes direct from a farmer). They will then sell them on to different retailers (for example, ten retailers might each buy 40 bags of potatoes from the wholesaler). The retailer will then sell the potatoes on to the customer (for example, in a café or hotel).

Wholesalers and retailers can be:

- national
- local
- specialist (for example, **organic**).

Cash and carry shops

Booker, Makro and Bestway are examples of cash and carry shops. They stock large quantities of items and sell them in bulk to smaller businesses. Many hospitality businesses will go to the cash and carry to buy non-perishable goods such as cleaning materials, toilet paper and goods in tins, packets and jars.

What are the benefits to a business of buying goods from a cash and carry?

Daily markets

Many hospitality businesses shop for fresh ingredients on a daily basis. Some chefs may go to the markets to choose their own produce, for example, fresh fruit and vegetables, meat and fish. They prefer to see what the goods look like – to feel and smell them – and to discuss where the items have come from. This makes sure that the best ingredients are purchased fresh every day.

Company nominated supplier

Hospitality businesses may be able to take delivery of their materials or goods before paying for them. They can do this by using a **nominated supplier**. They will be given an **invoice** by the supplier that needs to be paid for within an agreed time, usually 30 days. The supplier and the hospitality business will have a contract for a set period of time. This arrangement will suit both parties because the supplier can regularly supply goods to the hospitality business and the hospitality business can negotiate over the price they pay.

Advantages and disadvantages of types of suppliers

'Price' will be near the top of the list when a hospitality business is choosing a supplier. Businesses are always looking for the best price and best value for money. This does not always mean the cheapest, because businesses are also interested in the quality of the materials and goods they buy and the range and choice of items available.

Reliability and consistency are also important considerations when looking for a supplier. The level of service and the quality of the goods supplied to a business need to be of the same standard all the time.

Table 1.6 lists some of the pros and cons of using different suppliers.

Chefs often like to go to markets to choose their own ingredients. What are the advantages of doing this?

Key terms

Nominated supplier – a business's main or preferred supplier.

Invoice – a list of the items/goods that form the order being delivered. The invoice also lists the cost of the items/goods being delivered.

Table 1.6 The benefits and drawbacks for hospitality businesses of using different suppliers

Supplier	Advantages	Disadvantages
Company nominated supplier	• Hospitality businesses can negotiate the price they pay, especially if they are buying in bulk • Goods are available on **credit** • A wider range of items might be available which a hospitality business cannot easily source themselves	• If tied into a contract, a hospitality business might not be able to get goods or services from a cheaper supplier
Daily market	• Fresh goods are available every day – restaurants can offer a seasonal menu • Locally grown produce – appeals to customers	• A limited number of items may be available each day (the market may not have the ingredients needed) • Prices could be higher
Cash and carry	• Good for buying non-perishable items in bulk and at competitive prices	• Could involve travelling some distance to the cash and carry – involves time and transport, e.g. a van
Specialist supplier, e.g. organic	• Ideal for businesses that specialise in a particular area, e.g. organic restaurants and cafés	• Fewer specialist suppliers, therefore, prices can be higher

The purchasing cycle

The **purchasing cycle** is the system used in a business to place, receive and pay for orders of materials and goods from outside suppliers. The system is strictly managed so that each order is accurately placed, monitored and managed.

Before placing an order with a supplier, a business should start with a review of what materials they have in stock in order to decide what is needed. Effective management of purchases means that:

- only materials that are needed are bought
- wastage is kept to a minimum.

Purchasing order

Many suppliers take orders via their website, but they can be paper-based and orders are also placed by telephone. If ordering through the internet, a copy of the purchasing order should be saved by the person placing the order and a copy sent to the finance department for their records. Two copies of paper-based orders should also be made. Again, a copy should be kept by the person placing the order and a copy sent to finance.

Delivery note

This is a document from the supplier which describes the items being delivered. The business needs to check the items that have been delivered against the items on the delivery note and then against the purchase order.

Returns note

This document details any items that a business rejects. The business and the supplier must both keep track of items that need to be paid for and those that have been returned.

Credit note

If goods have been returned, the supplier may give the business a credit note. This explains that the business will not be charged for these goods.

Invoice

This document is sent to the business, itemising how much the business owes the supplier. It will need to be paid by a set date.

Statement

Once a month a supplier will send the business a statement which lists all the transactions that have taken place over the last month. This helps both businesses have a clear picture of what has been delivered and paid for and what is still owed to both parties.

Managing costs and revenue

Controlling costs and prices

All hospitality businesses need to control how much they spend on goods and services. If they spend too much money then there is a danger they won't make a profit. If a business does not make a profit, it will fail. Businesses need to work out how much they spend on goods (ingredients, equipment) and other costs (staff pay, business costs). They need to work out how much money they have to make in order to make a profit. They then decide on what price to charge for their products or services so that they make a profit.

Estimating profit

The main objective for a business is to make a profit. In very simple terms, profit is the money a business makes after it has paid its expenses and costs. A business needs to have a clear idea of how much money they need to charge for goods and services so they can make a profit.

There are a number of different types of profit.

- **Gross profit** is calculated as revenue (the income made from selling goods) minus all costs related to those sales (e.g. ingredients). See the worked example below.
- **Net profit** is the amount of money left after all of a business's expenses have been paid out of total revenue.
- **Gross profit margin** represents what is left of the income from the sales after the cost of goods sold has been paid. Gross profit margin is expressed as a percentage.

Link

See Unit 4: Costing and Controlling Finances in the Hospitality Industry for more information about costing and controlling finances in hospitality businesses.

Key term

Portion control – the amount of food that needs to be given to make sure that every customer receives the same amount.

Worked example: Working out gross profit margin

You make a fish pie for six people. The cost of all the ingredients is £35.

You decide to sell each portion for £9.99. The money you make from selling six portions is your revenue.

- Your revenue generated is £9.99 × 6 (as you have six portions).
- Your revenue is £59.94.

To work out the gross profit you take away the cost of the ingredients from your revenue.

- £59.94 (revenue) − £35 (cost of ingredients) = £24.94.
- Your gross profit is £24.94.

The gross profit margin is the gross margin as the percentage of revenue that remains after the ingredients are paid for.

- £24.94 (gross profit) ÷ £59.94 (revenue) × 100 = 41.6%.
- Your gross profit margin is 41.6%.

Activity 1.8   Gross profit poster

There are a number of factors that can impact on a business's gross profit. In a small group, design a poster that describes how each of the following things can impact on a business's gross profit.

- The amount of unused food that is thrown away (wastage)
- Stock being stolen by staff (pilferage)
- An increase in the cost of food items
- A decrease in the cost of food items
- Food not being used by the use-by date (poor stock control)
- Dividing a cake into six slices instead of eight slices and still charging the same price for each slice (**portion control**)

Compare your poster to others in your class.

A health and safety poster like the one shown in this photograph should be put on display in staff areas.

Assessment practice 1.4

1 Anna has ordered a dozen aubergines for her vegetarian café so she can make vegetable moussaka. She is not happy with the quality of the aubergines and wants to return the aubergines back to her supplier. Explain what Anna needs to do in order to return the aubergines. [2]

2 Explain how food being thrown away could affect a restaurant's gross profit. [2]

Controlling staffing

How staff behave towards customers has a big impact on a business. Customers will form a good or bad impression of a business depending on staff's appearance, knowledge, customer service and general attitude. Training and a consistent approach to customer service will help make sure that staff are aware of how to behave.

Every employee should complete an induction programme when they start a new job. This will include any training that they need in order to carry out their job effectively, including information on **policies** and **procedures**. Businesses can also use posters and staff noticeboards to display rules and reminders.

Whenever a group of people work together there will be times when not everyone gets along or will follow the workplace rules. In these cases, the best resolution is to follow company **grievance disciplinary** procedures. Using these polices can be difficult and upsetting, but by following the laid down rules the process should be clear and situations can be sorted out.

A business is also responsible for the health and safety of its staff, visitors and customers. It must make sure that all employees know their responsibilities for health and safety and that they act in accordance with guidelines to keep everyone safe.

Maintaining standards and quality

At business level

Hospitality businesses must maintain their standards and quality in order to keep **repeat business** and create new business. For example, to be rated as a four-star hotel, the hotel must provide a number of different products and services. These standards need to be maintained if the hotel wants to keep its four-star status.

To make sure that standards are maintained, a business needs to have the right procedures in place to monitor quality. Quality checks will need to be carried out as outlined in the business's procedures. Checks may include **mystery shoppers** who check the quality of the products, health and safety standards, the level of service and that communications **protocols** are being kept to. For example, a customer service procedure may state that the phone will be answered within four rings and the caller will be greeted with 'Good morning/afternoon, the Grand Hotel. My name is (receptionist's name). How can I help you today?'

Activity 1.9   Feedback from customers

There are many ways of collecting feedback about customer service. Research and list three methods.

At staff level

It is important to make sure that staff dress and communicate in the right way. This includes back of house staff as they will have contact with internal customers. Each department in a business will have a dress code that staff should comply with. Personal presentation is also extremely important. Personal hygiene, wearing the correct uniform, looking smart and tidy, excellent timekeeping and professional behaviour, as well as maintaining health and safety, all help to create a positive impression of staff members, and subsequently the business. Employees should also remember that customers may be able to hear them, even if they cannot see them, so they should be respectful at all times.

Importance of customer service

Customer service must be the main objective of any hospitality business, and excellent standards of service must lie at the business's core. If customers receive high standards of service when a business supplies them with goods and/or services, they will return and recommend the business to others.

What is the waitress doing wrong in this photograph in terms of the customer service she is providing?

Link

Go to Unit 7: Food and Beverage Service in the Hospitality Industry to find out more information about customer service and personal presentation.

Learning aim C   **TOPIC**   **C.1**

▶ Trends and issues affecting the hospitality industry and how the industry responds to these

Introduction

Trends and issues have a major impact on all businesses, and the hospitality industry is no exception. Local, national and even global events will have an impact on all hospitality businesses and how they operate, from burger vans to Michelin-starred country house hotels.

Write a list of the trends and issues that you think are currently affecting the hospitality industry. Share your list with others. Add to your list and keep it in your file.

The hospitality industry is always changing, evolving and looking for the next 'big thing', much like fashion or the music industry. It is vital that hospitality businesses keep a watchful eye out for new and up-and-coming trends that will influence their customers' buying habits.

What are the disadvantages to the UK's hospitality industry of people not choosing the UK as a holiday destination?

Link

Go to Unit 9: How the Hospitality Industry Contributes to Healthy Lifestyles for more information about healthy eating.

Take it further

Research how the hospitality industry can do more to handle food waste efficiently. You could visit the green hotelier website to get started. You can access this website by going to www.pearsonhotlinks.co.uk and searching for this title.

▶ Issues concerning the hospitality industry

There are a number of trends and issues that affect the hospitality industry.

Investment in tourism funding

A lack of investment in marketing and promoting the UK as a tourism destination, as well as the UK weather, result in people choosing to take their holidays in other countries as they go in search of guaranteed sunshine. This damages the UK's hospitality industry.

Healthy eating and lifestyle choices

We all need to be concerned about improving our lifestyle and making healthy food choices. The hospitality industry has to keep pace with these trends and offer its customers activities and facilities that support lifestyle choices. For most businesses, this means thinking about how to improve food choices on their menus, offering more healthy options and providing customers with information about what is contained in the food and beverages.

The licensing reform

The licence trade has received a lot of criticism in recent years because of the increase in alcohol-fuelled antisocial behaviour. In a bid to combat this, and alcohol-related crime, the government introduced early morning alcohol restriction orders and a tax on late-night licence holders (to contribute to policing costs) in 2012. The government is also currently looking at minimum pricing for alcohol. Any changes in the licensing laws will affect pubs and clubs, and their pricing strategy.

The National Minimum Wage

When the minimum wage increases there is a cost implication for all businesses. The concern for a lot of hospitality businesses is that they will not be able to meet the increase in pay as their profit margins are already small. There is also a concern that these costs will be passed on to the customer, making products and services more expensive.

Handling food waste

Waste food is an issue because it encourages pests such as rats. It needs to be handled correctly, with consideration for health and safety. Responsible hospitality businesses should also take steps to reduce food waste as much as possible by making sure they do not order too many supplies and by using supplies in date order. They can also serve portions that are not too large in order to reduce the amount of food left on the customers' plates. This in turn helps to reduce costs, which can be passed on to the customer in lower prices.

Customers are also increasingly aware of the impact of waste on our environment. They want to be reassured that businesses are doing their bit to help by recycling. Hospitality businesses could, for example, consider turning their organic waste (uneaten food) into green fertiliser. Customers will want to hear about practices such as this – it also makes for good publicity!

Activity 1.10   Current issues affecting the hospitality industry

In pairs, carry out research to find out the following.
- What is the current minimum wage?
- How much did the tax on beer reduce/increase in the last budget?
- Where can you get a licence to sell alcohol?
- How do the above things impact on the hospitality industry?

Link

Go to Unit 9, Learning aim B, Topics B.1 and B.2 for more information on trends and their impact on the hospitality industry. You will also find more information in Unit 5, Learning aim A, Topic A.4.

Factors determining success in the hospitality industry

There are many factors that can affect the success of a hospitality business. Many argue that location is the most important factor. Although this is true for a lot of businesses, there are other factors that need to be considered as well.

Product quality

As a rule, you pay more for high-quality items. For example, where and how an animal was reared will influence the quality of product and the price – prime cuts of meat cost more than other cuts. Some businesses market themselves as using 'only the best'. Their prices for products and services will reflect this, and customers paying for such a product or service will only expect the best. Poor-quality goods and services can have devastating effects for a business.

Pricing

There are lots of different pricing strategies that businesses use and the location, type of business and the types of items sold will all affect the price. The price has to match the market. This means, for example that a café in a tourism destination may charge more for a cream tea, because people will pay more, but they will not expect to pay the same price for a cream tea at their local café.

The effectiveness of distribution networks

How a business moves its products around the UK or globe will affect its success. The businesses being supplied with the goods will rely on the goods being delivered within the agreed time frame. This means distribution needs to be carefully planned, so that items go to the right destination via the quickest route, using the least fuel.

Innovative marketing

Technology has allowed hospitality businesses to target their products directly to their market via texts, emails and social media sites. Businesses can send special offers and information about new products or services which meet individual needs, directly to customers. Customers can shop 24 hours a day and from anywhere with an internet connection or phone signal; they can access information about products and services within minutes.

Large ships are used to transport produce throughout the world. Can you think of any other modes of transport that are used?

Technology means that customers can make bookings at any time of the day or night, wherever they are. Have you ever made an online booking? How easy did you find it to do?

Social issues and trends

As a service industry, hospitality businesses will be influenced by social issues and trends, and they need to be responsive to changing markets.

Population changes and the labour market

Statistics show that the UK population is getting older.

- The 2001 Census showed that the percentage of males aged 65 and over and females aged 60 and over was 14.9 per cent.
- The 2011 Census showed that the percentage of the population aged 65 and over was the highest ever seen at 16.4 per cent, or one in six people.

(Source: '2011 Census – Population and Household Estimates for England and Wales, March 2011'. Office for National Statistics licensed under the Open Government Licence v.1.0.)

Generally, the over 60s are fitter and more active than ever, and some are taking walking and activity holidays because they enjoy staying fit. In turn, this has led to more demand for hospitality businesses to meet the needs of walkers and outdoor activity tourists in key locations such as the Lake District, Peak District and along coastal pathways.

The increase in workers from countries in the European Union also impacts on the hospitality industry. It does so in two ways.

- There is an increase in the number of people available for employment.
- The culinary tastes of customers influence the styles of cuisine offered by chefs.

Contribution to community projects

The hospitality industry participates in a wide variety of community and charity projects on both small and large scales. Two particular large-scale projects of note include:

- the Hospitality Trust, founded in 2000, which supports people from the hospitality industry in Ireland who have fallen on hard times
- Hospitality Action, founded in 1837, which offers assistance to all who work, or have worked, within hospitality in the UK and who find themselves in crisis.

Small-scale projects include offering products and services for free, or allowing charities to use venues to host fundraising events.

Environmental issues and trends

The economic climate, the increase in food and fuel prices and the rise in unemployment have all affected how much money people have to spend on 'luxuries' such as eating out and taking holidays. The hospitality industry has had to work really hard to attract and keep customers.

Renewable energy

Part of any hospitality business's strategy should be to decrease the amount of money spent on energy and to increase its use of renewable energy. Solar power is a way to do this, however, the initial cost of solar panel installation needs to be considered as does the look of solar panels on the building. If a customer does not like the look of the premises, they may go elsewhere.

Discussion

Discuss the different types of hospitality business that benefit from the increase in UK-based holidays.

Take it further

Research Ashley Palmer-Watts's trip to Kenya to work with fish farmers. This is an example of how a UK-based charity, Farm Africa, is working with hospitality specialists to help fish farmers trade fish for other products so they can become self-sufficient. Go to the Farm Africa website to help you with your research. You can access this website by going to www.pearsonhotlinks.co.uk and searching for this title.

Activity 1.11

Renewable energy

In pairs, list as many different types of renewable energy as you can think of. Compare your list with others in your group.

Reuse and recycling facilities

Recycling is important, not only because it cuts down on the need for landfill sites for rubbish disposal, but it is also a sensible use of resources. Hospitality businesses need to play their part in recycling waste and work with local councils and waste disposal companies to dispose of waste in a sensible way. Hospitality businesses can reduce waste in a number of ways as shown in Figure 1.1.

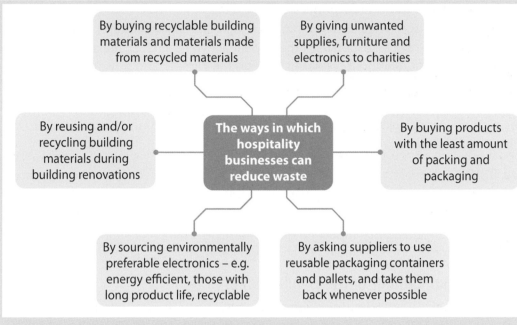

By buying recyclable building materials and materials made from recycled materials

By giving unwanted supplies, furniture and electronics to charities

By reusing and/or recycling building materials during building renovations

The ways in which hospitality businesses can reduce waste

By buying products with the least amount of packing and packaging

By sourcing environmentally preferable electronics – e.g. energy efficient, those with long product life, recyclable

By asking suppliers to use reusable packaging containers and pallets, and take them back whenever possible

Figure 1.1 The ways in which hospitality businesses can reduce waste

Reducing pollution, noise and waste

Pollution and noise are areas that the hospitality industry needs to manage. Some measures can be simple to enforce such as asking delivery vans, customers with cars, and taxis to turn off their engines rather than leaving vehicles idling while making deliveries, unloading luggage or waiting for customers.

Noisy customers leaving a hospitality premise and loud music can disturb those living and working in the surrounding area. Local councils in England, Wales and Northern Ireland deal with complaints about noise from pubs and clubs. The noise could be linked to antisocial behaviour such as disorderly or violent conduct and police may be called. In Scotland, councils regulate noise from pubs and clubs by imposing and enforcing planning and licensing conditions. Some councils may also have by-laws to control noise levels.

▶ Ethical issues and trends

Ethical issues for hospitality businesses influence customers' buying decisions.

Ethical concerns of potential and existing customers

Fairtrade, responsible sourcing and food production methods are all ethical concerns for hospitality businesses. In recent years there have been a number of food scandals which have affected customers' buying habits, even if only for a short time. Hospitality businesses need to be aware of current concerns and respond to them to keep their customers informed.

Animal welfare

Hospitality businesses must be aware of animal welfare – meat processing has also become a concern for many **consumers**. It is essential that businesses know where the food they serve comes from and that they have a good working relationship with suppliers.

Carbon footprint

Global warming and **carbon footprints** are often in the news – but what does it all mean?

- Global warming is the rise in temperature of the Earth's atmosphere.
- A carbon footprint is an estimate of the impact activities such as making a product, living a lifestyle or running a company have on the climate and how much they contribute to climate change.

Both of these issues have a direct impact on the hospitality industry. For example, it takes a lot of water to clean linen, bedding and towels. Most of this water needs to be heated and this uses a lot of energy.

Food miles

'Food miles' refers to the distance food is transported from the time of its production until it reaches the consumer. Food miles are one factor used to assess the environmental impact of food, including the impact on global warming. There are a number of ways that goods can be transported, including by ships and ferries, lorries, planes and trains.

Disposable packaging, cutlery and crockery

Many hospitality businesses use disposable packaging, **cutlery** and **crockery**, especially fast food restaurants – this creates waste and litter. A survey by the charity Keep Britain Tidy in March 2011 found that fast food wrappers are the most common type of litter, accounting for a third (33 per cent) of all litter observed during the study. Hospitality businesses need to work with customers and local councils and their service departments (refuse collection and street cleaning) to do as much as they can to stop littering happening.

Fairtrade

Fairtrade is a certification system that means farmers and workers in developing countries receive a fair price for their goods, as well as the Fairtrade Premium, which they can choose how to invest in their communities. Charities like Oxfam have done a lot to support such initiatives and you can now find Fairtrade products in all major supermarkets. Many hospitality businesses will also use and sell Fairtrade products and there is a continuing demand from the public to know this information about a business.

Equal opportunities for staff

Hospitality is one of the few industries where an employee can start in the kitchen or bar and work their way up to be the general manager or chief executive officer of a major company. Jobs can include accommodation and food as part of the salary.

All hospitality businesses should meet equal opportunities policy in order to:

- treat all staff fairly and equally
- make sure all new applicants and existing members of staff are treated fairly when applying for jobs
- make sure that suppliers and customers are also treated fairly
- use existing and future staff to the best of their abilities
- improve staff morale
- recruit, train and keep the skilled staff who will help the business to achieve its objectives
- make sure they do not discriminate against anyone.

If you see this Mark on products, it means they are Fairtrade.

Assessment practice 1.5

Mohammed would like to open a vegan café and wants to make sure that the business will operate in an environmentally friendly way. Describe four ways in which he can do this. [4]

How hospitality businesses respond to trends and issues

In some cases, responding to trends and issues will require a change in the way a hospitality business operates. A decision to use recycled stationery, or local suppliers, will change the way the business makes orders or which dishes end up on the menu.

Changes in methods of operation

Imagine that a restaurant chain requires all its businesses to use a supplier which offers fair trade products and responsibly sourced goods. They will write this change into their buying policy so that all businesses in the chain stick to buying ethically. This results in a change to how the business operates.

Development of new products

All businesses must try to meet their customers' needs and expectations and this means introducing new products and services, especially in line with new trends or fashions.

Figure 1.2 shows the process that a large restaurant chain would go through if it introduced a new menu in all its businesses.

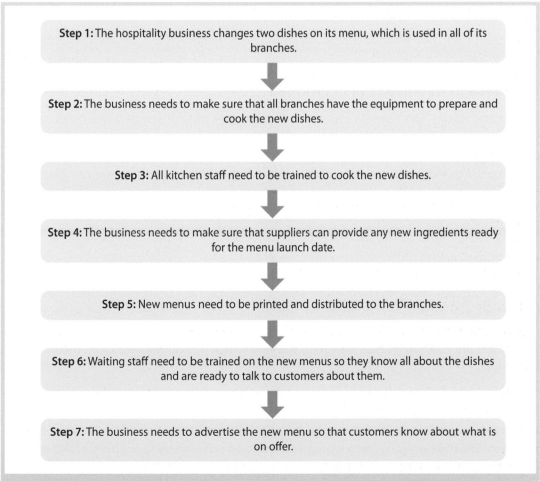

Step 1: The hospitality business changes two dishes on its menu, which is used in all of its branches.

Step 2: The business needs to make sure that all branches have the equipment to prepare and cook the new dishes.

Step 3: All kitchen staff need to be trained to cook the new dishes.

Step 4: The business needs to make sure that suppliers can provide any new ingredients ready for the menu launch date.

Step 5: New menus need to be printed and distributed to the branches.

Step 6: Waiting staff need to be trained on the new menus so they know all about the dishes and are ready to talk to customers about them.

Step 7: The business needs to advertise the new menu so that customers know about what is on offer.

Figure 1.2 For larger businesses, it can be a lengthy process to introduce new products.

Many restaurants and cafés use daily specials to add variety to their menu and to feature their use of seasonal food.

The size of the business and the type of product will affect how quickly a business can respond to customers' needs.

Changes in marketing or promotions

In today's technological world, the ability to connect instantly with your current and future customers is essential. The use of technology has changed the way hospitality businesses communicate with their customers to tell them about their products and promotions – emails, texts and tweeting are methods commonly used.

Instant contact with customers allows hospitality businesses to tell them about price changes, discounts and special offers, some of which might only be available for a limited period of time.

Changes in prices

All hospitality businesses are constantly looking for ways to be more competitive and pricing is one area that is key to a business's success. At the moment, the food area relies heavily on special offers to attract customers, for example:

- two for the price of one on main meals
- children eating for free
- two or three courses for a set price
- paying with discount vouchers.

These offers are designed to attract customers to eat out even if customers do not have much money to spare.

Increases or decreases in employees

Trends and issues can have an impact on the number of staff needed in a hospitality business. Innovation can sometimes result in the need for fewer members of staff, whereas some changes will result in growth for a business and the need to take on more staff. For example, modern booking systems mean that customers can book a table in a restaurant through a business's website – this allows restaurants to make a judgement call about how many staff they will need for each service, depending on how many tables and **covers** are booked and what the normal level of passing trade is.

Changes in policy

In order to make changes permanent and meaningful, new policies will often need to be written. For example, it may be that a hotel chain will set itself a target to reduce its carbon footprint and will decide on a number of ways to do this. These measures will be written into the business's policy on the environment and relayed to all the hotels in the chain.

You have already looked at some changes in policy with a view to businesses sourcing fairtrade goods. There are other policies that may need to be changed, not least those that concern the law. A recent change for all businesses is that employers in the UK have to offer their employees a workplace pension scheme by law. This started with the biggest employers in October 2012 and will be phased in over six years.

WorkSpace

▷ **Harry Tuma**

Trainee chef, Cornwall

My parents have always grown organic vegetables, so they never used chemicals on the soil or plants. I've not inherited my parents' love of gardening, but I do think it's important to know where our food comes from and how it is reared or grown.

When I was looking for a part-time job I got a job in our local pub. They use locally produced food and have a seasonal menu.

After two years at college studying for my A levels while working part time at the pub, I decided that I wanted to be a chef. I was lucky as the manager of the pub offered me an apprenticeship doing a Level 2 NVQ Diploma in Professional Cookery. I'm close to completing my apprenticeship and I'm confident that I made the right decision in training to be a chef.

I love going to work. I get to decide what the specials will be, based on what is in season and what our local suppliers have available. I've been to see where and how the fruit and vegetables are grown at the local farms and market gardens, so I know where the food comes from. Our fish is from sustainable sources and our meat is from a local farm. The food is fresh and of the best quality – we know and trust our suppliers and I know that we're using the best ingredients. The menu prices are not expensive and our customers get really good value for money.

About six months ago, I suggested that we add a section to the menu introducing our suppliers, so that our customers could also see where their food is coming from. The manager thought it was a great idea. Now our customers are always commenting on how important they feel it is to have confidence in what is in the food they eat. We're also seeing an increase in customers coming to the restaurant because they've heard about our food ethos.

Think about it!

1 Are there any other ways in which Harry could improve his skills?

2 How else could Harry and the team promote the seasonal and local nature of the produce they use?

3 Would a job like Harry's appeal to you? Why?

Assessment Zone

This section has been written to help you to do your best when you take the onscreen test. Read through it carefully and ask your teacher/tutor if there is anything you are still not sure about.

How you will be assessed

For this unit you will be assessed through an examination that lasts 1 hour and 15 minutes. The examination paper will have a maximum of 50 marks. The number of marks available for each question will be shown in brackets, e.g. [2], with the total for each question being shown at the end of the question.

There will be different types of question in the examination.

Disclaimer: These practice questions and sample answers are not actual exam questions and have been provided as a practice aid only. They should be used as practice material only and should not be assumed to reflect the format or coverage of the real external test.

A Questions where the answers are available and you have to choose the correct answer(s) that fit. *Tip: Always make sure that you read the instructions carefully. Sometimes you may need to identify more than one correct answer.*

Examples:

The AA assess and rate hotel and guest accommodation providers using a star-system. Identify one of these that is not an AA star-rating? [1]

A 1 star

B 3 stars

C 4 stars

D 5 stars

E 6 stars

Answer: E

Identify two of these that would not use the services of a Contract Food Service Provider? [2]

A School

B Hospital

C Cruise liner

D Armed services

E Fine dining restaurant

Answers: C and E

B Questions where you are asked to give a short answer worth 1 or 2 marks. *Tip: Look carefully at how the question is set out to see how many points need to be included in your answer.*

Example:

Explain one difference between a 1-star hotel and a 4-star hotel. [2]

Answer: The facilities and services offered would be different. The 4-star hotel is likely to offer more facilities and services, such as room service, en-suite bathrooms and a pool and gym.

C Questions where you are asked to give a longer answer – these can be worth up to 8 marks. *Tips: Make sure that you read the question in full, and answer all of the parts of the question that you are asked. It is a good idea to plan your answer so that you do not forget anything and remember to check your answer once you have finished.*

Example:

Saima owns a small restaurant that serves a range of British food. She received a number of complaints last week about the quality of the restaurant's food and waiting staff. Discuss why it is important to maintain standards and quality, and the possible impact on Saima's restaurant if she does not maintain them. [8]

Answer:

1–2 marks. The learner has given one reason why it is important to maintain standards and quality but this only shows limited knowledge.

If Saima does not maintain the standard and quality of the food and waiting staff in the restaurant, customers may decide not to come back to the restaurant and may not recommend it to their friends and families.

3–5 marks. The learner has given a number of reasons why it is important to maintain standards and quality and the possible impact on Saima's restaurant if she does not maintain them. However, for the higher marks, the learner needs to discuss what Saima could do to improve and maintain the standards and quality of the service she provides.

Saima must maintain the standard and quality of the food and waiting staff in the restaurant in order to encourage repeat business. It is important for Saima to please her customers and encourage them to visit the restaurant again. Her customers are unlikely to recommend the restaurant to their friends and families if they are unhappy with the food and service they received, which means it will be hard for Saima to create new business. If Saima continues to lose customers, her restaurant will make less profit and may not be able to continue operating.

6–8 marks. The learner builds on the answer for 3–5 marks by including examples of how Saima could improve and maintain standards and quality.

Saima must maintain the standard and quality of the food and waiting staff in the restaurant in order to encourage repeat business. It is important for Saima to please her customers and encourage them to visit the restaurant again. Her customers are unlikely to recommend the restaurant to their friends and families if they are unhappy with the food and service they received, which means it will be hard for Saima to create new business. If Saima continues to lose customers, her restaurant will make less profit and may not be able to continue operating. To help her maintain standards and quality she should put procedures in place to monitor quality and carry out regular quality checks. Checks may include mystery shoppers who check the quality of the food and beverages and the level of service, that health and safety standards are maintained and that communication protocols are being followed. For example, a procedure could be put in place that requires waiting staff to greet and welcome customers at the restaurant door and chefs could be required to check every plate of food that leaves the kitchen.

Hints and tips

- **Use the time before the test.** Make sure that you have got everything you will need. Check that your pen works properly and make sure you read the instructions on the front of your examination. Try to make yourself comfortable and relaxed.

- **Keep an eye on the time.** The examination will last 1 hour and 15 minutes, and you should be able to see the clock in the examination room so that you will know how long you have got left to complete the paper. As a rough guide, allow one minute for every mark on the paper. This means that a question work five marks should take you around five minutes to complete.

- **Read the questions fully.** Make sure you read the question through enough times to be sure that you understand what you are being asked to do. It is easy to misread a question and then write an answer that is wrong. Check you are doing what you are being asked to do. This is where many learners lose marks.

- **Plan your answers.** For longer questions, it is worth spending a minute or two writing down the key points that you want to include in your answer. If you are being asked to evaluate, you will need to think about positive and negative points. Using a plan will allow you to make sure you include both in your answer.

- **Read through longer answers.** Read through your longer answers to make sure your answer makes sense, and you have answered the question fully.

- **Check your answers.** Once you have answered all of the questions on the paper, you will probably have a few minutes to spare. Use this time to check your answers and maybe fill in any parts that you have left blank. You should try to answer every question on the paper.

- **Make sure you have completed the front of the paper.** Once the examination has ended, check that you have written your name and candidate number on the front of the paper. This is important so that you will gain the marks for your work.

How to improve your answer

Read the two student answers below, together with the feedback. Try to use what you learn here to improve your answers in your examination.

Question

Explain two ways in which other industries support the hospitality industry. [4]

Student 1's answer

A tour operator will have a contract with a hotel to sell the hotel rooms as part of a package holiday.

Feedback:

The learner has provided an example of how a single industry supports the hospitality industry. However, the question asked for two ways, so how 'industries' plural support the hospitality industry. The learner's answer does not address the question and the example provided does not give enough detail about how a tour operator supports a hotel/the industry and the ways it does this. The learner would only receive one mark for this.

Student 2's answer

A wide range of other industries support the hospitality industry. Tour operators, for example, will have a contract with a hotel(s) to sell hotel rooms as part of a package holiday. The contract with the tour operator means that the advertising and marketing is done by the tour operator and the responsibility for selling the rooms becomes part of the tour operator's role. The same sort of arrangement can be made with coach companies who offer tours when accommodation forms part of the tour.

A hotel may liase with local taxi businesses to offer a drop-off and pick-up service for their guests to identified locations in the local area.

Feedback:

The learner has understood the question and has used two clear examples to demonstrate how different industries provide support, services and products to the hospitality industry. The learner has explained the different services each type of business provides and identifies how they support different hospitality businesses.

The learner could also have referenced other industries, including banks, employment agencies, entertainment and leisure, and service providers (television, electricity, business services). The learner would receive full marks for this answer.

Assess yourself

Question 1

Give three examples of the advantages of being a sole trader. [3]

Question 2

Graeme owns a small restaurant and would like to create a training handbook for his staff. In it he would like to include a section on working skills. Analyse the result of poor working skills on a hospitality business to help Graeme decide what information to include in the handbook. [6]

Question 3

Employees are required to wear a uniform so that they look smart and tidy to create a good first impression on customers. Explain one other reason why a company dress code is important. [2]

Question 4

Explain one difference between internal and external customers. [2]

Question 5

People living longer is one trend that has affected the hospitality industry. Explain two other trends that have affected the hospitality industry. [4]

Answers can be found on page 310.

Introduction

What is it actually like to work in the hospitality industry? This unit will give you a chance to explore that question and to look at the working skills needed for a number of job roles within the hospitality industry.

You will learn about the importance of teamworking, customer service skills, appropriate conduct and personal appearance. Staff behaviour and presentation within the workplace can make or break a business. Making a good impression as well as using the correct communication skills are vital when you are working with customers and other team members. Where the right impression is given, customers will return, boosting a business's reputation and its profitability.

Assessment: You will be assessed by a series of assignments set by your teacher/tutor.

Learning aims

In this unit you will:

A understand effective working skills in the hospitality industry

B use working skills in a hospitality situation.

I left college in 2010 and I haven't looked back. I completed a catering course and then started on a management training programme run by a well-known fast food chain. I believe that knowing and understanding the skills needed to work effectively as a team member and having the ability to motivate my own team have been part of the reason for my success. I am extremely excited as 2013 has brought me excellent news; I have been successful as a restaurant franchisee! I am raring to go and meet and lead my new team.

Niall, *23-year-old restaurateur*

Working in the Hospitality Industry

BTEC
Assessment Zone

This table shows what you must do in order to achieve a **Pass**, **Merit** or **Distinction** grade, and where you can find activities to help you.

Assessment criteria			
Level 1	**Level 2 Pass**	**Level 2 Merit**	**Level 2 Distinction**
Learning aim A: Understand effective working skills in the hospitality industry			
1A.1 Identify working skills needed to work effectively in the hospitality industry, using examples from two different businesses.	**2A.P1** Describe, using examples from two different hospitality businesses, the importance to the businesses, customers and staff of having effective working skills in the hospitality industry. **See Assessment activity 2.1, page 62**	**2A.M1** Explain, using examples from two contrasting hospitality businesses, the benefits for the business, its customers and staff of having appropriate working skills. **See Assessment activity 2.1, page 62**	**2A.D1** Evaluate the consequences of poor working skills on a selected hospitality business, including the effect on its staff and customers. **See Assessment activity 2.1, page 62**
1A.2 Describe business procedures, legislation and regulatory requirements that contribute to consistent and reliable service provision in the hospitality industry.	**2A.P2** English Explain how business and professional policies and procedures, and legislation and regulatory requirements contribute to consistent and reliable service provision in the hospitality industry. **See Assessment activity 2.1, page 62**	**2A.M2** English Explain the impact of following business and professional policies and procedures, and legislative and regulatory requirements affecting service provision on a selected hospitality business. **See Assessment activity 2.1, page 62**	
Learning aim B: Use working skills in a hospitality situation			
1B.3 Demonstrate working skills in one hospitality situation.	**2B.P3** Demonstrate working skills in two hospitality situations to meet given business requirements. **See Assessment activity 2.2, page 68**	**2B.M3** English Apply communication and teamworking skills in addressing a work-related problem in a hospitality situation. **See Assessment activity 2.2, page 68**	**2B.D2** English Evaluate the effectiveness of own communication and teamworking skills in addressing a work-related problem in a hospitality situation, justifying areas for improvement. **See Assessment activity 2.2, page 68**
1B.4 Identify examples of teamwork skills that are important in the hospitality industry.	**2B.P4** Explain the use of teamworking skills in the hospitality industry and why they are important. **See Assessment activity 2.2, page 68**		
1B.5 English Use verbal and non-verbal communication skills in a team in one hospitality situation.	**2B.P5** English Use effective verbal and non-verbal communication skills in a team in two contrasting hospitality situations. **See Assessment activity 2.2, page 68**		

English Opportunity to practise English skills

How you will be assessed

This unit will be assessed by a series of internally assessed tasks. These tasks will be set by your teacher/tutor. You will be expected to show that you understand the skills needed to work in the hospitality industry and their importance. You will also need to prove that you have demonstrated these work skills in a variety of realistic hospitality situations. In order to meet all the criteria, you will need to show that you have researched two different hospitality businesses. These businesses could be a pub, restaurant, hotel, events organiser, a membership club, etc.

Your assessment could be in the form of:

- assignment work
- role play or work experience (supported by a log or diary and an observation record)
- a training handbook
- leaflets
- tasks and activities, which may include demonstration.

Job roles within the hospitality industry

Introduction

The hospitality industry is responsible for the employment of 1.9 million people in the United Kingdom (UK) today. It is a large industry, offering some excellent opportunities (Source: People 1st, 2013, 'State of the Nation Report 2013').

Think about all the different job roles in hospitality and the businesses they are found in. Produce a table to show as many job roles as you can think of and the businesses where they can be found.

Job roles

There are numerous job roles available in the hospitality industry and lots of opportunities for career progression. You can enter the workforce and train on the job to reach more senior or highly skilled positions. There is a wide variety of job roles in the hospitality industry: chef, **barista**, food server, bar person, receptionist, room attendant, marketing assistant, hotel/hostel housekeeper, food and beverage supervisor, hotel manager and events organiser.

Table 2.1 provides a little more detail about some of these job roles.

Table 2.1 Job roles in the hospitality industry

Job role	Responsibilities	Duties	Skills required for the job role	Work category in which the job fits
Room attendant	• To maintain the cleanliness and order of hotel rooms and public areas within a hotel	• To clean and maintain hotel rooms and public areas • To deal appropriately with guests • To follow and maintain health and safety	• Carry out room servicing • Clean and maintain a range of different service areas, floors and furnishings • Clean, maintain and collect linen for beds and bathroom areas • Create and promote a positive impression of yourself and your work area • Work safely and maintain a healthy and safe working environment • Follow procedures when carrying out work duties • Work effectively within a team	Operational

continued

Table 2.1 (continued)

Job role	Responsibilities	Duties	Skills required for the job role	Work category in which the job fits
Chef	• To prepare food • To plate food • To follow and maintain hygiene, health and safety procedures	• To cook, prepare and plate food • To maintain stock control • To maintain good standards of food hygiene, health and safety • To communicate effectively with other team members	• Comply with food hygiene regulations • Complete relevant paperwork • Work effectively within a team • Maintain a safe, hygienic and secure working environment • Maintain effective stock control • Prepare, operate and clean equipment • Produce basic food items and products • Set up and close kitchen • Create and promote a positive impression of yourself and your work area	Craft
Food and beverage supervisor	• Responsible for the management or supervision of a team of waitresses and waiting staff	• To take food orders • To deal with customer payments • To arrange staff rotas • To supervise staff • To follow and maintain health and safety	• Promote hospitality services and products • Work effectively within a team • Maintain a safe, hygienic and secure working environment • Develop relationships with customers • Deal with customer service problems • Prepare and clear service areas • Prepare and serve beverages • Provide leadership for the team • Complete and supervise practices for handling payments	Supervisory
Hotel manager	• Has overall responsibility for all aspects of the hotel	• To manage budgets • Responsible for recruitment • Responsible for staff training • Responsible for marketing strategy and activities • To maintain and follow health, safety and hygiene procedures	• Review the business • Contribute to the promotion of hospitality products and services • Contribute to the control of resources • Promote and develop working relationships with colleagues • Keep up to date with current legislation affecting the business • Effectively lead a team • Maintain the health, hygiene, safety and security of the working environment • Manage resources • Monitor and resolve customer problems and complaints • Plan the strategic development of the business • Plan/provide appropriate training for staff • Recruit, select and retain colleagues	Management

Would the job of a barista in a busy coffee shop appeal to you?

Case study: Dreaming bigger

Charmaine has worked as a pot wash assistant in a busy independent coffee shop since finishing school. She often visits her local chain coffee shop with her friend Martie. She loves the smell of coffee and all the different beverages that they make there. She likes to watch the staff on the barista machine making the coffees one by one for the customers. She would like to work in that role one day. Martie tells her that as she didn't get good grades in her exams at school, it is all just a dream.

1 Can you help Charmaine to find out how she could gain a job working as a barista?

2 What skills would she need?

3 Are there any existing training programmes that she could follow?

4 Can you think of any more job roles in the hospitality industry? What are their responsibilities?

▶ Hospitality industry businesses

The hospitality industry consists of seven main business types: hotels; restaurants; pubs, bars and nightclubs; hospitality services; membership clubs; events organisers; contract service providers. We will now look at some of these business types in more detail.

Hotels

Hotels vary by size, the number of people employed, the facilities available and price of a room. In 2011, hotels employed 262,000 people (Source: People 1st, 2013).

Whatever the style of hotel, all employees will need some common skills including:

• the ability to communicate well

• customer service skills

• the ability to work effectively within a team.

Employees also need to be able to use their skills to maintain health, hygiene and safety within the workplace. Roles such as an accountant or a chef would need more specific job skills.

Activity 2.1   Working in star-rated or budget accommodation

Discuss the key differences between star-rated accommodation and budget accommodation. What skills do you think staff would need when working in each of these types of business? Which skills are the same and which might be different?

Restaurants

In 2012, there were 75,600 restaurants in the UK compared to 71,800 in 2011 (Source: People 1st, 2013). The restaurant industry is, therefore, a growth industry. Restaurants can be grouped into the following categories:

• fast food businesses

• fine dining

• chain restaurants

• cafés and coffee shops

• grouped by cuisine, for example, Italian, vegetarian, Thai, etc.

Restaurant staff need:

- the ability to work in a team
- effective communication skills
- customer service skills
- the ability to maintain and follow good hygiene, health, safety and security practices in a workplace.

Bartenders would need more specific skills such as the ability to mix and prepare drinks and a knowledge of different beverages, as well as the ability to comply with the relevant legislation.

Pubs and bars

Pubs, bars and nightclubs have a licence to sell alcoholic and non-alcoholic beverages. The hours when they can do this may vary. Most bars and pubs also sell food. A public house could be:

- managed – the business and premises are owned by a **brewery** and staff are employed to run the business on their behalf
- a free house – the business and premises are owned and managed by the **licensee**
- tenanted/leased – the premises and business are owned by the brewery and rented by the licensee.

Staff working in pubs and bars need similar skills to bartenders working in restaurants. They need to be able to mix and prepare drinks and should have knowledge of different beverages.

Nightclubs

Nightclubs usually offer a place for dancing, with music as entertainment. Clubs usually charge an entrance fee and some encourage people to attend early by offering, for example, free entry before 10 p.m.

Typical job roles include:

- DJs – who are responsible for providing music and entertaining customers. They need up-to-date knowledge of current and past music depending on the type of club, for example, some clubs host 'back to the 80s' evenings. DJs also need a level of customer service skills so they can interact with customers who request specific music. They may also be the first person to spot any security issues and will need to use their communication skills to alert security staff.
- Security staff – who have an overall focus on the security of the club. This includes monitoring the doorway and the number of people allowed inside, as well as dealing with any security problems throughout the evening. Security staff are also responsible for making sure that the club is empty at the end of the evening before it closes.

Other job roles include: club manager, deputy manager, bar supervisor, bar staff and cleaning staff.

Contract catering/contract food service providers

Contract catering businesses offer catering services to businesses in which catering and hospitality are not their main focus. This includes hospitals, schools, care homes, prisons, the armed forces and many places of work. Contract catering usually operates by catering companies bidding (**tendering**) for a contract to provide the food and beverage services for a particular business. The contract catering business that provides the most appealing bid in terms of price, quality and service will win the contract with the business for a specified time period. Is a contract caterer responsible for the catering in your school/college canteen?

Key terms

Brewery – a place where beer is made on a commercial scale so that it can be sold to pubs, bars and restaurants.

Licensee – someone who holds a special licence to sell something, in this case alcoholic beverages.

Tendering – when a company is given the chance to win the contract to supply goods or services to another company.

Activity 2.2

Running a pub

Use the internet to find a selection of job adverts for pub and bar staff. What are the main responsibilities of staff in this area? What skills do they require?

Discussion

In a group, discuss what job roles you think might be available within membership clubs and event management businesses.

Unlike the staff who work in hotels, restaurants, pubs and clubs, people working for a contract caterer are less likely to work weekends or evenings. This is because many contract caterers only supply services during 'normal' working hours.

Typical job roles within contract catering include:

- chefs/cooks
- kitchen managers
- waiting staff
- management
- accounting staff
- cashiers
- cleaning staff
- marketing roles.

▶ Working skills in the hospitality industry

Introduction

In this section you will learn more about the different skills needed to work within the hospitality industry. By now you should have some idea of the skills that are important and whether or not you currently have them.

Consider your dream job within the hospitality industry and identify the skills you think you need in order to work in, and obtain, that role.

There are plenty of skills that it is beneficial to have when it comes to attracting an employer. Many of these skills are useful in lots of different jobs – these are known as 'transferable skills'. You may not realise it, but you probably already have several of the skills that employers like to see. By working in the hospitality industry, you can practise and develop these skills to suit particular job roles. There may be other skills that you will need to learn from scratch, but a willingness to do this will take you a long way.

There are five main categories of skills you need in order to be successful within the hospitality industry. These are:

- occupational skills
- personal skills/personal attributes
- working with others/teamwork
- interpersonal skills
- communication skills.

Case study: Communicate!

Lindsay worked as a kitchen assistant in a local restaurant. Her job role included preparing vegetables and other food items, as well as washing dishes. One day, Lindsay was late for work, which was not like her, and she had not made contact with anyone at work to say where she was.

1 What do you think the other staff should do about the dishes and the vegetable preparation?

2 What should Lindsay have done when she knew she was not going to make it to work on time?

▶ Occupational skills

Occupational skills are the skills needed to carry out a particular job role or set of duties. Table 2.2 shows specific job roles in the hospitality industry and the occupational skills needed for each role.

Table 2.2 Examples of occupational skills required in specific job roles within the hospitality industry

Job role	Occupational skills required

Chef	• Cooking skills
	• Knowledge of:
	  ▪ food preparation – cooking times, equipment, storage methods, suppliers, ingredients
	  ▪ food and nutrition
	  ▪ special dietary requirements and requests
	  ▪ menu planning
	  ▪ health and safety and hygiene legislation, regulations and practices
	• Ability to:
	  ▪ multi-task
	  ▪ work under pressure
	  ▪ practise and maintain time management skills
	  ▪ communicate effectively with other kitchen members and front of house staff

Waiting staff	• Food service skills
	• Strong communication and interpersonal skills
	• Excellent customer service skills
	• Knowledge of:
	  ▪ health and safety and hygiene legislation, regulations and practices
	  ▪ menu items and ingredients
	  ▪ special dietary requirements and requests
	• Ability to:
	  ▪ prepare and maintain food and beverage service area
	  ▪ multi-task
	  ▪ work under pressure
	  ▪ practise and maintain time management skills
	  ▪ communicate effectively with other front of house staff and members of the kitchen team
	  ▪ relay service timings
	  ▪ provide food and beverage services
	  ▪ memorise and relay customer orders accurately

Bar staff	• Beverage service skills
	• Strong communication and interpersonal skills
	• Excellent customer service skills
	• Knowledge of:
	  ▪ health and safety and hygiene practices
	  ▪ beverages, menu items and ingredients
	  ▪ legislation affecting job role, e.g. licensing laws
	• Ability to:
	  ▪ multi-task
	  ▪ work under pressure
	  ▪ practise and maintain time management skills
	  ▪ communicate effectively with other front of house staff
	  ▪ relay service timings
	  ▪ provide food and beverage services
	  ▪ memorise and relay customer orders
	  ▪ enforce the rules of legislation

continued

Table 2.2 *(continued)*

Job role	Occupational skills required

Housekeeper	• Accommodation skills
	• Excellent customer service skills
	• Knowledge of health and safety and hygiene practices
	• Ability to:
	  ▪ multi-task
	  ▪ work under pressure
	  ▪ practise and maintain time management skills
	  ▪ communicate effectively with other staff

Receptionist	• Front office skills
	• Excellent customer service skills
	• Knowledge of health and safety and hygiene practices
	• Ability to:
	  ▪ multi-task
	  ▪ work under pressure
	  ▪ practise and maintain time management skills
	  ▪ communicate effectively with other departments, internal and external agencies
	• Knowledge of hotel and restaurant facilities as well as local and surrounding area
	• Strong communication and interpersonal skills
	• Ability to provide reception/concierge services
	• Ability to memorise and relay customer orders
	• Knowledge of legislation affecting job role
	• Ability to enforce rules of legislation

Concierge	• Front office skills
	• Excellent customer service skills
	• Knowledge of health and safety and hygiene practices
	• Ability to:
	  ▪ multi-task
	  ▪ work under pressure
	  ▪ practise and maintain time management skills
	  ▪ communicate effectively with other departments, internal and external agencies
	• Knowledge of hotel and restaurant facilities as well as local and surrounding area
	• Strong communication and interpersonal skills
	• Ability to provide reception/concierge services
	• Ability to memorise and relay customer orders
	• Knowledge of legislation affecting job role
	• Ability to enforce rules of legislation

Activity 2.3   Now, it is your turn!

Identify five further hospitality job roles and produce your own table to show the specific occupational skills needed within each job role.

▶ Personal skills/personal attributes

These are skills that a person either has or needs to develop in order to act and behave correctly. They include:

- tact and diplomacy
- effective teamworking
- patience

- honesty
- initiative
- self-motivation.

Case study: The best response

Kate works as a waitress in a restaurant. Towards the end of one particularly busy shift, she went into the ladies' toilets to check that they were clean and well stocked with handwash and toilet rolls. She found a customer who was very distressed. She had been taken ill, and had been sick – she was very embarrassed and apologetic. Kate could have reacted badly, telling the customer that the smell was disgusting and leaving her to clean it up herself. Instead, Kate put a sign on the door closing the toilets for five minutes while she helped the customer to clean her dress. She reassured her that everything was fine and that there was no need to be embarrassed – it could happen to anyone. She then had a discreet word with the customer's partner who took her straight home. Finally, she returned to the toilet to clean it. No one was any the wiser and Kate could congratulate herself that she had responded well.

1 Which skills did Kate use in this scenario?
2 What might have happened if she had chosen to react badly?

▶ Working with others

Working with others is vital in order to succeed in the hospitality industry. Individuals must work effectively as a team and also cooperate across teams, working together to provide the customer with the best possible service. For example, if housekeeping and reception did not work together, then it is possible that a guest could be checked into a room that was not ready and had not been serviced. These sorts of problems can be **eliminated** if teams work together and communicate clearly between departments.

Effective teamworking skills

The skills needed to work effectively with others include the ability to:

- cooperate, for example, one chef cannot produce all the meals – they need others to help them prepare and cook
- communicate, for example, if reception know of a guest's early arrival, they can tell housekeeping who can prepare that room first
- realise that goals cannot be achieved without the help and support of others, for example, meals that have been carefully prepared by the chef can be spoiled if waiting staff take too long to serve them to the guests

Key term

Eliminated – completely removed or destroyed.

- know when to ask for help
- work independently to carry out tasks
- solve problems, for example, if the commis chef sees that the kitchen porter is late for work, and a delivery of frozen food has arrived, they can check it and put it away
- be self-reliant – to be reliable, dependable and honest
- keep good time management
- meet deadlines and goals, for example, a group booking of 40 people is scheduled to sit down for lunch at 1 p.m. – all the restaurant staff need to be ready for their arrival.

> ### Key term
>
> **Footfall** – the number of people who go into a business in a particular period of time.

Case study: A busy day

Tariq is working in a busy takeaway restaurant. It is half-term and his shift started at 2 p.m. **Footfall** is still high at 4 p.m. and Tariq is struggling to keep up with demand. Two things have happened that have affected the team: first, one member of staff called in sick and no one has had time to call another member of staff to take over the shift; second, one drinks pump has stopped working, meaning that service is taking longer than usual.

1 Discuss the effects these problems may have had on the team throughout the day.

2 What skills would the team need to have used to overcome the problems and work well as a team?

▶ Interpersonal skills

Excellent interpersonal skills help lead to excellent customer service skills.

Positive attitude and appropriate behaviour

A positive attitude and appropriate behaviour help to show customers and other team members that you care about the service you provide and your job role.

Whatever kind of day you are having, you cannot let this show to your customers or team members. Even if you are harassed or having a bad time, you still need to make your colleagues and customers your priority. A smile and a calm attitude will reassure your colleagues that you will do your best to help them and your customers that they are in good hands.

If you work in the hospitality industry, you are likely to be 'on display' to customers, so you need to behave in the right way. Be polite and show people that you are interested in helping them and meeting their needs. A waiter who looks bored and pulls out his mobile phone while customers are waiting will not create a good impression of himself or the business he works for.

First impressions last! Do you feel you always create a good first impression when you are dealing with customers?

Greeting customers

The way a customer is greeted by a member of staff can be a key part of the success of their experience. A simple 'Hello', 'Good morning' or 'Good evening' and a smile goes a long way. The first things a customer wants to see when they enter a restaurant, for example, are attentive staff and a welcoming atmosphere. This gives them confidence that the service they are going to receive will be first class.

Respect for customers

Customers can be shown respect by staff members if they:

- are **courteous**
- listen and show an interest in what the customer has to say
- offer and provide help and assistance when needed.

Case study: High spirits or antisocial behaviour?

Dave works for the front of house team in a contract catering business. It is a Saturday and his team are working together on an event. They have another event at the same venue the next day, so accommodation has been provided for the whole team, including the kitchen team.

The front of house team has gone out to socialise and party until late after the end of their shift, whereas the kitchen team need to be up early the next day so have gone to bed early. The front of house team has returned in the early hours of the morning, just a couple of hours before the kitchen team needs to leave for work. They are very noisy and think it's funny to knock on the doors of other customers in the hotel, as well as the kitchen team, to wake them up.

1 Discuss what type of customer Dave would be classed as – well behaved, difficult, etc.?

2 State the problems for the hotel as a result of the front of house team's behaviour.

3 Identify the issues that this may create between the front of house and kitchen team.

▌▶ Communication skills

Communication skills are essential within the hospitality industry. Staff have to be able to communicate effectively with customers to provide the best possible experience and with staff to make sure the workplace operates effectively. There are two types of communication: verbal communication and non-verbal communication. You will need to be skilled in both types.

Verbal communication (speaking)

When speaking to customers or colleagues you need to use suitable language, and at the correct tone, pitch and pace. This makes sure that the message you are conveying is clear and understood by the receiver. You should avoid the use of **jargon** as this may be confusing. Repeating what the customer has said back to them is important, because it allows you to check that the message has been correctly conveyed and received. Remember that areas such as a busy bar, restaurant or kitchen will be noisy. You should therefore make sure that you can be heard without shouting, that you speak clearly to be understood and that you listen and can hear when others are speaking.

Key terms

Courteous – polite and respectful.

Jargon – words or expressions that are used by particular professions (e.g. chefs), which are not commonly used elsewhere and which may be difficult for others to understand.

Link

Go to Unit 7: Food and Beverage Service in the Hospitality Industry for more information about communication skills.

Non-verbal communication

Non-verbal communication skills include:

- listening
- body language
- writing skills.

Listening skills

It is important that you listen carefully to what the customer has said as it will help you to interpret their tone (and possibly their mood). You can then be sure that any questions you need to ask are relevant to what has been said. When the conversation is drawing to a close, you should repeat any important information back to them – this will show that you care and want to provide them with the best service possible. Look attentive – show that you are listening.

Body language

You need your body language to convey a positive message to colleagues and customers. The following things contribute to positive body language:

- posture – stand tall and do not slouch
- facial expression – smile and do not frown (see Figure 2.1)
- hand gestures – gesturing can show that you are animated and interested in what you are saying
- eye contact – keeping eye contact shows you are being attentive.

What is your first impression of the expressions shown in Figure 2.1?

Activity 2.4	Body language

Create a table with two columns. In one column, make a list of the ways in which you can portray positive body language. In the other column, list the things you should avoid doing as they show negative body language.

Writing skills

You need to think carefully about the way you communicate in writing. If the tone of your writing is abrupt, this can cause as much offence as the spoken word. You also need to make sure that you write clearly and legibly so that your message is understood and can be read easily. A member of waiting staff must write clearly when taking a customer's order so that the kitchen staff prepare the correct dishes.

Communication styles

There are several styles of communication and you need to be skilled in each one. You also need to understand when to use each style. Communication can be carried out in the following ways.

- **Face to face** – communication in person. This involves showing the right body language. Many employees within the hospitality industry do not have English as their first language and, therefore, face-to-face communication may be helpful. This is because it allows you to show a colleague what you mean, draw instructions or a diagram if needed, or get someone who speaks both languages to help you to convey the message.

Figure 2.1 You often convey how you feel through your face. Imagine you were a customer being served by this person – what do each of these expressions convey?

- **On the telephone** – when using the telephone in a working environment you need to be specific and accurate. You should remember to speak clearly, at the correct pace and speed, answer the phone according to company guidelines, record information given and repeat back the message to make sure you have correctly understood what has been said. When answering the phone at work you must write down:
  - the details of the caller – name, number, time and date
  - the details of when the call is to be returned
  - the details of the message left
  - the name of the person who is to respond.
- **In writing** – by email, fax, letter or memo. You need to choose which is the best method depending on the situation. You should make sure that you write legibly so that others can understand what you have written. Use accurate spelling and make sure that the layout you have used is clear and easy to follow.

Activity 2.5   How to communicate

You are working in the role of head chef. Make a copy of the table below and complete it to show examples of when you might need to communicate face to face, by telephone and in writing.

Communication type	Example
Face to face	
Telephone	
In writing	

Case study: Strained relations

John joined a three-star hotel about four months ago as a waiter in the hotel restaurant. His supervisor, Jenny, is always disappearing during service and is often found chatting on her phone during working hours. The relationship between the kitchen and restaurant staff is often very strained. Waiters place orders that are either inaccurate or are not required. The chef gets irritated by this and it causes orders to be delayed. Customers often complain and John has to try to deal with a lot of complaints, although he has not been trained to do so. Jenny blames the kitchen for the mistakes and often tells the customer the fault is with the kitchen team.

1 What are the main communication problems in this scenario?

2 What training do the staff need?

3 What should John do about Jenny's behaviour and her lack of customer care?

 Discussion

Discuss in a group the most suitable communication method to deal with the following scenarios.

- The vegetable supplier calls to explain they will not be able to deliver stock at 7 a.m. tomorrow. It will be delayed until 9 a.m.
- Rosie asks you to restock the bar with gin and vodka, which she has ordered from the cellar.
- The table reserved for Morgan this evening has increased by two **covers**.

Key term

Cover – a place setting at a table in a restaurant.

Once you have completed the skills audit you should be able to identify the skills that you need to develop. You can transfer these skills into an action plan like that shown in Figure 2.3. The action plan will help motivate and focus you on developing your skills. An example of the type of information you could include has been added.

Skills needed	Date by when skill is required	Activities to help achieve this skill	Date by when activity needs to be completed	Achieved/ Progress?
1 Ability to work confidently within a group	June 2014	• Take part in a themed event.	• January 2013	• Achieved January 2013
		• Get a part-time job.	• As soon as possible	• Ongoing
		• Complete work experience.	• March 2013	• Achieved March 2013
		• Actively take part in discussions within a group at college.	• Daily in class sessions	• Ongoing
2				
3				
4				

Figure 2.3 An example action plan

▶ The effect of good working skills on hospitality businesses

Introduction

This section will help you to gain an understanding of the effects that good working skills can have on hospitality businesses.

Imagine yourself in the following three roles and list the possible benefits for you and your staff if you can display good workplace skills.

- The business owner
- The customer
- The member of staff

Benefits to businesses

Businesses that employ staff who consistently demonstrate good working skills will be well on their way to providing good customer service. The benefits that you, your staff and your business will receive through good working skills are outlined in Table 2.3.

Key term

Repeat business – when a customer returns to a business.

Table 2.3 Benefits of good working skills to a business and staff members

Benefits to the business	Benefit to self/staff member
• Improved efficiency in the workplace leading to increased profits and customer satisfaction • An ability to meet deadlines and targets, both short term (e.g. an event that is run successfully) and long term (e.g. the growth of the business) • A good reputation among customers, suppliers and staff • Increased staff morale, leading to a positive working environment • Increased sales and therefore increased profits • **Repeat business**/custom and satisfied customers recommending your business to other people • Improved workplace relationships contributing to a positive working environment and potentially increased efficiency • Competitive advantage	• Improved productivity when you and other staff use good working skills to work more efficiently • Increases potential career progression – good working skills should guarantee promotion to more senior roles in the hospitality industry • Transferable skills – the working skills you perfect can be used in other roles, both within the hospitality industry and other areas of business

Benefits to the customer

Customers' experiences of a business and its services and products will also be enhanced. If they can trust in the reliability of your business and the products and services you offer, they are likely to keep coming back.

Activity 2.8   Upskilling

You are the newly appointed manager of a restaurant in a busy city centre. All of the staff currently employed were recruited by the previous manager and from what you can see you feel that their skills are not up to scratch. Next door there is refurbishment work going on and there are rumours that a popular chain of gastro pub is about to take over the premises and set up alongside you.

Consider the above scenario and answer the following questions.

1 What training and development should your team undertake?

2 How can you combat the competition from the gastro pub?

3 What are the benefits of acting immediately and developing the workplace skills of your staff?

A team that works well together will bring benefits to each other, the business and its customers.

▶ The consequences of poor working skills on hospitality businesses and staff

Introduction

This section will help you understand the effect poor working skills can have on hospitality businesses.

If you or your colleagues displayed consistently poor workplace skills, what do you think the consequences would be for you, the business and its customers?

The skills of staff working in hospitality businesses can be key to a business's overall success. Where staff skills are not up to standard, this can have many negative effects.

▶ Damage to reputation

A good reputation is essential for success within the hospitality industry. It is important to make sure that all staff are trained to prevent them damaging a business's reputation. Once damage has been caused, it is difficult to rebuild reputation and regain customer confidence.

▶ Reduced profit and custom

If waiting staff have ignored a customer or if their food is cold or unappetising, the customer is unlikely to return. If this happens regularly, it will lead to a drop in the business's profit and sales. The customer may also tell others about their experience, which could lead to further loss of business and damage to the business's reputation.

▶ Negative publicity

Customers who read negative reviews or hear bad things about a business are unlikely to want to visit it. You can probably think of TV programmes which focus on problematic hospitality businesses and the problems they have due to customer dissatisfaction. Review sites such as TripAdvisor provide both positive and negative feedback about hospitality businesses and these sites are increasingly used by customers to find recommended places to visit. Employees should always provide the best service possible to avoid creating negative publicity for themselves or the business.

Key term

Market share – the amount of trade a company has in comparison to the entire trade that is available to trade in.

▶ Competitor advantage

Competitor advantage is gained by companies who have the edge over all other businesses within the market, and are those businesses which hold the largest **market share**. Businesses with poorly trained staff and employees who have poor workplace skills are unlikely to gain competitor advantage.

▶ Staff dissatisfaction

Businesses whose staff have poor working skills may not be offering them a suitable training programme. Businesses whose staff are not motivated are unlikely to retain their employees and this may lead to high levels of staff turnover. Staff who are unhappy and unmotivated are also unlikely to care about the service they provide to customers. Morale and motivation are important factors when retaining staff and making sure they are happy.

Negative effects of poor working skills include the following:

- staff who give the wrong information to customers about the product or service
- staff who do not give their full attention to the customer and show unsuitable behaviour and body language, including looking disinterested
- staff over-promising and under-delivering products and services to customers, for example, a hotel receptionist who offers guests a seaview upgrade when it is not available
- staff describing a product incorrectly, for example, telling a customer that a product such as a bread and butter pudding is served with raspberries and cream when actually it is served with custard
- staff providing a poor-quality product, for example, a customer books a five-star hotel and when they arrive it only equates to a three-star standard, as the room and public areas are unclean
- poor portion size, for example, if a member of staff in a school/college canteen gives one person three scoops of fries and then the next person is only given one, customers will complain or feel undervalued if they are not treated the same
- poor value for money – when customers feel that a product or service does not reflect good value for money they may complain or not return. This can cause dissatisfied customers, loss of profit and sales, and damage to the overall reputation of the business
- poor timing in the delivery or service provided – if a customer orders a ham salad roll in an empty café and has to wait for half an hour, they are unlikely to return. Some customers may not be able to wait this long to be served, for example, if they are on their lunch break
- faulty products, for example, if a customer hires a self-catering cottage for a short break and the oven is broken, they will not be happy that they cannot cater for themselves.

Would you feel cheated if you received the bottom portion?

Activity 2.9 | Training staff

Carla's Cupcakes is a new business employing two members of staff. Carla is working on a tight budget and as a new business owner she is nervous about investing in training for her staff.

1 Discuss how Carla could benefit if she did supply her staff with training.

2 What consequences might there be for her business if her staff are not given adequate training?

3 Suggest some ways that Carla could safeguard her investment in training if she does choose to train the two employees.

▶ Providing consistent and reliable service through procedures

Introduction

Economically, we are experiencing tough times and, to stay afloat, it is vital that all hospitality businesses, large and small, provide a consistent and reliable service for their customers. Businesses that do this are likely to have a good reputation, loyal customers and increased sales and profit. Having business guidelines and a set of rules to work with will help staff to offer a consistent and reliable service.

Name an example of a business that you regularly visit because they offer consistent and reliable service. Discuss these businesses with your whole group.

▶ Ways that businesses can provide consistent and reliable service

Providing consistent and reliable service is key to the success of any hospitality business and to providing customer satisfaction. This means making sure guests receive the same, if not improved, service every time they visit. We will look at how consistency and reliability can be achieved.

Monitoring customer service

Link

Go to Unit 7, Learning aim B, Topic B.2 for more information about monitoring customer service.

Hospitality businesses can monitor the service they provide by getting feedback from both staff and customers. This can be obtained through customer surveys and questionnaires, as well as during staff meetings. Acting on feedback is crucial, and it may show that staff training is needed. The financial cost of training staff may be less expensive than the loss of customers in the long term.

Activity 2.10   Monitoring customer feedback

Collect three different examples of businesses attempting to monitor customer feedback. Analyse the methods and identify similarities and differences between them.

Staff are a good source of customer feedback. Do you ask customers if they are happy with the service they are receiving?

Following policies and procedures

All hospitality businesses will have policies and procedures for staff to follow. Staff will be informed of these during an induction and possibly by a staff handbook and noticeboards in staff canteens. Examples of policies may include a customer service policy, lost property procedures and uniform standards. Larger hospitality businesses may have policies and procedures set by head office, which are then put in place in a number of businesses across their chain or brand. Some policies, such as a policy for **risk assessment** and a policy for health and safety, are written to put in place practical actions that are required as part of the law.

Meeting legal regulatory requirements and having ethical standards

Hospitality businesses must comply with **legislation** and **regulations** to stay within the law. Some of the legislation and regulations are shown in Figure 2.4.

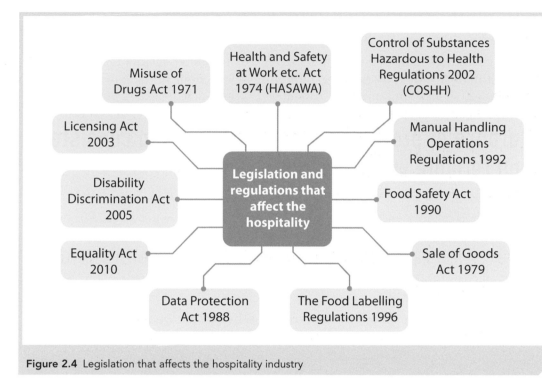

Figure 2.4 Legislation that affects the hospitality industry

We will look at some of these Acts in a little more detail in the next section.

Take it further

Carry out research into:
- The Food Labelling Regulations 1996
- the Licensing Act 2003
- the Manual Handling Operations Regulations 1992.

List at least four points for each Act or piece of legislation that affect the way you carry out a role in the hospitality industry.

As well their legal obligation to comply with laws and regulations, businesses also need to think about whether they will have a policy that discusses their **ethics** and ethical standards. How will their business and its goods/services impact on society, the economy and the environment? Owners and employees should aim to work with each other, their customers and suppliers in a fair, honest, equal and respectful way.

Ensuring procedures are followed

It is essential that all staff are familiar with policies and procedures so that they can follow and carry them out.

Key terms

Risk assessment – a proactive review of what can cause harm and what can be done to control or prevent hazards.

Legislation – a set of laws.

Regulation – a rule made by an authority.

Ethics – the moral principles that should underpin decision-making. Business ethics can provide moral guidelines for how business affairs are conducted.

Link

Go to Unit 3, Learning aim B, Topics B.1 and B.2 to find more in-depth information about the laws and regulations that affect the hospitality industry.

Link

Go to Unit 5, Learning aim A, Topic A.4 to find more in-depth information about ethics and ethical considerations.

Staff will need to know when they should:

- refer to someone in authority, for example, a supervisor or the owner of the business if a customer has a complaint or query they cannot deal with
- ask for help and assistance with questions that they cannot answer, for example, if a member of staff has missed the briefing for a new product or menu item, they should ask a colleague, so that they can give the customer accurate information
- treat all customers fairly and equally, for example, if a waiter accidentally spills wine on a customer, it should be policy to offer to dry-clean their clothing – and this should apply to all customers.

▶ Purpose of procedures that contribute to consistent and reliable working skills

Businesses put in place policies and procedures to make sure their staff work consistently and reliably, and that the best standard of service is provided. Business policies and procedures help to make sure that:

- staff comply with the standard of service required by the business – this is important so that all customers receive the same standard of service and to maintain the reputation of the business
- the **mission** statement set out by the business is being followed – a mission statement is set to guide a business to where it wants to be
- any external targets have been met – for example, some businesses set a time limit on food being served after it is ordered, and if the food is not served within the set time the customer will get their money back and eat for free.

Activity 2.11	Consistent and reliable customer service

Visit a local hospitality business to interview a member of staff to find out what policies and procedures they have to follow to provide consistent and reliable customer service.

Working in a busy cafeteria can be stressful and you may feel like cutting corners when it comes to following policies. Why is it important to follow them at all times?

Complying with legislative and regulatory service requirements in the hospitality industry

Introduction

This section covers **compliance** with legislation and regulations that apply to the hospitality industry. You will gain knowledge of how to comply with sales of goods, health and safety, data protection and equal opportunities. You will also explore why it is important to comply with the law and the possible consequences of **non-compliance**.

Meeting all legal and regulatory requirements

You have already learned that the hospitality industry is governed by many laws and regulations. Therefore, it is essential that all staff are trained in how to understand and carry out the requirements.

Sale of Goods Act 1979

This law states that the prices of products and services, as well as the alcoholic content of beverages, must be displayed. To do this, a menu or bar list should be available to customers to view before ordering. Staff must make sure they have a good knowledge of pricing and alcoholic content in order to give accurate information to the customer.

Health and Safety at Work etc. Act 1974 (HASAWA)

This Act states that employees have a responsibility to:

- ensure the health and safety of themselves and others
- maintain a safe system of work and to work safely
- cooperate with their employers and follow instructions
- not tamper with anything provided in the interest of health, safety and welfare.

Employees must be aware that they could be responsible if their actions result in injury or **accident**. For example, if a chef spills the contents of a saucepan and does not clean it up, and it results in another member of the kitchen team slipping, the chef could be to blame because they have not taken the correct precautions to prevent this from happening. That is, they have not made sure of the health, safety and welfare of others as required by the law under HASAWA.

There are lots of rules about health and safety in the workplace and they are there to protect both staff and customers. It is essential that any new employees receive training before starting work so that they are aware of, and can work within, the rules of health and safety in the workplace.

Key terms

Compliance – acting in a way that follows a set of rules, policies or standards.

Non-compliance – where rules are in place but they are not followed.

Accident – an unplanned event that may include injury or property damage.

What might happen if this spillage is not cleaned up?

Discussion

Give three examples where health and safety policy could be breached by employees in a restaurant.

Discussion

Describe three scenarios that would reflect a breach of data protection policy in a hotel.

Key term

Disciplinary – when an employer raises concern about the conduct, work standards or absence record of an employee.

Take it further

Suggest other prejudices that people might have that would be covered by the Equality Act 2010. You might find it helpful to visit the government website for the Act. You can access this website by going to www.pearsonhotlinks.co.uk and searching for this title.

Data Protection Act 1998

This Act is in place to protect any of the information that customers share with, or give to, a business. Businesses have a responsibility to make sure that personal information is not distributed. Employers should also make sure that computers are password-protected and that employees follow correct procedures when handling data of any kind. Staff who fail to keep information secure could be subject to **disciplinary** and/or legal action. An example of a breach would be a waitress giving the telephone number of a guest to another customer.

Equality Act 2010

The Equality Act 2010 dictates fairness and equality. This not only protects staff but customers too. Staff cannot let their own thoughts and feelings affect their role at work and they must make sure that all customers and colleagues are treated equally. For example, a business cannot refuse to employ a person because they are deemed to be 'too old'.

| Assessment activity 2.1 | *English* | 2A.P1 | 2A.P2 | 2A.M1 | 2A.M2 | 2A.D1 |

You work as part of an events management team. Lately, the staff seem to have been rather slack and the team is not working well together. They also seem to be oblivious to some of the policies and procedures they should be following. You are worried that this could lead to an accident or customer complaints. You have approached your boss about this and she has asked you to carry out some training with the staff. As part of this, your boss would like you to research two contrasting hospitality businesses. Using these businesses as examples, produce a training booklet that includes the following information.

1 The occupational and personal skills needed to work effectively in the hospitality industry and why it is important to have effective working skills – for the business, their customers and the individual members of staff themselves. You should explain the benefits for the business, its customers and staff of having appropriate working skills.

2 A section to identify and describe business procedures, legislation and regulatory requirements that contribute to consistent and reliable service provision. You need to explain how business and professional policies and procedures, and legislation and regulatory requirements, contribute to consistent and reliable service provision within the industry.

3 A section to explain in more detail the impact of following policies and procedures, and legislative and regulatory requirements on a business.

4 A section to evaluate the consequences of poor working skills on a hospitality business and the effect of this on both staff and customers.

Tips

- Speak to staff working in different hospitality businesses to learn what occupational and personal skills are required for work in their business and to find out what procedures, legislation and regulations their business complies with.
- Give real examples from industry experience, case studies, interview transcripts or handbooks acquired from real hospitality businesses.
- Use real articles and real news stories, or industry examples of the consequences of poor workings skills.

▶ Creating a positive first impression with customers

Introduction

It is important to create a positive first impression when you are dealing with customers. This section looks at how you can do just that.

Imagine walking into a restaurant to find the chef slumped on a stool at the bar with a glass of alcohol in his hand and chewing gum in his mouth. His chef's whites are an off-grey colour and his trousers are ripped at the bottom. There is a strong smell of body odour. Would you stay or would you go?

▶ Personal presentation

Most businesses, and this includes businesses within the hospitality industry, require staff to wear a uniform. Uniforms may differ according to the job role but the purpose is to:

- make sure all staff are smart and dressed to the same high standard
- make all staff easily identifiable to customers
- protect staff from potential harm, for example, in a kitchen environment if a heavy pan was dropped on a staff member's foot it might cause injury (this could be prevented by wearing suitable footwear and steel toecaps)
- promote a positive impression of the staff member and the business in which they are working.

Staff must also have a high standard of personal hygiene, including a fresh appearance; washing or showering daily; preventing any bad body odours; having clean, well-manicured hands with short, neat nails; and covering any cuts or wounds with a suitable waterproof dressing.

Link

Go to Unit 7, Learning aim A, Topic A.1 for more information about personal presentation.

Discussion

In groups, discuss how you would form an impression of a staff member working in the hospitality industry. What things would you focus on?

Activity 2.12   A good impression?

Visit two different hospitality businesses and decide if the impression given by staff meets the standards you would require if you were managing the team. Make notes and discuss your observations with the rest of your class.

Personal appearance

Staff in the hospitality industry need to pay close attention to their personal appearance. Here are some tips that you should bear in mind.

✓ Your uniform should be clean, ironed and in good repair.

✓ Your hair should be clean, neat and tidy. Male workers should be clean shaven.

✓ Make-up should be minimal, neat and tidy.

✓ Nails should be clean and cut short – nail varnish should not be worn.

✓ Teeth should be brushed and breath should be fresh.

✓ Your appearance should be fresh – you should shower and wash daily.

✓ Cuts and wounds should be covered with a clean and waterproof dressing.

✓ Staff should smile, show the right body language and posture, and have an overall happy manner and positive attitude when working.

✗ The amount of jewellery you can wear will depend on business rules and your job role. Generally the rule is that no piercings are allowed and only a wedding band should be worn.

✗ Perfume or aftershave is almost certainly prohibited in the kitchen area but in areas such as reception, minimal and not overpowering scents may be acceptable. Again, you should check the business policy.

✗ Chewing gum should be avoided at all times as it creates a poor impression. It can be noisy and sometimes means staff come across as disinterested.

Employers who set uniform standards should supply the staff members with enough sets of uniforms to last a working week. In some cases, the employer will often pay for the laundry of staff uniforms, making sure that they are clean, tidy and in good repair.

Activity 2.13   Staff uniforms

Visit three different hospitality businesses and find out who is responsible for the purchase, upkeep and laundry of staff uniforms. Present your findings in the form of a table.

During the visits, note down whether the staff you spoke to gave you a positive or negative impression.

Professional behaviour

Showing professional behaviour at all times will help you to give a professional image and create a positive impression. To do this, you should:

✓ take pride in your personal appearance and make sure you are always well presented, clean and tidy

✓ always present the right attitude, manner and level of maturity

✓ take pride in your work and the tasks you undertake

✓ be punctual and attend work as required

✓ work efficiently using effective teamwork and communication skills

✓ be helpful and supportive

✓ maintain your work area.

▶ Working effectively with customers and colleagues

Introduction

In any hospitality business it is important that you can work effectively with both customers and colleagues. You also need to be able to work as part of a team and to understand the consequences of poor teamwork. You are going to develop your knowledge of the different customer types, including both internal and external ones, and identify reasons why you need to work effectively with them.

Choose one hospitality business and list all the different customers you might have to deal with if you were working there. Try to describe how you and your colleagues should behave while you are in the work environment.

▶ Customer types

Customers can be internal and external.

Internal customers

Internal customers are people who work within a business, for example, team members, supervisors and managers. They are also people who carry out tasks which help the business to operate. An example of this would be a local food producer delivering food items to a hotel or a supplier delivering brochures to a travel agency.

External customers

External customers are people outside a hospitality business, including:

- **existing customers** – customers that a business already has
- **new customers** – people who are new to a business who have not been before
- **individuals** – people who choose to visit on their own
- **groups** – large or small, restaurants often attract groups of people for family or birthday celebrations
- **business people** – people who use a hospitality business while they are on business (an example of this would be a business person staying Monday to Thursday in a hotel while on business in the area for a week)
- **non-English speaking customers** – customers who are unable to speak English (could be visitors from abroad to a British seaside guest house or a foreign visitor at the airport)
- **people of different ages** – functions such as wedding celebrations at a hotel will often include a range of different people, particularly those of different ages

- **people from different cultures** – many restaurants and hospitality businesses will attract customers from different cultures
- **people of different gender** – both men and women will use hospitality businesses and services. Certain hospitality offers will be targeted towards men and others towards women. Examples include stag and hen party offers at nightclubs and bars.

Customers with special needs

There are many customers who may have specific needs or need assistance. These include the following.

- **Customers who may have a disability** – this could be a sight or hearing impairment or a physical disability, for example, a wheelchair user.
- **Customers with dietary needs or specific preferences** – this could be a person who requires halal meat or is a vegetarian or has a lactose **intolerance**.
- **Customers with small children or babies** – customers with small children and/or babies may need extra help, for example, you could offer to carry a tray for them in the restaurant or open doors if they have a pushchair. Restaurant staff need to make sure highchairs are readily available and, possibly, activities or toys for the children to play with while waiting for their food order.
- **Customers with learning difficulties** – these customers may need extra help as they may not understand menu items and could have difficulty ordering.

Businesses should make sure that staff are trained to deal with different customer needs so that they provide the best possible service for all customers.

How could the restaurant help this customer with her child?

| Activity 2.14 | Internal and external customers |

List examples of internal customers to the following businesses:

- a local fast food business
- a school or college canteen.

List the different types of external customers for:

- one branded restaurant
- one hotel.

Working effectively within a team of colleagues

Working effectively within your team is essential to the success of a hospitality business. The teams you are expected to work in will vary in size depending on where you work and the type of business. Teams that have good team members will be made up of people who:

- have a positive approach and attitude
- accept instructions and complete tasks willingly
- work and cooperate with one another
- offer help and assistance to others
- respect and understand one another
- show fairness across a team and consideration of others.

Remember

Teams that display effective teamworking and communication skills are likely to be more productive than those who do not.

You have been working at the Bear Hotel for three years. Last night was the staff Christmas party and as a result four of the housekeeping team have phoned in sick. The hotel was full last night and all 50 rooms need cleaning. There were 35 departures and 15 stayovers. Of the 35 departures, 25 of the rooms are booked by new customers arriving this evening. You have just two housekeeping staff to complete the tasks required.

Discuss how the remaining staff can work together to clean the rooms and ensure customer satisfaction.

Then, think about times when you have worked as a team. What went well? How could you have improved the efficiency of the team?

Key terms

Intolerance – when a person's body reacts badly to certain foods, causing them to become unwell.

Allergy – when a person has an allergic reaction to a food item. The reaction can sometimes be life-threatening.

▶ Communicating effectively

Not all jobs in hospitality are customer facing but it is important to remember that, even if you are not in direct contact with customers, you are still involved with them. For some staff this may be the only chance they have to create an impression.

For example, chefs often stay in the kitchen. However, if the presentation of a meal is substandard, if the portion size is small, if the food is cold and the quality is poor, the customer will leave with the impression that the chef does not care enough to make and present an attractive, good-quality product. Of course, there are times when it may be necessary for a member of the kitchen team to talk to a customer. An example of this would be when a customer with a particular **allergy** or concern about a menu item asks for a list of the ingredients or when a customer has a complaint to make about the food. All staff, whether working in the restaurant or kitchen, should know the ingredients of menu items, and the methods of preparation, cooking and serving. They should also have an awareness of the customer service policy in order to put it into practice.

All staff dealing with customer complaints must make sure they:

- show empathy – they should sympathise with the situation
- clearly explain things to the customer and avoid using jargon
- apologise where necessary
- ask for the customer's opinion and agree on a solution with them.

Can you think of any scenarios in which a member of the housekeeping team in a hotel would need to use these skills?

Activity 2.15   Customer types

Choose one local hospitality business and list all of the types of customer who visit it. Are all of these customers the same or might there be times when you need to communicate with some differently? Make a poster of the different communication styles you might need to use.

▶ Improving performance

Let's look at some ways of improving business performance.

- **Reflect on problems** – if you understand typical problems and the reasons why they happen you can put procedures in place to prevent them in the future. For example, if customers are queuing for too long at the food counter, increase the number of serving staff. By listening to customer feedback, it shows that you are prepared to update and improve procedures in your business.

- **Maintain standards** – it is important to keep up standards to make sure that all customers receive a consistent and reliable service but you should also aim to improve those standards.

- **Identify areas for improvement** – this can be done by either customers or staff. It is important to look at all feedback, whatever its source, and try to improve the overall experience of both customers and staff.

Assessment activity 2.2	*English*	2B.P3	2B.P4	2B.P5	2B.M3	2B.D2

Your boss at the events management team was very impressed with the booklet you produced for the rest of the staff. Your boss would now like you to develop the training by focusing on teamworking skills. Create a presentation to give the staff that explains which teamworking skills are used in the hospitality industry and why they are important. Include the benefits for the customer, the employer and the staff themselves.

Now she would like you to carry out some hands-on practical training with the staff that will help them to practise their working skills. Your boss has given you two case studies to role play for the staff. The case studies are based on the following two scenarios.

1 Preparing a meeting room where light refreshments will be served.

2 Dealing with a customer who has made a complaint at a hotel reception.

In the role plays you will need to:

- demonstrate working skills in the two different hospitality situations

- identify examples of teamworking skills and explain which teamworking skills are used in the hospitality industry and why they are important in the workplace

- demonstrate use of effective non-verbal and verbal communication skills when working in a team in both situations

- apply communication and teamworking skills to address the work-related problems.

Your boss would like you to prepare for the staff a plan for dealing with the problem followed by an evaluation of your own performance in the role play to assess how well situations were dealt with, any lessons that were learned and areas for improvement.

Tips

- Speak to staff in different hospitality businesses to learn about times when they use teamworking skills, verbal and non-verbal communication skills and when they use different workplace skills.

- Use this information to put together your role-play scenarios.

WorkSpace

▶ Johann Kingh

Staff member in a hotel concierge and reception team

I have enjoyed staying in hotels since I was a child. I went on many trips to foreign hotels with my mum and dad while my dad was on business. My mum and I often stayed at hotels for several days and I loved the atmosphere and environment. But the thing I always remembered was how good the staff were and how they always made a fuss of me and greeted me with a smile. When I left school and started thinking about what I could do next, I remembered how good these staff had made me feel and thought that I would like to return the favour to others. I signed up for a BTEC Level 2 in Hospitality course at my local college. Once I had completed it, I knew I needed to stay on and complete my Level 3 qualification, which I did. During both courses, I was lucky enough to complete work experience in two hotels and was excited by how much I had enjoyed dealing with people at work and customers in the customer service environment.

After completing my Level 3 qualification, I returned to my work placement provider and was lucky to find there was a vacancy within the concierge team. I thrive on providing excellent customer service and I'm extremely passionate about my work. I believe this is down to having such a good team and excellent communication between reception and reservations staff. Eventually, I hope to work in London in either the Dorchester or the Ritz hotel – I'm just not sure how to make this dream a reality.

Think about it!

1 Provide Johann with some guidance on how he may get to work at a prestigious hotel in London.

2 Suggest ways Johann can develop his skills and better his career prospects.

3 Identify how Johann could find out about vacancies and the application process at both the Ritz and the Dorchester.

4 Do you think that Johann would benefit from undertaking any further courses or training in order to get to his dream job and venue?

Introduction

An understanding of food safety and health and safety is essential when working in the hospitality industry. It is vital that businesses comply with food safety and health and safety legislation, as this keeps staff and customers safe. In this unit, you will learn about the importance of following and maintaining food safety procedures. You will also build your knowledge of the procedures for storing, preparing, cooking and serving food and will explore how food safety hazards can be prevented.

All hospitality businesses, both large and small, have to follow legislation that is designed to protect staff and customers by preventing hazards that could cause injury or ill health. You will learn how businesses comply with and enforce legislation, as well as learn about the different health and safety signs and relevant documentation that hospitality businesses must use.

Assessment: You will be assessed by a series of assignments set by your teacher/tutor.

Learning aims

In this unit you will:

A understand food safety when dealing with food in the hospitality industry

B understand safety legislation and regulations that control safe working practices in the hospitality industry.

> When I started this unit, I was surprised by how many things I needed to think about. I learned how important it is to follow safe practices as these keep both customers and the people you work with safe.
>
> I would like to open my own cake business and this unit has really helped me to understand the importance of following and maintaining food safety and health and safety practices.
>
> Jamelia, *BTEC Level 2 First in Hospitality student*

Food Safety and Health and Safety in Hospitality

3

BTEC
Assessment Zone

This table shows what you must do in order to achieve a **Pass**, **Merit** or **Distinction** grade, and where you can find activities to help you.

Assessment criteria			
Level 1	**Level 2 Pass**	**Level 2 Merit**	**Level 2 Distinction**
Learning aim A: Understand food safety when dealing with food in the hospitality industry			
1A.1 Identify procedures to maintain food safety when storing, preparing, cooking and serving food.	**2A.P1** Describe, using examples, procedures to maintain food safety when storing, preparing, cooking and serving food. **See Assessment activity 3.1, page 92**	**2A.M1** Explain, using examples, the importance of following appropriate procedures to maintain food safety when storing, preparing, cooking and serving food. **See Assessment activity 3.1, page 92**	**2A.D1** Analyse the benefits and potential consequences to hospitality businesses of complying with appropriate procedures for food safety when storing, preparing, cooking and serving food. **See Assessment activity 3.1, page 92**
1A.2 Identify potential food safety hazards in hospitality businesses when storing, preparing, cooking and serving food.	**2A.P2** Describe, using examples, potential food safety hazards in hospitality businesses when storing, preparing, cooking and serving food. **See Assessment activity 3.1, page 92**		
1A.3 Identify controls for potential food safety hazards in hospitality businesses when storing, preparing, cooking and serving food.	**2A.P3** Describe, using examples, controls and monitoring procedures for eliminating potential food safety hazards in hospitality businesses when storing, preparing, cooking and serving food. **See Assessment activity 3.1, page 92**		
Learning aim B: Understand safety legislation and regulations that control safe working practices in the hospitality industry			
1B.4 Give examples of legislation and regulations that require safe working practices to control risks in hospitality businesses.	**2B.P4** English Describe, using examples, how hospitality businesses enforce safe working practices to control risks to staff and customers. **See Assessment activity 3.2, page 100**	**2B.M2** English Explain how compliance with legislation and regulations is used to control risks to staff and customers, and its benefits to businesses. **See Assessment activity 3.2, page 100**	**2B.D2** English Evaluate how legislation, safety information and working practices are implemented in and benefit hospitality businesses. **See Assessment activity 3.2, page 100**
1B.5 Identify safety signs, information and documentation used in businesses within the hospitality industry.	**2B.P5** Describe, using examples, how safety signs, information and documentation should be used in two contrasting businesses within the hospitality industry. **See Assessment activity 3.2, page 100**	**2B.M3** Explain how safety signs, information and documentation improve safety in two contrasting businesses within the hospitality industry. **See Assessment activity 3.2, page 100**	

English   Opportunity to practise English skills

How you will be assessed

This unit will be assessed by a series of internally assessed tasks. These tasks will be set by your teacher/tutor. You will need to show that you have gained an understanding of food safety. You will need to demonstrate that you understand the importance of monitoring food safety when storing, preparing, cooking and serving food. In addition, you will need to show an understanding of the legislation and regulations that control safe working practices to prevent hazards.

Your assessment could be in the form of:

- written work, e.g. an induction booklet for new staff or training materials
- information leaflets, posters, booklets
- case studies of real businesses
- interviews/questionnaires completed by people working in the industry.

▶ Procedures to maintain food safety

> ### Introduction
>
> Within a hospitality business, all staff must be aware of, and comply with, food safety and health and safety procedures.
>
> Think about the tasks a chef has to complete during their working day. In pairs, discuss and prepare a list of these tasks. Put an 'S' next to all the tasks where you think the chef needs to consider food safety. Share your list with the rest of your class and discuss your findings as a group.

Hospitality businesses must be able to show what they do to make or sell food that is safe to eat. To do this, businesses have in place food safety procedures and policies.

▶ Food safety requirements and regulations

Food safety is essential to make sure that the food served to customers is safe to eat. **Legislation** and **regulations** exist to make sure this happens across all hospitality businesses. These laws and regulations cover all of the steps in food-related activities, including delivery, storage, preparation, cooking and serving.

All businesses within the hospitality and catering industry are required to produce and put in place **policies** and **procedures** to see that legislation and regulations are properly enforced. They state how they will make sure standards are set, monitored and maintained; they must also state how and when training will be given to all staff.

Food safety legislation often includes key requirements that businesses must **implement** to ensure effective **compliance** with the legislation. These requirements include the following.

- All staff must receive relevant, regular and accurate food safety and health and safety training. Records of any training must be kept.
- All staff must practise and demonstrate a high standard of personal safety and hygiene. This includes regular and appropriate hand washing, for instance, between dealing with raw and cooked foods as well as after going to the toilet, and using oven gloves when picking up hot pans.
- Staff must comply with legislation and regulations governing the organisation.
- Staff must follow and comply with organisational policies written to meet legislation.
- All records required by legislation are made, monitored and maintained. The types of records that should be kept include temperature records, cleaning records, records showing that the business uses reputable suppliers and maintenance records including a pest control contract.

Local authorities are responsible for making sure legislation and regulations are enforced. To do this, businesses can be inspected by environmental health officers every six months, or more often if required. These inspections look at all aspects of health and safety and food safety to make sure standards are being met. Businesses can be inspected more often if they have previously given, or still give, some area of concern to the environmental health officer or if a complaint has been made by a member of the public. In this case, an officer must visit the premises even if the business has been seen recently. During a visit the environmental health officer looks at several things, including:

- food samples
- food safety records and documentation
- safe food storage
- the cleanliness of the kitchen and dining area.

Table 3.1 gives some examples of good practice and poor practice when working with food safety standards.

Table 3.1 Examples of good practice and poor practice in food safety standards

Good practice		Poor practice or unhygienic standards	
Regular washing of hands	✔	Not washing hands after handling raw meat	✗
Cleaning as you go	✔	Leaving spoilt food to attract pests	✗
Wearing correct uniform (see Figure 3.1)	✔	Wearing dirty uniform	✗
Using oven gloves when moving hot pans	✔	Using a tea towel or cloth instead of proper oven gloves	✗
Following correct lifting procedure	✔	Not taking proper care when working at height	✗

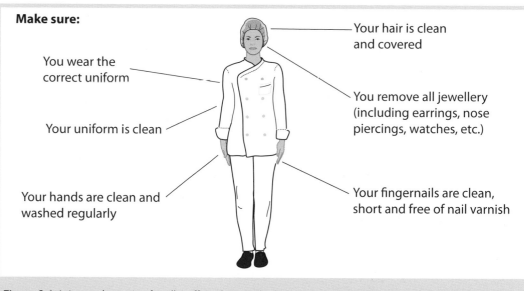

Make sure:

You wear the correct uniform

Your uniform is clean

Your hands are clean and washed regularly

Your hair is clean and covered

You remove all jewellery (including earrings, nose piercings, watches, etc.)

Your fingernails are clean, short and free of nail varnish

Figure 3.1 It is good practice for all staff working in the hospitality industry to carry out correct personal hygiene and consider food safety when preparing for work.

▶ Systems for controlling/monitoring food safety

There are many systems of monitoring that take place within a hospitality business to ensure food safety. Monitoring is essential, for example, in kitchens. Systems in place for monitoring in kitchens include:

- the head chef monitoring and recording items produced by others to make sure they meet acceptable standards and quality
- temperature logs of equipment, such as fridges and freezers

Take it further

Research PAT testing and make a list of the typical equipment you would find in a professional kitchen that would need to be PAT tested. Visit the Health and Safety Executive (HSE) website to get you started. You can access this website by going to www.pearsonhotlinks.co.uk and searching for this title.

Key terms

Hazard – something that could be dangerous.

Eliminated – completely removed or destroyed.

Systematic – to do something methodically, according to a fixed plan or system.

Hazard Analysis and Critical Control Point (HACCP) – a system used by food businesses to look at how they handle food, to help them put in place procedures to prevent food safety hazards and to make sure the food they produce is safe to eat.

- cleaning schedules and completed cleaning documentation
- maintenance records and requests, e.g. records to show that the ventilation system has been cleaned
- records relating to health and safety equipment, e.g. records to show that fire safety equipment has been checked and that PAT testing of small, portable electrical appliances has been carried out
- contractor agreements, e.g. there may be a cleaning/maintenance contract for large pieces of equipment or extraction systems
- documentation to show that deliveries have been checked
- stock rotation practices
- food waste records
- photographic specifications to make sure that presentation is standardised across all businesses (often used in large chain companies).

The process of monitoring makes sure that food safety **hazards** are reduced or **eliminated** before they become an issue. Regular checking, reviewing and monitoring will make sure that problems are highlighted early and effective controls are implemented.

HACCP monitoring

Hospitality businesses are required to have a **systematic** preventative approach to food safety and to safeguard against potential hazards. Businesses use the principles of **Hazard Analysis and Critical Control Points (HACCP)** to do this. HACCP is a system that helps businesses develop procedures for food safety management.

HACCP puts in place procedures to control hazards. These reduce the risk of food safety hazards by noting areas where food safety may be problematic. HACCP requires businesses to:

- look at what their business does and what could go wrong at all steps in food-related activities – where there are potential hazards
- decide the areas they need to focus on to prevent hazards or reduce them to a level that is acceptable – where hazards can be controlled
- decide any critical control points (CCPs) – these are the essential points where the hazard must be controlled (for example, the most common CCP is cooking)
- the maximum or minimum limits at which the hazard must be controlled (these limits vary depending on the hazard)
- put in place procedures to control the hazards – to eliminate the hazard or reduce it to a safe level
- decide what to do if something does go wrong
- monitor procedures and keep records to show procedures are being carried out and are working.

In a restaurant, the HACCP process might examine each step or stage in the production of a meal. Table 3.2 shows the steps in food production, from the initial delivery stage of ingredients through to the sale of the finished product. You will see that each step is examined, potential hazards or risks highlighted and some measures outlined to eliminate or reduce these risks.

Table 3.2 The steps in an HACCP plan covering food production

HACCP step	What should be covered in the plan?
Delivery	Checks to make sure the quality of the product is correct, to look for any defects with packaging and to make sure the temperature of the product on delivery is correct.
Storage	The temperature different products should be stored at, the location of the storage and what materials should be stored where.
Preparation	How, where and when the food will be prepared.
Cooking	The time between preparing food and cooking it, the method of cooking, cooking time and the temperature at which food is cooked.
Hot-holding after cooking	The length of time food can be held, e.g. in a buffet, and the temperature at which it should be held (hot food should be held at 63°C or above).
Cooling after cooking	The length of time food should cool for, the correct temperature during the cooling process, the method of cooling to be used and storage after cooling.
Reheating	That the food item must only be reheated once. Items that are reheated must be reheated thoroughly and reach a minimum temperature of 75°C for two minutes.
Chilled storage	The **FIFO** approach of labelling food with the correct date to make sure food stocks are held for a minimum time. The labelling of foods is key to effective food storage.
Serving	Methods of food service need to be considered in advance. Foods to be served cold should be stored in the fridge for as long as possible to avoid them becoming too warm and to avoid the risk of **contamination**. Hot foods should be served quickly to stop the food cooling down.

You can find out more about HACCP by visiting the Food Standards Agency website. You can visit this website by going to www.pearsonhotlinks.co.uk and searching for this title.

▶ Storage of food

Storing food items correctly makes sure that they remain safe to eat. There are several methods that can be used to store food. We use these methods to reduce **bacterial growth** on the food, to prevent contamination and to reduce the rate at which food **spoilage** occurs. In addition, storing food correctly will remove possible risks of **infestation**.

Cross-contamination

Cross-contamination is when bacteria from one food item are transferred to another. It can be direct or indirect. Direct cross-contamination happens when there is contact between raw and cooked food, for example, during preparation or when the foods are stored. Indirect cross-contamination can happen when bacteria are transferred from hands or equipment onto a food item. For example, cross-contamination could happen when a member of staff who has handled raw bacon for a breakfast meal takes cooked toast from the toaster and serves it to a customer without washing their hands in between the two tasks.

Key terms

Bacterial growth – growth of germs. Some bacteria are harmful and can cause food poisoning. Bacteria need food, time, temperature (between 5–63°C) and moisture to grow.

FIFO – 'first in, first out'.

Contamination – in food, any substance that has the potential to cause the customer harm or illness.

Spoilage – food that is no longer safe to eat. It will look, smell, feel and/or taste wrong.

Infestation – the presence of pests in a food premises, particularly in large numbers, or when difficult to remove.

Cross-contamination – can occur when bacteria that may cause disease are transferred to food, for example, from hands, kitchen equipment or from other foodstuffs (e.g. blood dripping from raw meat onto a trifle that has been stored below it in the refrigerator).

Activity 3.1   Dealing with food hazard problems

Make a copy of the table below. Identify five potential problems that you may come across in a food premises and list them in the table. Complete the table by explaining in the 'Possible action' column how you could reduce the problem. An example of a problem and possible actions has been provided to help you get started. Make sure you fully explain each action. Then, discuss your ideas as a whole group.

Problem	Possible action
Example: A member of staff spots a rat outside, near the bin area.	*Example:* • The staff member should report what they have seen to the manager or supervisor as soon as possible. • Pest control should be contacted and called out for an immediate visit. • All staff should look for signs of infestation, both inside and outside the building. • All staff should ensure usual high standards of practice in all aspects of food safety. • If the problem is related to un-emptied bins of waste being held on the premises for too long, a waste disposal company should be contacted to empty them. • Staff should make sure that all waste is stored securely, in containers with secure fitting lids, to avoid further infestation.

Infestation

Infestation by pests is a common problem that environmental health officers have to deal with.

Common food pests include:
• rodents, such as rats and mice
• insects, including flies, ants and cockroaches
• insects that infest stored products such as flour and grain
• birds.

Signs that there is a pest infestation include:
• footprints, smears and marks
• sightings
• droppings, egg cases, skin and webs
• holes in food and in packaging
• disturbed equipment or food items, damage to skirting boards.

Common food pests: insects and rodents

Food handlers are responsible for reporting signs of a pest problem to their supervisor immediately. This is essential as uncontrolled pest infestations may lead to:

- contamination of food items and spread of harmful bacteria
- damage to stock and premises
- food waste
- customer complaints and business loss.

A pest problem can also lead to fines, prosecution and business closure if identified by Environmental Health.

▶ Storage methods

The hospitality industry relies on food being stored safely. Businesses cannot always know exactly how much food will be needed, but they rely on not wasting stock as this costs them money. Uneaten food may need to be kept so that it can be reused in the future. A roadside burger van business, for example, will only be able to carry a limited amount of stock. On an average day, the owner might carry 100 uncooked burgers. However, if they sell just 80 burgers, they will want to safely store the remaining 20 uncooked burgers for future use.

All food items intended for storage should be covered or wrapped, and clearly labelled with the exact contents and date. This will help with **stock rotation** and stock control. Chefs need to know which items have gone past their use-by date so that they are thrown away and not used.

Food storage methods include:

- chilled storage
- frozen storage
- dry storage.

Chilled storage

Chilled storage refers to storing food in refrigerators within safe temperature limits (at, or below, 8°C). A refrigerator temperature should, ideally, be within the 0 to 8°C range – with a target temperature of 5°C – to prevent bacterial growth and make sure that food is safe to eat. Foods that have been cooked must be cooled as quickly as possible ready to be refrigerated. To do this, you could reduce the portion size or spread the food out on an open tray.

To avoid cross contamination, raw and cooked foods should be stored separately. Raw foods, especially meat, should always be placed towards the bottom of the refrigerator. This ensures that blood cannot drip down and contaminate any food items below.

All foods requiring chilled storage should be:

- kept at the correct temperature
- well wrapped
- clearly labelled
- kept away from the cooling unit
- stock rotated.

Refrigerators should not be overstocked and the door should always be kept closed. An open fridge door allows the temperature inside the refrigerator to rise and bacteria to multiply.

? Did you know?

Flies are unable to eat solid food; they have to soften and liquefy food to consume it. They do this by vomiting saliva onto food and treading it in to aid the liquidising process. Once food is suitably liquefied, they suck it up with their proboscis.

Flies excrete their own body waste onto food and, as they are attracted to decaying materials and faecal matter, they can also transfer bacteria from these sources to food. Because of this, uncovered food items are particularly at risk of contamination by flies.

Key term

Stock rotation – a process of making sure that items of stock with the shortest expiry date are used before ones with a longer expiry date. Products that need to be used first are stored at the front of the storage area.

Foods that need to be chilled

Key terms

Thaw – melt.

Freezer burn – occurs when frozen food has been damaged due to air reaching the food. On meat it shows as a greyish brown discolouration. It generally occurs when food is not wrapped in air-tight packaging. Although unsightly, freezer burn is not a food safety risk, but it does affect the food's quality and taste.

Did you know?

All items should be stored in line with the food manufacturer's guidelines. However, different organisations may have their own policies about the length of time that frozen food products can be kept. It is, therefore, important to get to know the policies when starting work in a new business.

Discussion

Why should you not re-freeze items that have already been defrosted? What can happen?

Frozen storage

Freezing preserves foods, giving them a longer shelf life. The temperature of a freezer must be at -18 C or below. If a freezer temperature is allowed to rise, foods will start to **thaw** and bacteria will be able to multiply. Foods stored within the freezer should be:

* stored at the correct temperature
* well wrapped – to avoid **freezer burn**
* clearly labelled
* stock rotated.

Freezers should not be overstocked and the door should always be kept closed. An open door or broken seal allows the temperature inside the freezer to rise and bacteria to multiply. Raw foods should be stored at the bottom of the freezer to avoid cross contamination.

Foods that need to be frozen

Defrosting frozen foods

Some frozen foods need defrosting before they are prepared or cooked. Some foods can be cooked straight from frozen and this information will appear in the manufacturer's instructions on the food label. If there are no instructions you must assume that the product should be completely defrosted before it is used.

When defrosting food items you should:

* plan ahead to make sure there is enough time for the food to thaw at the bottom of a refrigerator – this is the ideal method to defrost food as it keeps it at a safe temperature
* keep raw and cooked items separate in the refrigerator
* place a tray underneath the item to catch any liquid from the defrosting process
* make sure the food item is fully defrosted before cooking it
* cook defrosted products within 24 hours
* cook defrosted items thoroughly, using a temperature probe to make sure that the core, or the thickest area, has been heated to the required temperature (this would be heated to at least 75°C for 30 seconds)
* not re-freeze items that have already been defrosted.

Dry storage

The types of food that you would expect to find in a dry storage area are cereals, rice, flours and canned/tinned produce, unless the packaging states otherwise.

Foods requiring dry storage need to be stored:

* in a cool, well-ventilated area
* in a suitable container with a lid, and clearly labelled

Foods that need dry storage

- raised off the floor and away from the walls. This protects them from damp (condensation from the walls) through air circulation and also prevents pest infestation
- using FIFO stock rotation, with new items placed at the back of the shelf to allow those with the shortest expiry date to be used first.

Storage times and date labelling

All foods should be stored in line with recommended manufacturer guidelines, or company policy. Packaged food items will always have dates labelled on the item's packaging. These dates will be either 'use-by' dates or 'best-before' dates.

Use-by dates give clear dates by when the food item must be eaten. These dates are applied to **high-risk foods**. High-risk food products include items such as a pre-prepared chicken salad, ham sandwich, fresh cream cake, freshly prepared trifle and cooked chicken drumsticks. These items are similar in that they do not need to be cooked further before being eaten so they can be eaten straight away. They can also be easily infected by bacteria.

An example of a best-before label. Use-by dates are shown in a similar place.

Best-before dates show the date by which a product is at its best. The product can be eaten after the date, but the quality of the product is not guaranteed. People should use their common sense when eating foods after the best-before date: if either the smell or the appearance of the food is not as it should be, the item should be thrown away.

Monitoring stock levels

All hospitality businesses should carry out regular stock checks. This may be done internally by recording stock levels on a stock sheet. Alternatively, external auditors may come in to complete the same process. Records should also be made of any waste or damaged stock. Monitoring stock levels helps businesses know how much product they need to order and may also show up any differences in the products, such as a problem with a supplier or with stealing.

Key term

High-risk foods – include pre-prepared food items that can be eaten without further cooking, and which may easily become infected with bacteria.

Take it further

Look at three different food items, all with best-before dates. Make notes to feed back to your group to explain any specific manufacturers' guidelines about how each item should be stored.

Activity 3.2	Storage: chilled, frozen or dry?

Sort the following items to show how they should be stored: chilled, frozen or dry.

- cheese
- ham
- baked beans
- eggs
- lettuce
- cornflakes
- raisins
- mushrooms
- custard powder
- chocolate
- sugar
- oven chips
- opened mint sauce
- carton of orange juice
- onions
- brown rice
- assorted biscuits
- milk
- fillet steak
- carrots
- ice cream

▶ Preparing food

When preparing food items, it is important to follow safe procedures to maintain food safety. The temperature of the food item is likely to be different from its temperature during storage, with the risk of bacterial contamination higher. The **danger zone** is the temperature at which bacteria are able to grow. Food items are, therefore, most at risk of bacterial contamination when their temperature is within the danger zone. The danger zone is between 8°C and 63°C (see Figure 3.2). As a food handler you must make sure that items spend the minimum time at these temperatures.

Good food safety

When preparing and cooking food items it is essential that you use the correct surfaces and equipment to make sure that good food safety is being followed. In a kitchen there are dangerous pieces of equipment such as knives and food mixers. It is important that all staff receive training on how to use this equipment if they are involved in preparing food. Simple procedures for how to use equipment safely can be displayed beside the equipment. In addition, always follow manufacturers' instructions.

Make sure the power is turned off on electrical equipment before changing tools. It is also important that different knives and utensils are used for raw and ready-to-eat foods and that they are washed thoroughly after they have been used.

One way of making sure that food is prepared on the right surfaces is to use colour-coded chopping boards and knives when you are using different types of food. Using colour-coded equipment prevents the risk of cross contamination. Table 3.3 outlines the colour of the board that should be used for different types of food.

As well as working on the correct surfaces and using suitable equipment, it is important that you follow good hygiene practices to keep food safe. Hospitality businesses usually have a procedure for staff to follow. Examples of good practices include:

- keeping yourself and your uniform clean
- washing your hands regularly (take a look at the hand cleaning techniques poster on page 83)
- wearing hats or covering hair
- removing body piercings and jewellery
- covering any cuts with a waterproof dressing
- not smoking in the food and drink service area
- not coughing or sneezing over food as this spreads germs

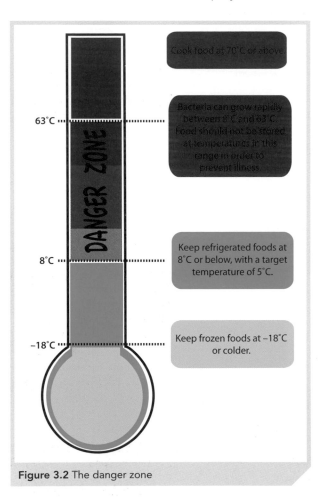

Cook food at 70°C or above

Bacteria can grow rapidly between 8°C and 63°C. Food should not be stored at temperatures in this range in order to prevent illness.

63°C

DANGER ZONE

8°C

Keep refrigerated foods at 8°C or below, with a target temperature of 5°C.

–18°C

Keep frozen foods at –18°C or colder.

Figure 3.2 The danger zone

Table 3.3 Colour-coded chopping boards and knives and the foods they should be used for

Colour	Food
Yellow	Cooked meats
Red	Raw meats
Blue	Raw fish/seafood
Green	Fruit and salad
Brown	Vegetables
White	Dairy/bakery items

Chopping boards are colour-coded according to what they are used for.

- avoiding unhygienic habits – do not lick your fingers, pick your nose, ears or teeth and do not scratch your hair
- keeping the work area clean and tidy
- wearing suitable clothing
- following food safety training, e.g. keeping raw and cooked food items separate
- informing your manager or supervisor if you are ill or have been ill recently.

The importance of hand hygiene cannot be overestimated. Figure 3.3 shows the steps involved in correct hand washing.

Link

See Unit 7: Food and Beverage Service in the Hospitality Industry for further information about when you should wash your hands.

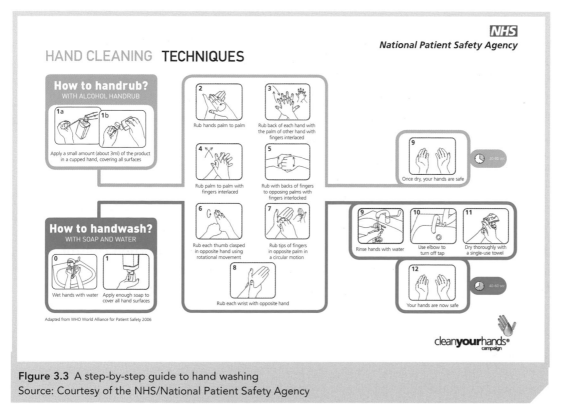

Figure 3.3 A step-by-step guide to hand washing
Source: Courtesy of the NHS/National Patient Safety Agency

Remember

When you are washing your hands, it is essential to:
- wash your hands with the hand washing product supplied by your employer
- wash your hands for a minimum of 40 to 60 seconds
- wash every part of your hands – both your palms and the backs of your hands and in between your fingers
- wash your hands regularly – particularly after you have handled raw ingredients such as meat or poultry.

Link

See Unit 6: Planning, Preparing, Cooking and Finishing Food for further information about how to prepare food safely.

Cooking food

Many foods that we eat are cooked by applying heat to them for a length of time. Cooking is a critical stage in food preparation, when **pathogenic bacteria** within food items should be destroyed or reduced to safe levels. Food that is not cooked correctly may still contain pathogenic bacteria and may cause **food poisoning**.

Different food items have different cooking requirements. Some items only need a short cooking time whereas some may need longer. The temperature at which they must be cooked may also vary. As a food handler, you must be aware of correct cooking temperatures and timings for different food items.

Table 3.4 Temperature/time ratios for cooking

Temperature	Time
70°C	For at least two minutes
75°C	For at least 30 seconds
80°C	For at least six seconds

Source: Food Standards Agency. © Crown copyright 2013.

When cooking, food is safe if it has reached a high enough temperature for a long enough period of time. Table 3.4 shows some examples of safe time/temperature ratios. You should use a clean temperature probe to check the **core temperature** of the food. Insert the tip of the probe into the middle of the food (or into the thickest part) and read the temperature. You should make sure that the required temperature is met for the required length of time. If you are cooking meat, you should also check that when you pierce the meat at its thickest part any juices released are clear and not blood tinged.

As the thickness of food items varies, you should follow recipe or food packaging guidelines for cooking times and temperatures. Time plans are useful to show the sequence of cooking tasks and how long each task will take. Dishes with long cooking times should be cooked first and those with short cooking times should be cooked and finished last. Preparation of raw foods can be time-consuming, so it is a good idea to allow for some things to take longer to prepare and cook than expected.

Equipment used in cooking is wide and varied. The piece of equipment needed depends on the food being cooked. Generally, heavy and thick cooking pots conduct heat more evenly and produce the best results. Equipment must be clean, safe and in good working order.

Key terms

Pathogenic bacteria – microorganisms that can cause illness.

Food poisoning – a gastric illness caused by eating pathogens in food. Symptoms include vomiting, diarrhoea, severe stomach pains and a raised temperature.

Core temperature – the temperature at the centre or thickest part of food. When probing, be careful not to spear through the food and touch the pan or pot with the probe as this will give a false reading.

Portion control – the amount of food that needs to be given to make sure that every customer receives the same amount.

Serving food

Food should be served quickly and safely to reduce potential contamination risks. It should always be served in clean dishes and it is important to keep some food items separate. For example, you would not serve rare beef on the same carving board as a vegetarian tartlet.

Suitable service utensils should be ready and clean to use. For **portion control**, the same sized utensils should be used to serve all customers. Some food businesses insist that disposable blue gloves are worn during service. It is important to remember that gloves should be changed as needed, and at the same intervals that you would wash your hands if you were not wearing gloves.

If food items are being kept hot in a hot-holding area, they must be stored at 63°C or above. The legal limit for keeping food in the hot-holding area is four hours and temperature checks should be made every two hours.

Throw away any food remaining in the hot-holding area after four hours, along with any items that fall below the correct temperature. Complete temperature monitoring sheets to show how long the food has been kept and at what temperature. Food held for two hours that has not previously been reheated can be cooled and reheated for service the following day until the four hour hot-holding limit has been reached.

Activity 3.3	Food safety interview

You have an interview with the head chef of a kitchen for a food handler position.

In pairs, discuss the questions you think the head chef might ask during the interview, based on the following three areas:

- the importance of following food safety regulations and procedures
- food safety control and the steps people need to follow
- how food and safety controls can be maintained and reviewed.

In pairs, role play the interview. The person playing the head chef should take notes on the interviewee's answers and provide feedback afterwards. Pairs should then swap roles and repeat the role play.

Discussion

Discuss with an industry representative the importance of following food safety procedures when cooking, preparing, storing and serving food.

TOPIC   A.2

▶ Food safety hazards in hospitality businesses

Introduction

Food safety hazards can happen in any food business. A good knowledge of different food hazards is essential to ensure a safe and healthy working environment for staff and customers.

Visit a local food business. From your observations, can you spot any potential food hazards?

▶ Microbiological, chemical and physical food hazards

A hazard to food is anything with the potential to cause harm. Food hazards can be categorised into three different types: microbiological, chemical and physical (foreign bodies).

Table 3.5 describes these types of hazards.

Table 3.5 Different hazard types

Hazard type	Description
Microbiological hazards	Microbiological hazards include pathogenic bacteria, viruses, moulds and yeasts. These are dangerous as they can cause food poisoning or food-borne diseases and should be prevented from entering food items. Bacteria are everywhere and can therefore be difficult to control. Places where food is prepared are ideal for bacteria to grow. Some bacteria can be helpful, e.g. in the production of cheese, but others can be harmful – even deadly – and these bacteria are known as pathogenic bacteria. Effective cooking is essential to make sure that pathogens are destroyed. Food must be cooked at the right temperature and for enough time otherwise harmful bacteria may survive the cooking process.
Chemical hazards	Chemical hazards found in food include cleaning substances, **pesticide** residues – on items such as fruit and vegetables – and bait used to kill pests, poisonous plants and wild mushrooms. All these substances may cause problems such as: <ul><li>making food taste unpleasant</li><li>skin irritation</li><li>a burning sensation</li><li>sickness</li><li>long-term damage to the human body.</li></ul> You must also make sure that toxic chemicals, e.g. cleaning fluids, do not get into food after it has been cooked and while it is being stored.
Physical hazards (foreign bodies)	Physical hazards are non-food items that are present in food. In large factories there are many production lines operating with each one carrying different food types. There is a risk that food items or even pieces of machinery could fall off one production line and land on another. This could result in cross contamination; for example, whole nuts could end up in a product marked as containing 'no nuts'. If the customer has a nut allergy then they could have an allergic reaction. Other examples of items that could contaminate food include: <ul><li>screws, nuts and bolts</li><li>glass shards</li><li>hairs</li><li>plasters</li><li>packaging</li><li>pests and droppings.</li></ul>

Food hazards can enter a product at any point in the delivery of food to the customer: from production, during purchase or delivery, throughout the preparation and cooking of the food, or during the serving stages. Therefore, to make sure the food is safe to eat, food handlers need to be extra careful at all stages of the process.

Activity 3.4 Food hazards: microbiological, physical and chemical

Sort this list of potential food hazards into microbiological, physical and chemical.

- A screw
- A strand of hair
- Salmonella
- A cigarette butt
- Mould

- Hand sanitiser
- Yeast
- Shattered glass
- A finger nail
- E. coli

- Dirt/earth
- Bleach
- An earring
- Washing-up soap

- Rat droppings
- Disinfectant
- Plastic packaging.

▶ Business hazards

In Unit 1, we looked at the structure of the industry and its different sectors. It is important to be aware of the environment in which you are working, and the common hazards associated with it, as every workplace has its own set of food safety hazards.

Although the need for food safety remains the same, its management varies in different hospitality businesses. Many factors affect this, including menu choice and the size and structure of the business. Therefore, when learning about food and health and safety within the hospitality industry, it is important to investigate a broad range of businesses.

Activity 3.5 Hazards in hospitality businesses

Hazards can be found in every hospitality sector. Copy the following table and complete it by researching and filling in the common hazards found in each of the sectors.

Hospitality sector	Common hazards found in the sector
Hotels	
Restaurants	
Pubs, bars and nightclubs	
Cafés and coffee shops	
Fast food outlets	
Contract food service providers	
Hospitality services	
Membership clubs	
Event catering	

Then, in small groups, select one local food business per group. List the hazards that may be relevant to the business. Then think about how these hazards could be controlled. Present your findings to other groups to share information about a number of different businesses.

Link

See Unit 1, Learning aim A, Topic A.1 for more information about the different hospitality businesses.

In Activity 3.5 you may have researched and identified hazards such as those from using knives, slippery floors and hot food and drinks. A very serious hazard in the workplace is fire. Fires can be caused by a variety of hazards, including smoking, gas, hot substances such as oil and faulty electrical equipment.

Activity 3.6 — Preventing fires

What other hazards in hopitality businesses that prepare and serve food could cause fires? What can be done to prevent fires? Carry out some research in pairs and put together a poster and short presentation of your findings.

▶ Controls and monitoring procedures

Introduction

This section looks at the importance of controls and monitoring procedures for food safety hazards within the kitchen and restaurant environment. This stage is critical to make sure that the food we serve is safe to eat.

In small groups, think about what you have already learned in this unit and name at least five occasions where you would need to monitor food safety. Report back to the other groups and then, as a whole group, identify any common themes.

▶ Controlling and monitoring food hazards

Several controls are needed to help reduce hazards to safe levels. Controls should be realistic, effective and understood by all food handlers. Food handlers should know which controls they are responsible for. Food controls should be monitored on a regular basis to make sure they remain efficient.

Using reputable suppliers

Hospitality businesses buy food and ingredients from suppliers in a number of ways – daily, weekly, or monthly depending on the style, size and location of the business and the type of food being bought. For example, fresh fruit and vegetables may be bought on a daily basis, whereas frozen foods might be purchased once a week.

It is best practice to use suppliers with a good reputation. As a food provider, you should be confident that you are able to trace food items back to their original source. For example, when fast food chains sell beefburgers, they should be able to trace the meat back to the exact farm and cattle that the meat came from. In addition, these suppliers are also likely to have the approval of local environmental health services as safe and hygienic operators. Suppliers should know their products and should use correct storage and delivery procedures.

Take it further

In January 2013, the first incidents of horse meat being found in processed meat products were reported in the UK and Irish media. In groups, use the internet to research these incidents and discuss the following questions.

- What was the role of suppliers in these incidents?
- What protocols (codes of correct behaviour) were breached?
- What health risks, if any, were involved?
- What measures could be put in place to make sure this does not happen again?

Checking food deliveries

On arrival at the hospitality business, food deliveries must be checked by the stores assistant. The first thing a stores assistant needs to check is the temperature of the food. Food items may be delivered as:

- **ambient** items or products, which can be stored at room temperature. This would include tinned food and dry items, such as cereals
- chilled items, including high-risk foods, which should be checked to make sure their temperature is between 0 and 8°C
- frozen food, which should be at −18°C or below.

Where items are not at the correct temperature, the delivery should not be accepted. These items must be returned to the supplier and replacements organised.

- Food must be carefully checked to make sure it is fresh and safe to bring into the kitchen.
- Check the smell – it should smell fresh.
- Look for insect or bird damage on fruit and vegetables.
- Inspect all packaging – it must not be damaged.

The vehicle used to transport the food items should also be checked to make sure it is suitable for use, clean and that any refrigeration in the vehicle is adequate for the goods being transported.

Finally, visual checks of individual items within the delivery should be made to make sure they are clean, with no signs of damage, tampering or food spoilage.

Labelling

A stores assistant should check that processed and packaged foodstuffs are properly labelled with:

- a product code
- the item's weight
- a use-by or best-before date
- details of the food production company
- a description of the food item
- a list of the ingredients
- allergy warning notices.

Use-by and best-before dates should be checked to make sure the food will still be within date when the kitchen is ready to use it. The business may need to use up existing stocks first.

Checking against the delivery note and order sheet

The order should come with a delivery note, which should be prepared by the supplier to show exactly what is being delivered. This note should match what was ordered. The stores assistant should check the actual food items delivered against the delivery note for quantity and quality.

From time to time, as the customer, you may need to reject orders, and return them to their source. In such circumstances, you must make sure that you record the return on the delivery note, and that the driver signs the delivery note – both to show acceptance of the return and that the item will be returned to the supplier.

Key term

Ambient – relates to the immediate surroundings. Ambient temperature is the temperature in a room or surrounding an object.

Remember

Keep raw and cooked foods separate at all times! Once deliveries have been checked they should be stored correctly. There will be different storage areas for raw and cooked foodstuffs. Remember that foods should also be stored at the correct temperature.

Link

Go to Topic A.1 in this unit for more information about the safe temperatures at which to store food and to recap on storage methods.

Remember

Remember that you need to cook foods correctly to make sure that harmful bacteria are reduced to safe levels. Food that is not cooked properly can cause food poisoning. If there is any doubt, checks should be made, for example, using a temperature probe. Correcting lack of cooking can be as simple as returning the food item to the oven.

Link

Go to Topic A.1 in this unit to recap on how to maintain a hygienic working environment when dealing with food.

Limiting food handling

The more often that food is handled, the higher the risk of contamination and bacterial growth; therefore, handling of the food should be kept to a minimum.

Clean equipment, premises and good personal hygiene

Good personal hygiene, particularly regular hand washing, is essential for a high level of food safety. Dirty premises and equipment and food debris can encourage food pests and contamination. Higher room temperatures and a lack of natural ventilation provide ideal conditions for certain pests, so these should be monitored. Regularly check all dry goods for pest infestation and store them in pest-proof containers. Bins should also have pest-proof lids. There is also a higher risk of physical hazards (foreign bodies) entering food products when equipment and premises are poorly maintained and/or dirty.

All businesses have standards for cleanliness. One of the easiest ways to monitor cleaning is to set up a cleaning schedule. This should outline how often an area should be cleaned and the cleaning method to be used. The person cleaning the area must sign and date the schedule to show that the task has been completed.

Figure 3.4 Would you want your food prepared and cooked in this kitchen?

Activity 3.7	The role of a stores assistant

With a partner, research the role of a stores assistant. Use your findings to develop a basic job description for a stores assistant working in a kitchen environment.

▶ Reasons to follow food safety procedures

Introduction

This section looks at the importance of following food safety procedures, and the reasons why we need to follow them. You will learn about the different practices and procedures that need to be followed, the benefits of doing so and the drawbacks of not doing so.

In small groups, using the knowledge you already have, think about the importance of following good safety practices and procedures. Then discuss the consequences of not doing so.

▶ Food safety practices and procedures

There are a number of reasons why we need to follow correct food and health and safety practices when working within the hospitality industry. One of these is the importance of avoiding food poisoning outbreaks. Unlike other food safety issues, this is something that only becomes known after the event has occurred, when it is too late to take steps to stop it. All you can do is investigate the cause of the outbreak and put procedures in place to prevent it happening again. However, it is much better to make sure that those procedures and practices are in place from the start by analysing potential hazards and being aware of activities that are critical to food safety.

By following good food safety practices and procedures, you are likely to:

* reduce the possibility of a food poisoning incident/outbreak
* reduce any harm that may result to either the customer or the business
* be confident that all those working within the business are aware of food safety practices and procedures, and how to implement them.

Table 3.6 shows the benefits of following food safety practices and the drawbacks if they are not implemented.

Table 3.6 The benefits of following food safety procedures and the drawbacks of not doing so

Benefits of implementing food safety practices	Drawbacks of not implementing food safety practices
<ul><li>The business will have a good reputation.</li><li>The business will have a happy, motivated workforce.</li><li>The business will effectively use their resources.</li><li>There will be a safe and secure working environment.</li><li>The business will keep up good relationships with suppliers.</li></ul>	<ul><li>There will be unhappy customers.</li><li>The business will suffer damage to their reputation.</li><li>The business may receive negative publicity.</li><li>The business will have an unhappy staff.</li><li>The business may face fines, prosecution and imprisonment.</li></ul>

Assessment activity 3.1

Your uncle owns a restaurant where you work at weekends and during school holidays. He is planning to open a second restaurant and has asked you to help train new staff. He would like you to produce some training materials on food safety for new staff members. He wants the materials to be informative, easy to read and colourful.

1 Research the types of training materials used by hospitality organisations to train and inform their staff. Identify the ways in which the training materials are useful and informative, and where there is room for improvement.

2 Create training materials for the staff at your uncle's new restaurant that:

a) explain how they should maintain food safety in the restaurant

b) analyse potential food safety hazards when:

- storing food
- cooking food
- preparing food
- serving food.

The materials should also include an outline of the controls and monitoring procedures that are in place to eliminate these food safety hazards.

3 Your uncle would like you to give a presentation to the restaurant's staff about the importance of complying with food safety procedures to maintain food safety and the results of not doing so when:

- storing food
- preparing food
- cooking food
- serving food.

Tips

- Speak to staff working in different hospitality businesses to learn what policies and procedures their organisation complies with.
- Give real examples from industry experience, case studies, interview transcripts or handbooks acquired from real hospitality businesses.
- Interview catering staff at your centre and ask them to provide real examples of food safety hazards when storing, preparing, cooking and serving food.
- Use real articles and real news stories, or industry examples of breaches of protocols (codes of correct behaviour).

Learning aim B　　　**TOPIC**　　**B.1**

▶ Safety legislation regulating working practices

Introduction

The key to working in, and remaining employed in, the hospitality industry is being able to understand and practise both food safety and health and safety in the workplace. There are several working practices, pieces of legislation and regulations that help to keep employees and customers safe. If you work in the hospitality industry you need a good understanding of such practices and how non-compliance can not only affect you but also others around you.

Choose one of the following pieces of legislation that is relevant to the hospitality industry and identify the main points covered:

- Health and Safety at Work etc. Act 1974 (HASAWA)
- Food Safety Act 1990.

Safety legislation

All employees should be familiar with basic safety legislation in order to carry out their job roles in a safe and healthy manner. The Health and Safety at Work etc. Act 1974 (HASAWA) is the main piece of legislation covering health and safety. The Act states that health and safety is the responsibility of both the employer and the employee, and that everyone has a duty to keep themselves and others safe. The Act sets out separate responsibilities for both the employee and employer. These responsibilities are outlined in Table 3.7.

Table 3.7 Employers' and employees' responsibilities under HASAWA

Employers' duties	Employees' duties
• Make sure a safe and healthy workplace is provided. • Carry out risk assessments to highlight any areas of work that could cause harm. • Put in place precautions to prevent harm from occurring and explain how these risks will be controlled. • Provide adequate health and safety training in relation to all work duties. • Provide correct equipment, materials and protective clothing to enable staff to carry out tasks, and make sure it is looked after. • Make sure there are toilets, drinking water and places to wash. • Provide first aid equipment and training where appropriate. • Provide an accident book. • Prepare a written health and safety policy. • Have insurance that covers you and your employees in case you are hurt or get ill at work.	• Be careful about your own safety and that of others. • Comply with law, training and workplace rules. • Follow the training you have received. • Do not tamper with anything that is provided in the interests of health, safety or welfare. • Report anything that you feel may cause injury or harm to yourself or others.

HASAWA is enforced by the Health and Safety Executive (HSE) along with local authorities. You can find out more information about HASAWA by going to the HSE website. You can access this website by going to www.pearsonhotlinks.co.uk and searching for this title.

Another piece of legislation that regulates working practices in hospitality is the Food Safety Act 1990. The Food and Safety Act 1990 states that businesses should not provide food that:

• is unfit for people to eat

• could cause danger to someone's health

• is of poor quality.

Simple rules include:

• using the FIFO system for all food products

• making sure that cold food is never stored in areas that are warmer than 8°C

• keeping hot food at a minimum of 63°C before it is served.

Food must also be labelled and advertised accurately. You can find out more information about the Food and Safety Act 1990 by going to the Foods Standards Agency website. You can access this website by going to www.pearsonhotlinks.co.uk and searching for this title.

Link

You can refer back to HACCP by looking at Topic A.1 in this unit.

▶ Safety regulations

There are several safety regulations with which hospitality and catering employees should be familiar. We have already discussed some of these earlier in the unit, for example HACCP procedures. There are, however, several other regulations that you should be familiar with and these are outlined in Table 3.8.

Table 3.8 Safety regulations which relate to hospitality and catering

Safety regulations	Main features
Food Labelling Regulations 1996	These regulations are set out by the Food and Safety Act 1990 and identify the information which must, by law, be included on food labels, for example a use-by date, a best-before date and nutritional information.
Regulatory Reform (Fire Safety) Order 2005	This is the main law relating to fire safety. It states that business owners or people who have some level of control must carry out fire risk assessment in the premises to identify risks and hazards. They must also take steps to reduce or eliminate the risk of fire.
Manual Handling Operations Regulations 1992	These regulations set out measures that should be followed to reduce manual handling risks in the workplace. The regulations apply to lots of activities, including lifting, lowering, carrying and pushing. More information can be found by going to the HSE website. You can access this website by going to www.pearsonhotlinks.co.uk and searching for this title.
Provision and Use of Work Equipment Regulations 1998	These regulations cover the use of any equipment by an employee at work, including hammers, knives and ladders. It states that employers must make sure equipment is suitable for use, maintained and inspected, and that protective devices and controls, such as emergency stop devices, are provided. It also states that equipment should only be used by fully trained operatives. Within the hospitality industry certain equipment can only be used by people aged over 16 years and who have received full training, including: • wrapping and packing machines • slicing machines • mincing machines.
Personal Protective Equipment at Work Regulations 1992	These regulations require the provision and use of protective equipment for hazardous tasks, e.g. the use of goggles when using cleaning chemicals, helmets, gloves and high-visibility clothing.

Activity 3.8 | Researching safety regulations

In pairs, research the main features of the following safety regulations that also affect the hospitality industry.

- Food Premises (Registration) Regulations 1991
- Reporting of Injuries, Diseases and Dangerous Occurrences Regulations 1995 (RIDDOR)
- Working Time Regulations 1998

Make a poster of your findings.

A male worker complying with manual handling regulations by lifting a box correctly with bent knees and a straight back

▶ Enforcing compliance with legislation

Hospitality businesses must comply with health and safety legislation, and they do so by following the guidance outlined in the regulations we covered in Table 3.8. This list is not complete and it is important that all hospitality businesses properly understand their responsibilities for health and safety. Compliance is necessary to control hazards and prevent injury or ill health to members of staff and customers. This tends to be the responsibility of those in supervisory and management roles but employees have a responsibility to take care of their own health and safety, and the health and safety of others.

Health and safety law is jointly enforced by the HSE and local authorities. The HSE and local authorities provide advice and guidance on what the law requires concerning health and safety, conduct inspections and investigations, and take action where necessary.

Health and safety officers are responsible for monitoring compliance with health and safety law. They provide advice to businesses and employers to increase awareness of health and safety in the work environment.

The powers of a health and safety officer include the ability to:

- enter the premises without previous arrangement
- question employees and safety officials
- investigate health and safety within the organisation (this includes looking at paperwork)
- remove samples from the premises and take photos for future evidence
- issue informal warnings, improvement and **prohibition** notices
- prohibit the use of specific items of equipment
- prosecute a business or any individual who has broken health and safety law.

Trading standards officers also have enforcement responsibilities but they focus on consumer products. They advise businesses and enforce legislation that governs the way products are bought and sold. This includes food labelling, ingredients, weights and measures. Failure to comply with legislation can result in: prosecution, closure and fines.

Compliance is monitored by the local authority and can be observed during routine inspection or if a complaint has been made by a member of the public.

Key term

Prohibition – when someone is forbidden to do something. For example, a restaurant must not serve food to customers that is past its use-by date.

Research

Can you list ten duties of an employer and employee in relation to safety regulations? You could visit the HSE website to get you started. You can access this website by going to www.pearsonhotlinks.co.uk and searching for this title.

Activity 3.9   Monitoring legislation and regulations – a survey

You are going to investigate how hospitality businesses enforce legislation and regulations that affect them. Prepare a list of questions that you can use to interview people in existing businesses. Visit two contrasting businesses – perhaps one in the commercial sector (for example, a pub or restaurant) and one in the service sector (for example, this could be your school/college canteen). Use your questions to interview staff members to find out how they enforce legislation and regulations to control hazards, and how they monitor and control this enforcement. Discuss your findings with the whole group.

▶ Safety signs, information and documentation used in businesses

Introduction

All employees need to be familiar with safety signs, information and documentation that may be found in the hospitality industry. You may be the only person who is able to help people out of a hotel in the event of a fire or other emergency. This information will have been provided and discussed with you during an induction or during training and it is critical that you understand it.

Think about the different safety signs that you have seen in the past week. Draw examples of the signs you saw and then jot down what information you think the sign was giving you. At the end of the unit come back to your drawings to see if you were right and how 'safety aware' you now are.

▶ Safety improvement measures

The safety of customers, staff and anyone near the workplace can be improved and kept going by putting certain measures in place. These measures, along with good practice, lead to safe working environments and conditions.

Safety signs

Safety signs are a good way of alerting others to a potential danger. Many of the signs used to get across health and safety messages are pictorial; this helps visitors and guests who might not speak English. There are specific colours used in certain signs to make sure that people who are colour blind can see them and understand the message.

- Red signs show that something is prohibited (something you must not do). They often have a red diagonal line over the symbol on the sign.

- Blue signs give an instruction that is mandatory (something that you must do or something that must be in place).
- Yellow signs give a warning (a hazard or danger). These signs are inside a black triangle.
- Green signs often show a positive action; usually where to go in emergency situations.

Figure 3.5 shows some of the most common safety signs.

No smoking

Wash your hands

Danger of fire

Electrical hazard

Fire exit

First aid box

Fire safety assembly point

Figure 3.5 Common safety signs

When putting up safety signs, it is important to alert people to whether the hazard is permanent or temporary. For example, if you have dropped food on the floor making it slippery, a temporary wet floor sign should be put on the area. You would not expect it to be there several days later when the floor had been cleaned and is safe to walk on. An example of a permanent sign is one placed where drinking water is available. This tells people that it is safe to drink from the water supply. This would be a permanent sign unless there was a fault or problem, which would need to be reported to a supervisor immediately.

Safety information and documentation

Hospitality businesses must have information and completed documentation on health and safety within their workplace available in order to comply with health and safety legislation, and to manage and control health and safety issues. This information and documentation will cover aspects such as food safety, manual handling, first aid and fire drills. The HSE provides free information guides and leaflets about legislation, regulations and how to carry out procedures and practices. These include first aid books and literature about personal protective equipment (PPE). To access the HSE website go to www.pearsonhotlinks.co.uk and search for this title.

? Did you know?

The most common accident in the workplace is a slip, trip or fall.

Maintaining records

It is good practice and a legal requirement for businesses to record and log details relating to health and safety. In the case of fire safety, for example, businesses should have fire evacuation procedures in place, a record of fire drills undertaken, fire risk assessments, records of fire alarm checks and fire training records for nominated fire marshals. It is good practice for businesses to also have, for example, an accident record book, first aid staff training and treatment records, manual handling risk assessment forms and training records, personal protective equipment literature, HACCP plans and food hygiene policies and records.

COSHH

The Control of Substances Hazardous to Health Regulations 2002 (COSHH) cover chemicals that can be dangerous to a person's health and control how they can be used. They require employers to assess the risks from hazardous substances and take suitable precautions.

Under COSHH regulations:

- chemicals must be clearly labelled (see Figure 3.6 for examples of labels you might see)
- dangerous chemicals must be securely stored and only issued for use to people who have received adequate training
- PPE must be provided.

Figure 3.6 Warning labels that you will find on containers of hazardous chemicals and substances. Labels such as these are required under the COSHH Regulations.

COSHH states that when using chemicals you must:

- follow manufacturers' instructions
- never mix chemicals or store them in a different container or leave them unlabelled
- store chemicals appropriately and securely.

Employers have a legal responsibility to carry out a COSHH risk assessment. This involves gathering information about the hazardous properties of substances used in the business, the work and the working practices. An employer then needs to:

- evaluate the risks to health
- decide on the necessary measures to comply with Regulations 7–13 of COSHH
- record the assessment (if the business has five or more employees)
- decide when the assessment should be reviewed.

Use of risk assessments

A risk is anything with the potential to endanger or cause injury – the chance that the hazard may harm somebody. A risk assessment is an important step in protecting employees and businesses and is necessary to comply with the law. It is a careful review of what, in the workplace, could cause harm to people. It looks at whether enough precautions are in place to prevent harm and how dangers can be eliminated or reduced. A risk assessment considers where there might be hazards, who is likely to be at risk from them and how they might be harmed. Once different risks have been identified they should be evaluated. The risk can be given a risk level – normally high, medium or low. These levels reflect what could go wrong and the likelihood of it happening. Businesses can then decide whether the existing precautions are good enough or whether more could be done to prevent the risk from causing harm. For example, trailing cables would be considered a risk and could be controlled by fixing them to the floor using brightly coloured tape to alert people to their presence.

Risk assessments should be carried out for all areas of a hospitality business, for example, for food preparation, for food and beverage service, for housekeeping and for front of house duties.

Typical risks/hazards in hospitality include:

- spilt oil on the floor
- incorrect stacking of food items in the stores
- faulty electrics
- chefs bumping into each other carrying hot pans/liquids.

Under HASAWA, all employers must carry out risk assessments. It is also essential to make sure that risk assessments are monitored and updated. By doing this, new hazards (which were not a problem on the original date of the risk assessment) can be identified and tackled.

Remember

As an employee you have a responsibility for the safety of yourself and others. Therefore, if you see something that could cause harm, you must report this to your supervisor.

Did you know?

If a business employs five or more people, they must have a written and recorded risk assessment.

Activity 3.10 — Hazard spotting

Identify at least five hazards that may be found in each of the following areas in a hospitality business and the problems that could occur:

- food preparation area
- food service area
- bar area
- reception
- housekeeping.

As a starting point, you could watch an episode of Fawlty Towers and identify the potential dangers within the hotel.

Choose one of the areas and create a risk assessment.

Risk assessments that are carried out effectively can help to prevent accidents, improve the safety and wellbeing of the workforce and make sure a business complies with the law. Figure 3.7 shows an example of a completed risk assessment form.

Company name: Carey's Café   Date of risk assessment: **27/7/13**

What are the hazards?	Who might be harmed and how?	What are you already doing?	What further action is necessary?	Action by who?	Action by when?	Done
Slips and trips	Kitchen/food service staff and customers may be injured if they trip over objects or slip on spillages.	■ Good housekeeping – work areas kept tidy, goods stored suitably, etc. ■ Kitchen equipment maintained to prevent leaks onto floor. ■ Equipment faults leading to leaks reported promptly to manager. ■ Drainage channels and drip trays provided where spills more likely. ■ Staff clean up spillages (including dry spills) immediately using suitable methods and leave the floor dry. ■ Suitable cleaning materials available. ■ Good lighting in all areas including cold storage areas. ■ No trailing cables or obstruction in walkways. ■ Steps and changes in level highlighted.	■ Consider changing floor surface with better surface roughness.	Manager	27/8/13	14/8/13
			■ Remind staff to maintain good standard of housekeeping.	Manager	27/8/13	1/8/13
			■ Repair damaged floor tiles by the dishwasher in the kitchen.	Manager	27/8/13	26/8/13
			■ Ensure suitable footwear with good grip worn by staff.	Manager	27/8/13	1/8/13
Manual handling Handling heavy items such as flour sacks, ingredients, boxes of meat, trays of crockery, kegs etc	Kitchen staff and food service staff may suffer injuries such as strains or bruising from handling heavy/bulky objects.	■ Ingredients bought in package sizes that are light enough for easy handling. ■ Commonly used items and heavy stock stored on shelves at waist height. ■ Suitable mobile steps provided and staff trained to use them safely. ■ Handling aids provided for movement of large/heavy items. ■ Sink at good height to avoid stooping. ■ Staff trained in how to lift safely.	■ Ensure team working for moving heavier items (e.g. pots).	Manager	27/8/13	14/8/13

Figure 3.7 An example of a completed risk assessment
Source: Contains public sector information published by the Health and Safety Executive and licensed under the Open Government Licence v1.0

Assessment activity 3.2   *English*   2B.P4 │ 2B.P5 │ 2B.M2 │ 2B.M3 │ 2B.D2

Your uncle was so impressed by the material you produced on food hygiene that he has asked you to develop a training booklet covering health and safety issues. He is interested to see how health and safety is enforced in two contrasting hospitality businesses. He is hoping that you can produce a booklet that will:

• describe how hospitality businesses enforce safe working practices and comply with legislation and regulations

• explain how compliance with legislation and regulations is used to control hazards and prevent injury or ill health to staff or customers.

Develop a training booklet, making sure that:

1 you include a section on how safety signs, information and documentation are used in two contrasting hospitality businesses

2 you provide information to show how these things improve safety in your two contrasting businesses

3 you evaluate how compliance with health and safety legislation, regulations, safety signs, information and documentation are carried out in order to control hazards and prevent injury/ill health. Your uncle wants you to evaluate how compliance benefits businesses so that staff understand its importance. You could focus on one of the hospitality businesses to do this.

Tips

• Discuss your businesses with your teacher/tutor to make sure they will be contrasting enough to show your depth and understanding of the different safety signs, information and documentation.

• Give real examples within your training booklet to inform and emphasise the importance to new and existing staff.

WorkSpace

▶ Nadia Khan

Assistant manager of a hotel restaurant

I completed my BTEC Level 3 Diploma in Hospitality five years ago and joined my current company, a hotel, on a trainee management scheme. I've always enjoyed working in busy environments with lots of people, particularly customers.

I'm responsible for a team of 12 people, which includes both full- and part-time staff. Although I have routine responsibilities and duties to complete, working in hospitality and catering is anything but routine.

My day starts with making sure that staff are ready for work, deliveries have been received and food preparation can proceed. I then check front of house to make sure that the correct set-up for breakfast service is in place to open on time to customers. Once breakfast has been completed, it's time to think about lunch and dinner. However, that's just a small part of my job. I also have to deal with conferences, room service and maybe the occasional wedding or other function. There is no feeling as good as knowing that you and your team helped to make someone's special day happen.

I also make sure that we comply with food safety and health and safety legislation. To make sure I was fully up to date with relevant legislation and requirements, I completed my Level 4 Food Safety Certificate. With food hygiene there's always the risk that if something goes wrong it can have fatal consequences – and I wasn't prepared to let that happen on my watch! To make sure that the whole team is as efficient as possible, I run regular training in food hygiene and its importance, and undertake spot checks in the kitchen environment. I then work with the head chef to make any necessary improvements. As the kitchen is the chef's domain, I need good communication skills to make sure these suggestions are agreed and implemented. Sometimes I find myself having to be assertive to get things done.

Organisational skills are key to my job as I have to collate, update and make available the food hygiene documentation for both the kitchen and restaurant should environmental health officers request it.

Think about it

1 List the documentation Nadia will have to provide to environmental health officers.

2 Name the powers that an environmental health officer has when carrying out a visit to a hospitality business.

3 Explain the benefits of compliance with food safety for the hotel and the consequences of poor practice.

4 Evaluate how safety legislation is implemented in the hotel restaurant. Can you think of any other ways Nadia can make sure legislation is implemented?

Introduction

Finance is at the heart of business; it is a key part in any business's strategy to survive, make a profit and be successful. This unit will help you to understand the theory behind making a profit and what products and services are the most profitable. It is also essential that all business operatives have an understanding of the costs involved in running a hospitality business. Although all businesses incur costs, it is vital that these costs are monitored and controlled, so that a healthy profit can still be made.

Assessment: You will be assessed by a series of assignments set by your teacher/tutor.

Learning aims

In this unit you will:

A understand how hospitality businesses control costs

B understand the use of selling prices and break-even analysis for a hospitality event

C be able to use an income statement (profit and loss account) to measure the success of a hospitality event.

‘When my aunt got married three years ago, she let me help with the planning. Since then I've wanted to work as a wedding coordinator. Weddings are expensive and it was a real learning curve to see how she budgeted and how much everything cost. This unit really helped to develop my understanding of finances in real-life situations and I now feel equipped to work out calculations and plan and balance budgets.

Jenny, *BTEC Level 2 First in Hospitality student*’

Costing and Controlling Finances in the Hospitality Industry

4

BTEC
Assessment Zone

This table shows what you must do in order to achieve a **Pass**, **Merit** or **Distinction** grade, and where you can find activities to help you.

Assessment criteria			
Level 1	**Level 2 Pass**	**Level 2 Merit**	**Level 2 Distinction**
Learning aim A: Understand how hospitality businesses control costs			
1A.1 Identify, using examples, the difference between fixed and variable costs for a given hospitality business.	**2A.P1** Describe, using examples, the difference between fixed and variable costs for two contrasting hospitality businesses. **See Assessment activity 4.1, page 114**	**2A.M1** English Compare the importance of accurately identifying types of costs and controlling them in two contrasting hospitality businesses. **See Assessment activity 4.1, page 114**	**2A.D1** Evaluate the impact of inaccurately identifying costs and the consequences of not controlling them in two contrasting hospitality businesses. **See Assessment activity 4.1, page 114**
1A.2 Outline how costs are controlled in a given hospitality business.	**2A.P2** English Explain how different costs are controlled in two contrasting hospitality businesses. **See Assessment activity 4.1, page 114**		
Learning aim B: Understand the use of selling prices and break-even analysis for a hospitality event			
1B.3 Maths Calculate a selling price for a product/service for a selected hospitality event, with guidance, using given information.	**2B.P3** Maths Calculate an appropriate selling price for a product/service for a selected hospitality event, using given information. **See Assessment activity 4.2, page 127**	**2B.M2** Maths English Assess how changing selling prices will affect the break-even point of a product/service for a selected hospitality event. **See Assessment activity 4.2, page 127**	**2B.D2** Maths English Evaluate the importance of break-even analysis for a selected hospitality event. **See Assessment activity 4.2, page 127**
1B.4 Maths Calculate breakeven for a product/service for a selected hospitality event, with guidance, using given sets of data.	**2B.P4** Maths Calculate breakeven for a product/service for a selected hospitality event, using given sets of data. **See Assessment activity 4.2, page 127**		
1B.5 Outline the uses of breakeven in a selected hospitality event.	**2B.P5** English Explain how break-even analysis can be used to help ensure the success of a selected hospitality event. **See Assessment activity 4.2, page 127**		

continued

Assessment criteria (continued)			
Level 1	**Level 2 Pass**	**Level 2 Merit**	**Level 2 Distinction**
Learning aim C: Be able to use an income statement (profit and loss account) to measure the success of a hospitality event.			
1C.6 Maths	**2C.P6** Maths	**2C.M3** Maths English	**2C.D3** English
Prepare an income statement (profit and loss account) for a selected hospitality event, with guidance.	Prepare an accurate income statement (profit and loss account) for a selected hospitality event. **See Assessment activity 4.3, page 131**	Analyse the impact of expenses incurred on the success of a selected hospitality event. **See Assessment activity 4.3, page 131**	Justify recommendations for improving the net profit of a selected hospitality event, in relation to an analysis of a profit and loss sheet. **See Assessment activity 4.3, page 131**

Maths Opportunity to practise mathematical skills   English Opportunity to practise English skills

How you will be assessed

This unit will be assessed by a series of internally assessed tasks. These tasks will be set by your teacher/tutor. You will need to show that you have gained an understanding of costing and controlling finances. You must show that you understand how businesses control costs, that you are aware of how selling prices and break-even analysis are used and that you are able to use an income statement to measure success.

Your assessment could be in the form of:

- written work/report
- calculations
- income statement
- break-even analysis
- presentations
- work book
- annotated examples from industry.

Costs involved in running a hospitality business

Introduction

Hospitality businesses that are successful and grow every year do so because they successfully manage how they spend their money. In this unit, you will learn about the costs involved in running a hospitality business, and understand how to request the financial information you will need to plan for different costs. Hospitality businesses have to spend money on things such as rent and ingredients, and these are known as costs.

Pick a hospitality business you are familiar with. Write down all the different costs you can think of that the business will be liable for. Compare your list with those of other group members.

Types of costs

The two main costs within the hospitality industry are fixed costs and variable costs.

1 **Fixed costs** are often referred to as overheads and indirect costs.

These are the costs of running the business despite the number of products and services sold. These costs remain the same. A restaurant must pay the rent or mortgage owed every month on the building, whether they have one customer or ten.

Fixed costs will vary considerably depending on the size of the business and its location. A small café in a village will have much smaller **overheads** in terms of the rent or mortgage it pays for its premises compared to a large gastro pub in a busy city centre, where rent is likely to be very high and the building bigger.

2 **Variable costs** are often referred to as **direct costs**.

Variable costs will change depending on the volume of product being made. They are directly related to the number of items sold or produced, so they are also called direct costs. The cost of fish for a fish pie would be twice as much if there were 16 pies rather than 8. This fish can be directly linked to the fish pie (the product), so it is a direct cost.

How well a business understands and controls their costs will result in either success or failure. Table 4.1 shows some more examples of fixed and variable costs.

Key terms

Overheads – the everyday running costs of the business, e.g. electricity, gas, water and telephone bills.

Profit – the amount of money a business makes after taking all its costs into consideration – occurs when income is more than expenditure.

Cover – a place setting at a table in a restaurant.

Table 4.1 Fixed costs and variable costs

Fixed costs (indirect)	Variable costs (direct)
Rent	Food or drinks used to prepare items for sale
Labour costs, e.g. permanent staff wages	Labour costs, e.g.
Rates	• Wages – temporary staff • pension contributions – for permanent staff

continued

Table 4.1 (continued)

Fixed costs (indirect)	Variable costs (direct)
Insurance	Advertising/promotional activities
Office costs, e.g. telephone and internet	Travel expenses
Heating	Laundry costs, e.g. table linen, bed linen, etc.
Lighting	
Water	
Leasing of equipment	

Activity 4.1   Fixed or variable?

Sally's tea shop sells cups of tea, coffee and cream cakes. She has two assistants who help on Saturdays. Identify Sally's fixed and variable costs.

Calculating simple costs

Cost of products, ingredients and other items

In order to work out costs you need to know the cost of products, ingredients and other materials, such as packaging costs, used as part of the product. Hospitality businesses will then use these costs to calculate simple menu and recipe costings.

Portions and recipes for dishes and drinks

When calculating costs, you also need to think about how portions are measured out. Meat is usually costed by its pre-cooked weight (for example, 8 oz sirloin steak); vegetables are usually costed by volume (for example, a side order); and pies, quiches and cakes are costed by the slice. When you calculate the cost of a portion, you need to know both the cost of the ingredients and the size of the portion or serving. It is important to get portion sizes right – too small and the customer may feel cheated (and not return); too large and the **profit** on the dish will go down.

When planning for a restaurant, you need to understand how many **covers** per day you expect to be serving, the typical breakdown of menu options and the volume of ingredients that need to be bought. You also need to think about the price you will charge, based on either single unit purchases and bulk purchases.

Link

Go to Topic B.2 in this unit for more information about how hospitality businesses cost recipes and make money on each dish.

Worked example: Calculating price per portion

A chef makes a cottage pie that can serve 50 portions. The ingredients cost £20. To work out the price per portion the chef would divide £20 by 50.

£20 ÷ 50 = 0.40 or 40 pence per portion

Buying strawberries when they are in season can make a big difference to the price you pay for them.

Costing for meals or functions

You might need to plan and calculate costs for lots of different types of meals and functions. A mobile catering company or restaurant will cater for different types of functions, for example, weddings, birthdays, anniversaries, bon voyage parties, drink receptions and barbeques. As well as calculating the cost of ingredients, these businesses also need to work out costs for drinks and services (staff wages, music, venue, etc.).

Functions will incur different costs depending on the type of function. For example, whether it is a daytime or evening function requiring a smaller lunch or bigger evening meal, the type of meal that is needed (for example, a buffet or sit-down meal with several courses) and the number of guests to be served.

Services provided

Businesses also need to plan the cost of any additional services they will provide. For example, room service in a hotel or crockery, cutlery and plates at a wedding function.

Did you know?

The time of year or season can affect how much you will pay for particular ingredients. Seasonal purchasing, that is, buying fruit and vegetables in bulk when they are in season, can dramatically reduce the cost of a dish.

Carry out some research into seasonal fruit and vegetables. Find out when they are likely to be more plentiful (in season) and, therefore, cheaper to buy.

Activity 4.2　A good opportunity?

Andy is planning a surprise birthday party for his wife. There are 25 guests due to attend and he has decided on a three-course meal consisting of:

- a starter of prawn cocktail at £2.95 per head
- a main course of steak Diane, salad and chips at £10.25 per head
- a dessert of chocolate torte at £3.50 per head.

Andy has asked to hold this in his local hotel for a room hire fee of £50. He has also booked a magician to entertain his guests at a cost of £150.

The cost of staff at the party has been covered as part of the meal costs and, therefore, Andy does not need to pay extra for this.

1 Calculate the total cost of the function to make sure that Andy understands what the party is likely to cost.

2 Calculate the cost per head for the birthday function.

▶ Controlling costs

Introduction

Controlling your costs is critical to financial success. Cost control helps to maintain profits. When costs are not controlled, this may result in damage to profitability and can lead to businesses being unable to pay their costs.

Think of three ways that a catering business could control their costs. Discuss your ideas with a partner.

▶ Controlling ordering methods and systems

Ordering supplies for a hospitality business needs planning and exactness. Order too much and you have wasted supply and money; order too little and you are unable to provide what you advertised to customers.

It is difficult to predict how many customers will order meals each day. Therefore, a lot of businesses use ordering methods and systems to work out how much of something they need to order.

Forecasting sales

One method is forecasting. Forecasting is used to predict future activities within a business. It involves estimating sales and costs to plan how to meet future demands. It also sets a budget for spending and **revenue** over a future period of time.

Sales can also be estimated by using financial information from the previous year of sales as guidance. You can look at what has sold well or not so well. If you have been consistently selling roughly 100 portions of lasagne each week for several months, you have a good idea of how many portions you will sell in the future. By forecasting sales you can, therefore, decide on the volume of ingredients to order from your suppliers.

Checking prices

Hospitality businesses buy food or ingredients from a range of suppliers, and businesses must look for reputable suppliers to meet their needs. They should not rely on just one supplier. It is good business to check prices regularly across lots of suppliers, as this lets you know what is happening within the wider market. You might find that you can get the same quality ingredients for less money with another supplier; or you might find that you have a good deal with your current supplier.

Managing relationships with suppliers

Positive relationships with suppliers will benefit hospitality businesses, as they are more likely to provide you with updated pricing structures and, where possible, discounts. For example, they may tell you that you can save more if you increase the size of your

Key term

Revenue – the income of an organisation, especially a large amount.

order of a product which you can store for some time (such as flour or sugar). Where a saving has been made, the business may be able to pass the discount on to the customer to encourage loyalty and repeat business. For example, if a public house gets 50 per cent off wine at a cash and carry, they may be able to offer customers a promotion to buy two glasses and get the rest of the bottle for free.

Large businesses will have a list of approved suppliers and it may be difficult to use alternative suppliers without them being approved. This may be because a discount has been agreed with the approved supplier, and the finance department may need to negotiate with any suppliers that you wish to use.

▶ Controlling deliveries

Using purchase specifications

Link

Go back to Unit 1, Learning aim B, Topic B.1 to recap information on the purchasing cycle.

Purchase specifications are used by companies to specify the exact type and quality of an item they wish to buy. They tend to be used by larger businesses where standards need to be the same across all of their outlets. This is a very precise method of working and makes sure that no matter what the venue, a chicken wrap purchased in one café, is the same in all cafés. Purchase specifications are an ideal way of preventing substandard products being used.

Checking product quality

It is important to control deliveries to make sure the products that are delivered are:

- of good quality
- reflect the quantity ordered on the delivery note and order requisition
- in date, to allow enough time for them to be used and prevent wastage.

It is important to check that products are delivered on time, that they are of good quality and that the complete order has been delivered.

Controlling storage

Controlling storage is important not only in food safety but also to the finances of a business. This is because any wasted items will incur a cost.

Using stock rotation

A system of stock control and stocktaking is essential to avoid having too much of an item, which can lead to waste and reduced profit. Not having enough of an item means you will not be able to make certain dishes.

Remember that stock must be rotated. Make sure that stock with the most recent use-by date is placed at the front of the storage area, so that it is used before stock which has been purchased more recently. Any food that is past its use-by date must be thrown away. A familiar method of stock rotation in hospitality and catering businesses is 'first in, first out', also known as FIFO.

Controlling the issuing of goods or resources

Businesses can further control their costs by controlling the issuing of goods and resources. For example, if a housekeeper issues resources to a chambermaid for a period of one month, they will know that they must make their cleaning materials last for one month before they will be issued more. If cleaning materials were issued as and when required, there would not be as much control over what, and how much, was being used. This may be further controlled by limiting the access of stock and storage areas to named members of staff.

Serving meals at set times of the day

Another example of controlling goods and resources is to have set times of the day when meals are served. This controls labour costs. For example, if a hotel sets a period of time during which breakfast is served (between 7 a.m. to 9.30 a.m.), then it may be possible for waiting staff to clock off at 10.30 a.m. after clean down. They could then return for lunch service later on in the day.

Preventing wastage

Preventing waste is also key to controlling costs in a hospitality business. Methods to control waste include:

- correct portion control
- precisely weighing and measuring ingredients.

When food or ingredients have to be thrown away, be sure to recycle as much as possible. All staff should be aware of which bins to use when throwing away different items, that is, food waste, glass, plastic and tins. A number of supermarkets and restaurants donate their food items to charities and homeless shelters. Not only does this help to reduce the amount of food that is wasted, but it is also good for a business's public relations.

Case study: Hambilton Hall

Hambilton Hall is a countryside hotel with 120 bedrooms, four large function rooms and a separate spa and pool facility. The company employs 50 staff on both a full- and part-time basis. Janos Stavos is the general manager. The finance manager has concerns about an annual event that is held at the hotel.

In 2011, the Women's Institute held their summer tea at the hotel. Fifty guests attended at a cost of £9.95 per person. The same event in 2012 was attended by 52 guests at a cost of £10.50 per person.

1 What was the total bill for 50 guests in 2011?

2 What was the total bill for 52 guests in 2012?

3 In 2011, food costs for the event totalled £6.50 per person. What was the total food cost for the event?

4 In 2012, the cost of food increased by 20 per cent, to £7.80 per person. How much did the total food cost differ in 2012?

5 What reasons can you give for the rise in food costs?

Assessment activity 4.1 — *English* — 2A.P1 | 2A.P2 | 2A.M1 | 2A.D1

Your teacher/tutor has asked you to attend your department's open evening for prospective new learners and their parents. To showcase what your class has been learning, she has asked you to produce an information leaflet that explains how hospitality businesses control costs. She would like you to pick two different hospitality businesses and compare and contrast their costs and how they are managed. You will also need to consider the issues that arise if a business does not manage their costs correctly.

To complete this task effectively, you will need to arrange interviews with people from your chosen businesses to find out the relevant information.

In your leaflet you will need to include the following information.

1 Produce an illustrated report to explain the differences between fixed and variable costs. Then, describe how the fixed and variable costs for your two businesses differ.

2 Include a section that explains why accurately identifying costs and controlling them is important. Describe how each business does this.

3 Explain how you assess whether costs have been controlled properly. Evaluate how well both businesses have accurately identified and controlled their costs. What would happen if either business failed to do this? Explain what the outcome and impact could be.

Tips

- Before you interview people, make sure you know what information you will need from them. Prepare a questionnaire and make sure you have asked everything you need to know before leaving the interview.
- Use real examples from your interviews as well as case studies to show the differences between fixed and variable costs, and also between the businesses you have chosen.
- Remember that some information may be better presented in table or graph format. Tables and graphs will help your reader to understand the numbers and will make the differences easier to see.

WorkSpace

▷ Naseem Khan

Finance assistant

I have worked as a finance assistant in the Bear Hotel for six months. When I started I had no prior knowledge of finance procedures but had worked in both housekeeping, issuing resources and as a stores assistant in a local food factory. The Bear Hotel is a small independent hotel with just 12 bedrooms and one function room, which is busy for weddings and other events.

On a daily basis I have several tasks to perform.

I am responsible for inputting figures into the relevant spreadsheets for the key areas in the hotel, including the kitchen, restaurant, bar and function room. This helps to keep up to date the systems which show how much stock is held by each area and orders that have been made. I am also responsible for keeping track of waste and calculating the cost of waste in each of the key areas. I then pass all of this data on to the accountants and finance manager – they then complete the other more in-depth parts of financial and management accounting.

I didn't think that I would like working with figures all day but I have surprised myself and found that I am now even more interested in this side of how the hotel works. I'd like to learn more about how pricing is calculated and how problems with finances can be overcome. Because there is such a small team at the hotel I feel that now is the time to expand my knowledge.

Think about it!

1 Why should Naseem tell his line manager if he thinks that the chef is overspending?

2 What might his line manager do if the chef has been overspending?

3 Why is it important to record wastage and what should Naseem do if he notices an increase in wastage in a particular area?

▶ Generating revenue and making a profit

Introduction

Revenue is the amount of money that the business earns. This must be greater than the costs the business incurs for it to survive.

Hospitality businesses make money by offering products and services to customers. With a partner, make a list of the products and services offered by the hospitality industry.

▶ Methods of generating revenue

Hospitality businesses make money (revenue) in two ways.

1 They sell products, for example, dishes on a menu or cocktails in a bar.

2 They provide services, for example, room service or butler service in a hotel.

The formula used to calculate revenue earned for each type of item sold by a business is:

Revenue = number of sales × price per unit

Worked example: Calculating revenue

Betty owns a tea room. She wants to work out her revenue for the week. Betty has sold 1,000 cream teas costing £8 each.

Revenue = number of sales (1,000) × price of a unit (£8)

1,000 x £8 = £8,000

Activity 4.3   Ways to make money

Choose three hospitality businesses with which you are familiar. Make a copy of the table below and then make a list of all the products or services they sell or provide to generate revenue.

Then, identify areas where you think they could generate more revenue. How could the businesses make more money?

An example has been provided to get you started.

Hospitality business	Product	Service	Area for improvement
Café	Sandwiches, soups, pies, cakes and beverages including tea, coffee and soft drinks	Most items are available to take away	The business could consider catering for outside functions

Types of costs

All businesses must spend money to succeed. The types of costs incurred by a business can be many and varied, depending on the type and size of the business.

Expenditure

There are many different types of business **expenditure**. Expenditure refers to all of the money a business pays out – the costs it incurs in order to offer products and services. You have already learned that these costs will either be fixed costs or variable costs.

Expenditure includes overheads that a business might have. In Topic A.1, we identified overheads as a fixed cost. Overheads include money paid for rent and rates, heating and lighting, gas and electricity.

The formula for working out the total costs of a business is:

Total costs = fixed costs + variable costs

So, if Betty's fixed costs are £1,500 a week and her variable costs are £2,000 a week, her total costs are £3,500.

Key term

Expenditure – money that a business spends.

Link

Go back to Topic A.1 in this unit to recap information about the types of costs businesses have to cover.

Calculating profit or loss

There can be two main outcomes of offering products and services. These are:

- a profit is made
- a loss is made.

A profit is made when the revenue is more than the expenditure – when there is more money coming in than there is going out. A loss is made when expenditure is more than revenue – when the amount of money coming in is less than the monies being paid out.

Profit or loss is calculated using the following formula.

Profit/loss = revenue – expenditure

Worked example: Calculating profit

Betty's revenue from selling 1,000 cream teas in a single week is £8,000. She now wants to work out her profit.

To calculate her profit, she needs to add together her fixed costs (rent, lighting, equipment) and variable costs (prices of ingredients) and then deduct this total from her revenue. Her fixed costs for the week are £1,500 and her variable costs are £2,000.

Profit = revenue (£8,000) – total costs (£1,500 + £2,000)

£8,000 – £3,500 = £4,500

As the figure is positive, Betty has made a profit.

Case study: Event catering

Little Bites Doughnuts is a small doughnut van that moves from one event to another, making and selling doughnuts and hot drinks. During the Royal Welsh Show, the owners pay a pitch fee of £15,000. The event lasts for five days.

To make sure of a speedy service, one staff member is employed to work a ten-hour day at £5.75 per hour.

A coffee and a doughnut costs £0.98 to make.

The selling price of a coffee and a doughnut is £5.50.

During the five-day period the van is expected to sell 1,500 coffee and doughnut deals.

1 List the fixed and variable costs of the business.

2 Calculate revenue of expected sales during the five-day period.

3 Subtract any costs you have totals for from the revenue.

4 Do you think the van will make a profit or loss at the show?

▶ Calculating appropriate selling prices for products or services

Key terms

Gross profit – the amount of money made from selling a product after the cost of producing that product has been deducted.

Net profit – the amount of money made from selling a product after all costs (expenditure) have been deducted from the gross profit.

Cost of sales – the cost of producing a product.

Introduction

In this section, you will learn about **gross profit** and **net profit**. You will also find out how hospitality businesses calculate appropriate selling prices for their goods and services by considering factors such as tax (including value added tax), service charges and discounts.

▶ Gross profit

A business will make profit when it has more money coming in (revenue) than going out (expenditure).

Gross profit is the money made from selling a product (sales revenue) after the cost of producing that product has been deducted. The cost of producing the product is also known as **cost of sales**, that is, variable costs.

The formula for calculating gross profit is:

> Gross profit = revenue − cost of sales

Worked example: Calculating gross profit

Fred operates a burger van business. He wants to work out what his gross profit is for the month of July.

Fred spends £5,000 on ingredients (burgers, buns, onions). This spend is Fred's 'cost of sales'.

His revenue for the month is £20,000.

Gross profit = revenue (£20,000) − cost of sales (£5,000)

£20,000 − £5,000 = £15,000

So, the business's gross profit is £15,000.

Activity 4.4 Calculating gross profit

You work in a local coffee shop. In small groups, write a list of as many cost of sale items the shop has as you can think of.

If the revenue of the coffee shop is £50,000 and the cost of sales total £20,000, work out the shop's gross profit.

▶ Net profit

Net profit is the amount of money made after all the outgoings (expenditure/fixed costs) other than cost of sales have been deducted from the gross profit figure, for example, rent, electricity, gas, lighting, wages.

The formula for calculating net profit is:

> Net profit = gross profit − expenditure (overheads)

Worked example: Calculating net profit

A wine bar sells its house wines at £5.00 a glass. The price the business pays for the wine is £1.50 a glass. The business has overheads of £50,000 a year and sells 50,000 glasses of wine a year.

Gross profit = revenue (50,000 x £5.00) – cost of sales (£1.50 x 50,000)

Gross profit = £250,000 – £75,000 = £175,000

Net profit = gross profit (£175,000) – expenditure (£50,000)

Net profit = £175,000 – £50,000 = £125,000

So, the business's net profit is £125,000.

Take it further

If the wine bar increased the price of a glass of wine to £6.00 a glass, how would this affect the gross and net profit?

Activity 4.5   Calculating net profit

If the gross profit of a business is £20,000 and all expenses except the cost of sales total £10,000, what is its net profit?

Calculating appropriate selling prices

When businesses calculate the selling price of their products and services they need to make sure that the price enables the business to make a net profit. Pricing a product or service is not always straightforward.

It is important not to price products and services too high or too low. Reasons for this are listed in Table 4.2.

Table 4.2 Potential problems with incorrect pricing

Pricing too high	Pricing too low
• If a product or service's price is too high, it might not attract enough custom (sell enough), leading to the same problems as if the pricing was too low.	• The business may make a loss on the product or service. • Sales may not be able to cover the business's expenses. • The business could fail to make a profit. • Lack of profit might lead to bankruptcy. • This could eventually lead to business closure.

There are several factors that may affect selling prices and these include:

1 adding and subtracting tax, for example, value added tax (VAT)

2 adding a service charge

3 subtracting discounts.

Adding and subtracting tax

Value added tax (VAT) is a tax on all goods and services that are considered to be non-essential. The tax is collected by Her Majesty's Revenue and Customs (HMRC). Some food products are **exempt** from VAT but many hospitality products and services are subject to VAT; that is, it has to be paid.

All food and drink sold in hotels and restaurants is subject to VAT. Catering businesses which are not subject to VAT charges are those that are non-profit making, for example, those providing school and hospital meals. These are essential services, so are exempt from VAT.

There are two ways of charging for VAT in hospitality. Some businesses will include VAT within their pricing system, whereas others will add it to the total cost at the end.

Key term

Exempt – If a product is exempt from VAT, you do not have to pay VAT on it.

Did you know?

VAT is charged at 20 per cent in the UK and at varying rates in other countries.

In the UK, some items are exempt from VAT, e.g. school books, whereas in Ireland, books are charged with VAT. This makes it expensive to buy school books in Ireland.

Adding service charge

Some hospitality businesses add a compulsory service charge to a customer's bill. This is a charge for the service provided by waiting staff. Other businesses encourage the customer to leave a gratuity/tip for the service they received. This service charge is passed on to the staff in addition to, or as part of, their wages.

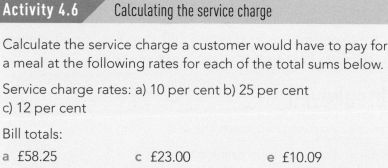

Activity 4.6 — Calculating the service charge

Calculate the service charge a customer would have to pay for a meal at the following rates for each of the total sums below.

Service charge rates: a) 10 per cent b) 25 per cent c) 12 per cent

Bill totals:

a £58.25   c £23.00   e £10.09
b £43.23   d £109.87

You can see on this bill that a service charge of £1.39 has been automatically added to the total the customer has to pay.

Subtracting discounts

A discount on the bill may be given if a customer is using a discount voucher or if the customer has made a complaint due to poor service or quality. Discounts are normally applied to the final bill.

Discounts are often given for promotional events and large groups. In these cases, the business will be receiving less than the usual total revenue.

Many websites such as Groupon, lastminute.com and LateRooms.com offer promotional deals to attract more custom. It is better for a hotel to sell rooms at a discount rather than have them sitting empty. You will find that customers may have paid different prices for their room, depending on the time they booked their stay and the method of booking.

▶ Using break-even analysis

Introduction

You have learned that a business makes a profit when revenue is greater than expenditure, but it makes a loss when revenue is less than expenditure. Between these two situations there is a point called **breakeven**. This is when income and expenditure are the same.

▶ Breakeven

Breakeven is reached when a business has made enough money from selling a product or service (revenue) to cover the costs involved in making the product or providing the service. In other words, at this point you have not made a loss but you have not made a profit. If a business exceeds the break-even point, they will be making a profit.

> Breakeven is when total revenue = total costs

If it costs an Italian restaurant £2.00 to produce a pizza, taking into account its fixed and variable costs, and the restaurant sells each pizza for £2.00, then they have reached break-even point. If the restaurant sells each pizza for £5.00, then they will have made a profit of £3.00 on each pizza. They have exceeded the break-even point.

▶ Calculating breakeven

The break-even point can be calculated two ways. The first is using a formula.

The formula used to calculate the break-even point is:

$$\text{Break-even point} = \frac{\text{fixed costs}}{\text{selling price per unit} - \text{variable cost per unit}}$$

Worked example: Calculating breakeven

Sara is thinking about opening a fish and chip shop business. She is aiming to sell a portion of fish and chips for £1.30. It will cost Sara 80p to make each portion of fish and chips (Sara's variable cost per portion). She reckons her fixed costs will be £100 per week.

Sara wants to know how many portions of fish and chips she would need to sell in a week before she would start to make a profit. Using the break-even formula:

$$\text{Break-even point} = \frac{\text{fixed costs (£100)} = £100}{\text{selling price per unit (£1.30)} - \text{variable cost per unit (80p)} = 50p} = 200 \text{ portions}$$

It is important that a hospitality business knows its break-even point – then they have a good idea of how much to charge in order to make a profit.

Activity 4.7 — Calculating break-even point

If a single room in a hotel sells for £50 per night, the variable cost is £3 and the fixed cost is £300. What is the break-even point? Use the formula to calculate it.

The break-even point can also be calculated by drawing a chart. Carry out Activity 4.8 so that you understand how the chart has been created.

Activity 4.8 — Working through a break-even chart

Study the break-even chart in Figure 4.2 and read through the list of features in Table 4.3. Ask your teacher/tutor if there is anything you do not understand.

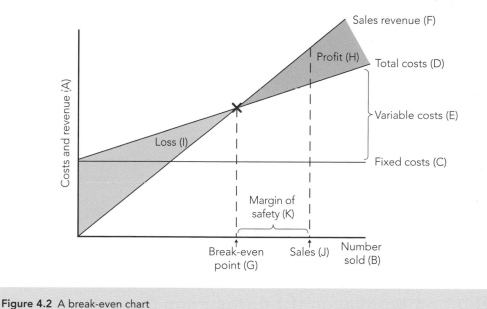

Figure 4.2 A break-even chart

Table 4.3 Features of a break-even chart

Feature	Explanation
A – Costs and revenue	The vertical axis shows the amount of money spent as costs and received as revenue.
B – Number sold	The horizontal axis shows the number of products that could be sold.
C – Fixed costs	This line is horizontal because the fixed costs never change no matter how many products are sold.

continued

Table 4.3 *(continued)*

Feature	Explanation
D – Total costs	This line shows the fixed costs plus the variable costs. It starts at the left-hand side where the fixed cost line meets the vertical axis. At this point, there are no sales so the variable costs are zero. The line is then drawn to show how variable costs increase in direct proportion to the number of items sold. It then shows the total cost for each level of sales.
E – Variable costs	The difference between the fixed costs line and the total costs line is the variable costs. This gap widens as the level of sales increases.
F – Sales revenue	This line starts at the zero point since no sales means that no income is being earned. The sales revenue is calculated by multiplying the price charged by the number of items sold.
G – Break-even point	This is the point where the sales revenue line crosses the total cost line and shows the number of sales needed for the business to break even.
H – Profit	To the right of the break-even line, sales revenue is greater than total costs, so the business is making a profit. The distance between the two lines shows the amount of profit for each level of sales.
I – Loss	To the left of the break-even line, sales revenue is less than expenditure and the business is making a loss. The distance between the lines shows the amount of loss at each level of sales.
J – Sales	This shows that sales are higher than the number required to break even.
K – **Margin of safety**	This is the amount by which sales would have to fall before the break-even point is reached.

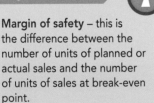

Key term

Margin of safety – this is the difference between the number of units of planned or actual sales and the number of units of sales at break-even point.

Effect on breakeven if figures change

Breakeven can be affected by:

- the selling price – raising or lowering the price a product/service is sold for
- changes to fixed or variable costs, for example, an increase or decrease in the cost of rent, fuel bills, wage bills, raw materials, etc.

If a restaurant specialising in seafood is unable to access fish locally due to shortages, they may need to pay more to source fish from further afield. This means that the restaurant's variable costs will increase. The restaurant will either have to increase the selling price of the fish dish (which could mean fewer dishes are sold) or earn less money on each dish. The restaurant will have to sell more to break even.

It is important that hospitality businesses are aware of what can affect their break-even point and are prepared to make changes as, and when, required.

Table 4.4 summarises the likely impact of different changes on the break-even point.

Table 4.4 The effect of changes in sales or costs on the break-even point

Factor/Change	Effect on the break-even point
Increased sales	Increase in the margin of safety.
Decreased sales	Decrease in the margin of safety, whereby if sales fall below break-even point the business will make a loss.
Increased costs	Number of sales needed to break even increases, so the profit level would fall and has the potential to become a loss.
Decreased costs	The break-even point would be lower and so the business makes a profit.

▶ Using break-even analysis

Using break-even analysis is a very useful tool. It allows businesses to:

- monitor short-term survival
- identify the break-even point in unit sales/revenue – the minimum sales needed to avoid a loss
- calculate a margin of safety – this identifies the number by which sales can fall before the business makes a loss
- identify profit/loss made
- monitor and consider the effects of changes to both fixed and variable costs
- consider the effects of selling price.

Break-even analysis does, however, assume that all of the goods produced are sold.

Activity 4.9	Heaven Sent Spa

Heaven Sent Spa offers a spa package for £25 (its selling price).

The spa has fixed costs of £350 per week.

The spa has variable costs of £6 per week.

On average, the spa will see about 50 customers per week.

1 Calculate the break-even point for Heaven Sent Spa using the break-even formula.

2 How many treatments do they need to carry out to make a profit? Are there any suggestions you could make to them about their pricing or future offerings?

3 What would be the result if their fixed costs were to rise to £500 per week?

4 What would be the effect of a decreased selling price to £20 per person?

▶ Preparing an income statement (profit and loss account)

Introduction

Financial statements are important to all businesses and in this section you will learn about the purpose of a profit and loss account.

Research what a profit and loss account is and identify the types of financial data needed for the account to be completed.

Key term

Income statement – this shows the money that has come into a business and the money that has gone out over a fixed period of time (usually a year). In this way, a business can see if it has made a profit or a loss. It is also known as a profit and loss account.

Remember

The revenue is the money that comes into a business (from sales) and the cost of sales are the business's variable costs.

▶ The purpose of an income statement (profit and loss account)

Businesses will use an **income statement**, also referred to as a profit and loss account, to show how they have performed financially over the course of a period of time, usually a year. However, an income statement can be prepared for a specific event or function.

It is a financial document that sets out a company's revenue and cost of sales for the given period. It provides a clear picture of the amount of profit or loss that a business has made and is a record of both the sales and costs over the given period.

A business owner(s) can use a profit and loss account to help them make future business decisions. It can also be used by potential investors or creditors who may be thinking of investing money in the business, for example, a new business partner or a bank.

An example income statement is shown in Table 4.6.

The top three lines of the statement are known as the trading account.

The bottom section lists the expenses.

This figure is found by subtracting the total expenses from the gross profit.

Table 4.6 Income statement (profit and loss account)

	£	£
Income from sales (sales revenue)		50,000
Cost of sales	15,000	
Gross profit		35,000
Expenses/overheads		
Wages	25,000	
Utilities	5,000	
Net profit		5,000

Activity 4.11 Checking the income statement

Work through the income statement carefully and make sure you understand all the calculations. Ask your teacher/tutor for help if you are unsure.

▶ How to complete an income statement

A profit and loss account in correct terms should be named a trading, profit and loss account. We will work through each section of the income statement so it is clear how to complete one.

The top section of the income statement shows a business how much gross profit they have made. This section is also known as the trading account.

Sales revenue

Sales revenue is the money coming into the business from selling goods and services, for example, accommodation, food and beverages and leisure facilities. Sales revenue is calculated as shown in the worked example. You have already learned the formula for calculating revenue.

Worked example: Calculating sales revenue

Samia owns a boutique hotel that has ten rooms. She prices the rooms at £40 per night. Over the course of the year, Samia has 9,000 room bookings. She wants to work out her sales revenue for the year.

Sales revenue = number of sales (9,000) × price per unit (£40) = £360,000

Cost of sales

The cost of sales is the cost of producing the product or service. So, if Ishmael runs a business selling ice creams, his cost of sales will be the total he needs to spend to buy the cones and the ice cream.

Gross profit

You have already learned that gross profit is the money made from selling a product (sales revenue) after the cost of producing that product has been deducted (cost of sales).

Worked example: Calculating gross profit

Sarah runs a business selling chefs' whites to hospitality businesses. It costs Sarah £10 to buy each set of chefs' whites. She sells each set for £35.

Gross profit = revenue (£35) − cost of sales (£10)

£35 − £10 = £25

Introduction

The word 'enterprise' has more than one meaning. It can be used to describe an undertaking, a business and a willingness to take on new challenges. In this unit, you will explore 'enterprise' in the context of the hospitality industry.

Hospitality businesses come in all shapes and sizes, from the sole trader operating a burger van to the huge multinational companies operating hotels all around the world. To be successful, companies need to be enterprising and to be enterprising they must continuously develop their products and services to meet the needs of their customers. They need to respond to the trends that affect how they operate and the factors that influence their success.

You will investigate different types of hospitality businesses and examine the common factors that make them successful.

You will learn that you too can be enterprising and you will be given the opportunity to plan an idea for a realistic hospitality business start-up in your local area, based on your research. You will then present the business model and plan.

Assessment: You will be assessed by a series of assignments set by your teacher/tutor.

Learning aims

In this unit you will:

A understand how trends and the current business environment may impact on a hospitality business start-up

B plan an idea for a new hospitality business

C present a business model for a hospitality business start-up.

My parents got me excited about food and the flair of presentation from a young age. I'm keen to open my own restaurant so I'm working in a local fine dining restaurant to learn about business and the industry. I love learning about the different dishes on the menus and helping customers to make their choices. The restaurant owners work really hard to make the business a success. It's good to see first-hand the challenges involved in running a business. This is the best kind of learning experience.

Ankur, BTEC Level 2 First in Hospitality student

Enterprise in the Hospitality Industry

5

BTEC Assessment Zone

This table shows what you must do in order to achieve a **Pass**, **Merit** or **Distinction** grade, and where you can find activities to help you.

Assessment criteria			
Level 1	Level 2 **Pass**	Level 2 **Merit**	Level 2 **Distinction**
Learning aim A: Understand how trends and the current business environment may impact on a hospitality business start-up			
1A.1 Identify factors of the business environment that can affect a hospitality business start-up.	**2A.P1** Outline how the business environment can affect a hospitality business start-up. **See Assessment activity 5.1, page 146**	**2A.M1** Explain how changes in the current business environment are likely to affect a hospitality business start-up. **See Assessment activity 5.1, page 146**	**2A.D1** Maths Assess the current risks, opportunities and trends in the business environment for a hospitality business start-up. **See Assessment activity 5.1, page 146**
1A.2 Identify current trends that may affect a hospitality business start-up.	**2A.P2** Maths Explain how current trends will affect a hospitality business start-up. **See Assessment activity 5.1, page 146**	**2A.M2** Maths Compare how two trends have affected a hospitality business start-up. **See Assessment activity 5.1, page 146**	
Learning aim B: Plan an idea for a new hospitality business			
1B.3 Identify four features of successful hospitality businesses.	**2B.P3** Describe, using relevant examples, features of successful hospitality businesses. **See Assessment activity 5.2, page 157**	**2B.M3** Compare features, strengths and weaknesses of two successful hospitality businesses. **See Assessment activity 5.2, page 157**	**2B.D2** Maths Justify how the initial plan for a new hospitality business idea has potential for success in relation to existing local hospitality businesses. **See Assessment activity 5.2, page 157**
1B.4 Maths English Prepare an initial plan for a new hospitality business idea for the local area.	**2B.P4** Maths English Prepare a realistic initial plan for a new hospitality business idea suitable for the local area. **See Assessment activity 5.2, page 157**	**2B.M4** Maths Explain how the initial plan for a new hospitality business idea has the potential to respond to market needs. **See Assessment activity 5.2, page 157**	

continued

Assessment criteria *(continued)*

Level 1	Level 2 **Pass**	Level 2 **Merit**	Level 2 **Distinction**
Learning aim C: Present a business model for a hospitality business start-up			
1C.5 Outline the choice of format selected for a hospitality business start-up.	**2C.P5** Explain the reasons for the choice of format selected for a hospitality business start-up. **See Assessment activity 5.3, page 165**	**2C.M5** English Present a realistic business model for a hospitality business start-up, explaining how the format and business model will enable it to carry out its activities successfully. **See Assessment activity 5.3, page 165**	**2C.D3** English Present a realistic business model for a hospitality business start-up, explaining how the format and supporting evidence justifies the initial business idea. **See Assessment activity 5.3, page 165**
1C.6 English Produce, with guidance, a business model for a hospitality business start-up.	**2C.P6** English Produce a realistic business model using sources of help and support for a hospitality business start-up. **See Assessment activity 5.3, page 165**		
1C.7 English Present, with guidance, a business model for a hospitality business start-up.	**2C.P7** English Present a realistic business model for a hospitality business start-up. **See Assessment activity 5.3, page 165**		

Maths	Opportunity to practise mathematical skills	English	Opportunity to practise English skills

How you will be assessed

This unit will be assessed by a series of internally assessed tasks. These tasks will be set by your teacher/tutor. You will explore current affairs and trends in the business environment and will reflect on the impact that changes in the environment could have on businesses in the hospitality industry. You will come up with your own business idea and give reasons for choosing it. When presenting your business idea, you should show that you have considered current market trends and influences, and that there is a market for your business – one that you have researched.

Evidence for this unit is likely to be presented in a portfolio. You could place your evidence under these suggested section headings to meet the assessment criteria:

- idea for the hospitality business start-up
- research for the hospitality business start-up
- initial plan for the new hospitality business idea
- format of the hospitality business start-up; reasons for choice
- business model
- presentation
- observation records and/or witness statements.

▶▶ Finding information

Introduction

The success of almost any hospitality business will depend largely on its plans for development. Businesses must develop constantly in order to maintain or improve sales, improve customer satisfaction and remain profitable. Businesses need lots of information to help them do this. In this section, you will look at different sources of business information and decide if the information is reliable.

Imagine that you have won the lottery and can afford to start your dream restaurant. In pairs, discuss the types of information you would need to know to help you open a successful business. When you have finished, compare your list with those of other pairs.

Key terms

Market intelligence – primarily external data collected and analysed by a business about markets that it anticipates participating in (used to make decisions).

Competitive intelligence – the action of defining, gathering, analysing and distributing intelligence about products, customers and competitors.

Market research – research that gathers and analyses information about moving goods or services from producer to consumer.

Activity 5.1

Hospitality facts

Use the internet, trade journals or newspapers to find the answers to the following questions.

1 How many people does the hospitality industry in the United Kingdom (UK) employ?

2 Representatives of the hospitality industry are campaigning for the rate of VAT to be lowered for the hospitality industry. Why are they campaigning for this? What would they like the rate to be?

How well a business is performing financially can be affected by a lot of different factors: food and health trends, the economic climate, a business's location, menu price and people's perceptions of the quality of the food and service. These all play a part in how successful a business will be. How a business advertises itself to customers and the ways that customers find out information about a business can also affect its success, especially that of a business start-up.

▶ Sources of information

Business operators in all industries need information about the markets in which their business operates. This kind of information is essential and it is often referred to as **market** or **competitive intelligence**. This type of information can be found:

- on industry and financial websites
- in annual financial statements and reports from competitors
- by speaking to people at business networking events
- in professional and trade journals
- in broadsheet and local newspapers.

These sources of information can help a hospitality business to carry out **market research** so they can:

- acquire an understanding of customers' needs, expectations and opinions on a huge range of issues
- make informed decisions about the type of products that customers want and the price they will pay for them
- anticipate future customer needs – hospitality businesses continuously adjust their products and services to remain successful.

▶ Reliability of sources and bias

Although it is vital to use external sources of information to make business decisions, you must bear in mind that the source of the information should be checked for:

- validity – is it true and up to date?
- reliability – can you trust the content?
- bias – is it subjective? Does it offer one person's opinion without offering an alternative view?

It is important to assess the validity of information by checking:

- who has produced the information
- why they have produced it (in other words, what is the purpose of the information)
- whether the information gives just one point of view.

Imagine that a property development company publishes an article stating that a redevelopment project in an area of previously high unemployment is set to bring hundreds of new jobs, new development opportunities and economic growth to an area. The article might tempt someone wanting to invest in a new restaurant to buy something in that area.

However, after doing further research, no supporting evidence is found to suggest that the redevelopment will have that impact. The article has been sponsored by the company carrying out the redevelopment to encourage unsuspecting **entrepreneurs** to invest. This is so that the property development company's plans have a greater chance of success. We can see that the article is not reliable and is biased. It has been published purely to get more businesses to invest in the area and is not based on fact.

Discussion

Would a report be biased if it urged restaurant operators to buy locally produced food? Discuss your thoughts as a group.

Key term

Entrepreneur – a person who organises, operates and assumes the risk for a business venture.

TOPIC **A.2**

▶ Size of hospitality business and type

Introduction

In Unit 1, you learned that hospitality businesses can range in size. In this section, you will learn how businesses can be categorised by size and type.

In pairs, write your own definition of a micro business, a small and medium enterprise and a large hospitality business. Give an example of each one in your local area.

Take it further

To access the People 1st, 'State of the Nation Report, 2013', go to www.pearsonhotlinks.co.uk and search for this title.

▶ Micro hospitality businesses

A micro business is one employing fewer than 10 people. In 2012, approximately 81 per cent of hospitality businesses were categorised as micro businesses (Source: People 1st, 2013, 'State of the Nation Report 2013').

▶ Small and medium enterprises (SMEs)

There is no standard definition of what makes a business 'small', however, generally a small business is defined as a business with 10 to 49 employees. In 2012, approximately 16 per cent of hospitality businesses in the UK were classified as small (Source: People 1st, 2013).

A medium business is defined as a business employing 50–249 employees. In 2012, only 2 per cent of hospitality businesses were classified as medium-sized (Source: People 1st, 2013).

Activity 5.2

Large hospitality businesses

Research, identify and list as many hospitality businesses in the UK as you can that employ more than 250 people.

Micro hospitality business

Fewer than 10 employees

A small business

10–49 employees

A medium-sized business

× 5

50–249 employees

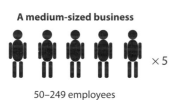

A large business

× 5+

250+ employees

Scale: 1 person = 10 employees

Figure 5.1 The number of employees in micro, small, medium and large hospitality businesses

Discussion

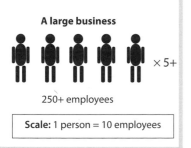

Why do you think so many people start up new hospitality businesses? Why do you think so many new businesses are unsuccessful?

Large hospitality businesses

A large hospitality business is defined as a business employing 250 or more employees. In 2012, only 0.4 per cent of hospitality businesses in the UK were classified as large. Yet, they employ just over 40 per cent of all hospitality staff (Source: People 1st, 2013).

Large hospitality businesses include companies such as Whitbread, McDonald's, Hilton Hotels & Resorts, J D Wetherspoon and Compass Group.

Although large businesses tend to be established and known for providing a particular food service, they also need to be aware of trends and changes within the current business environment. Economic and social change can have both positive and negative effects on businesses. For example, since smoking bans were introduced in enclosed workplaces across the UK during 2006–2007, pub chains have had to re-focus their target markets. As a result of these changing economic and social influences, many pub operators have recognised the importance of serving quality, value-for-money food aimed at the family market.

Figure 5.1 recaps the number of employees in micro, small, medium and large businesses.

Start-ups and existing hospitality businesses

According to People 1st, in 2011, 20,925 new businesses started in the hospitality and tourism industries, whereas 19,285 stopped trading (Source: People 1st, 2013). The number of hospitality businesses closing is higher than the average for the UK economy as a whole, which suggests that the hospitality industry is a bit more unstable than other industries. Although people are starting up businesses, this may suggest that not as many understand how to make their businesses successful.

Research shows that there were just over 180,000 individual businesses operating in the hospitality industry in 2012. The greatest number of businesses were found in the restaurant and pub, bar and nightclub areas (Source: People 1st, 2013). This may be as a result of current big trends in the food service area: pop-up restaurants, street food and food trucks.

Street food and food trucks are big trends in the hospitality industry at the moment.

▐▶ Current business environment factors that affect the hospitality industry

Introduction

Hospitality business operators read trade press and newspapers so they can keep in touch with what is happening in the business world. Among the things they need to know are proposed changes to the law. In this section, we will consider the political, economic, social and technological factors that impact the hospitality industry.

Reports in 2013 revealed that horse meat was found in some of the meat products sold in supermarkets. Discuss as a class the impact this discovery had on the hospitality industry.

Activity 5.3 Factors to consider when opening a restaurant

Imagine that you have opened a fine dining restaurant using the money from a lottery win. Consider how the factors listed below might affect your restaurant.

- The government increases the rate of VAT from 20 per cent to 22 per cent.
- The UK economy grows and we come out of the recession.
- A new hotel opens up in the area.
- A multinational company moves its head office to the area.

▐▶ National factors

All businesses are affected by things that happen in the country in which they operate.

Political issues

The government can influence the hospitality industry in many ways. How it runs the economy, the laws and regulations it introduces and policies on issues such as immigration, transport and public health will all have an impact on hospitality businesses.

- The introduction of the Working Time Regulations 1998 and the National Minimum Wage have affected how hospitality businesses organise their staff and how much they pay them.

The Working Time Regulations define employees' maximum weekly working time, the pattern of work and holidays, and the rest periods staff must be given daily and weekly. The National Minimum Wage is set by the government, and hospitality businesses must pay their staff at least the agreed pay rate for any work they do.

- The government has a responsibility for the health of the public.

In recent years it has focused on reducing obesity and binge drinking. The determination to do this has had an influence on the hospitality industry. For example, Jamie Oliver's campaign for healthier school lunches led to the government introducing minimum standards for school meals in England from 2008. They also stopped the sale of confectionery and canned drinks.

- The Licensing Act 2003 gave pubs the opportunity to apply for 24-hour licences.

Level and type of government support for hospitality businesses

We learned in Unit 1 that in 2013 the hospitality industry was the UK's fourth largest employer – directly employing over 2.68 million people. This means that it is an important industry.

Taxation

In 2012, the hospitality industry contributed £39.6 billion in tax **revenue** to the Treasury (Source: 'The Agenda for 300,000 New Jobs' (2013), a report by the British Hospitality Association). Tax is used to pay for many things including education, health care (the NHS) and defence. How much tax we all pay (the tax rate) is set by the Chancellor of the Exchequer (the finance minister of the UK). Any changes in tax rates can have an enormous impact on the industry.

The economy

The 'state of the economy' is often reported on by the media. Economic factors such as the level of employment, inflation, exchange rates and the cost of loans can influence demand for hospitality products and services. We will look at each of these things in turn.

In an **economic recession** or a period of low economic growth, people have less **disposable income** than in a time of **economic boom**. Hospitality businesses need to adjust their products and services to account for the changes in demand. Customers become more interested in value for money in a recession, and many businesses lower their prices or offer money-off vouchers to encourage people to buy their goods.

Activity 5.4   Special offers

Customers are increasingly seeking value for money and the hospitality industry often resorts to offering discounts, special offers and 'promotions' to convince customers that they are getting a good deal.

In groups of three or four, using the internet or the local press, find examples of two special deals offered to customers by a hotel, restaurant or pub. Do you think the promotions offer value for money? Explain your conclusions.

Level of employment

Levels of employment will affect customers' discretionary income. In times of high unemployment those without jobs will have less money to spend on hospitality products.

Inflation

Inflation is the rate at which the prices for goods and services increases and as a result the amount of goods or services you can buy decreases. As inflation rises, every pound buys a smaller percentage of a product.

Link

Go to Unit 9: How the Hospitality Industry Contributes to Healthy Lifestyles for more information about how hospitality businesses contribute to healthy lifestyles.

Take it further

In groups of four, prepare a short presentation for the rest of your class, which explores one or two of the government's recent health policies.

You can access helpful websites by going to www.pearsonhotlinks.co.uk and searching for this title.

Key terms

Revenue – the income of an organisation, especially a large amount.

Economic recession – a general slowdown in economic activity over a period of time.

Disposable income – the money left over from someone's wages after they have paid their taxes and basic living costs.

Economic boom – an increase in the level of economic activity, and of the goods and services available in the market place.

Suppose that in 2012, a loaf of bread cost £1. In 2013, the same loaf costs £1.22. The rise in price is due to inflation. In 2013, your £1 does not buy you as much as it did in 2012, meaning that the purchasing value of money has fallen.

Inflation can affect the hospitality industry in two ways.

1 Rising prices of food, beverages and fuel can lead to a rise in the cost of running a hospitality business.

2 Rising prices also leave customers with less disposable income and this can have a negative impact on customer spending.

Exchange rates

The exchange rate is the price of foreign currency that £1 can buy. If the current exchange rate is two US dollars to the pound, then £1 is worth $2.

The exchange rate is important to the hospitality industry, as many customers come from overseas. If a hotel has a lot of customers from America and the US dollar is strong, then customers are likely to spend more money. Imagine the exchange rate for US dollars in April is £1 to $2 and in June the exchange rate is £1 to $1.50. In April, a hotel room costing £100 would cost an American traveller $200. However, in June the same hotel room would only cost $150.

Cost of loans

If we borrow money from the bank or the building society, we have to pay interest on the loan. This is known as the cost of borrowing money. If interest rates are high, it will cost individuals and companies more to borrow money. If interest rates are low, it will cost them less to borrow money.

Hospitality businesses are deeply affected by the cost of loans for two reasons:

1 High interest rates mean customers have less disposable income and low interest rates mean they have more disposable income.

2 High interest rates mean the cost of borrowing money is high for hospitality businesses and this will add to their costs. On the other hand, low interest rates will lower their costs.

Rising fuel prices will increase the amount a contract caterer has to pay to travel to and from events and has a negative impact on their business running costs.

▶ Local factors

Location of business

Where to locate a business is a crucial decision for hospitality businesses. Typically, businesses will look to open in locations that maximise their revenues and minimise costs. For example, they will be keen to open in an area where the government offers incentives to operate, where labour costs are low, transport systems are good and demand for their business is high.

The location of the business can also affect its seasonality. Places such as Newquay in Cornwall and the Isle of Wight have an extremely busy tourist trade in the summer, but some hotels do not open in the winter.

Where a business is located can have a huge effect on its chances of success. What do you think happens to seaside businesses in the winter?

Requirements for resources

Operators will also need to think about the availability of resources when choosing a location for their business. This includes the availability of suitable premises and equipment, suppliers for food and beverages, staff and customers. Some country house hotels struggle to recruit and retain staff, because the cost of getting to work is so high. With a growing trend to buy food locally, restaurants in farming areas often benefit from local supplies, which adds a unique selling point to their menu.

▶ Impact of factors

All the factors that we have looked at can have a positive or a negative effect on hospitality businesses. It is important that businesses are aware of these factors, decide how they will impact their business and try to take advantage of opportunities or overcome negative effects. Some examples are as follows.

- If there is a rise in pensioners' monthly income, then restaurants, bars and hotels may focus their product development on the needs of the aging population. For example, a local pub might offer special rates on lunchtime meals.
- If a new nightclub opens in a university town, existing clubs may decide to target a new market segment (for example, discos for the over 30s) or put on special offers to try to stop students visiting the new nightclub.
- If the British pound (£) is weak against the US dollar ($), a hotel in London might invest more in a marketing campaign that targets American customers.

Businesses must consider the relevance of the factors to their business. For example, a government report outlining plans to deal with obesity might not have a big impact on a fine dining restaurant, as people tend to dine in this type of establishment for a treat. However, it may well have a big impact on a fast food restaurant.

▶ Risks and opportunities in the current business environment

As you have just learned, it is important for businesses to gauge the impact of issues and trends in the business environment if they are to survive. Businesses must constantly consider the risks and opportunities they face, and they can do so by carrying out a SWOT analysis. A SWOT analysis looks at the following.

- **S** – strengths (internal)
- **W** – weaknesses (internal)
- **O** – opportunities in the external environment
- **T** – threats in the external environment.

A SWOT analysis can help a business to explore:

- what the business does better than the competition
- what competitors do better than the business
- whether the business is making the most of available opportunities
- how a business should respond to changes in its external environment.

The result of the analysis is a list of positive and negative factors that the business can address.

Activity 5.5

Impacting factors

Consider the factors that are impacting a local nightclub in your area. In pairs, put together a short presentation to feed back to your class.

Activity 5.6

A SWOT analysis

Complete a SWOT analysis for your college/school canteen.

▶ Trends affecting hospitality businesses

Introduction

We tend to understand a trend as the current fashion or a change in customer behaviour. As the hospitality industry is very customer-focused, it is essential that businesses understand current trends, as they influence what customers buy. In this section, we will examine the types of trends that affect the hospitality industry.

Discuss the factors that have contributed to the growth of the following areas:

- budget/niche hotels
- coffee shops
- online booking systems (restaurants and hotels)
- products/services aimed at the 50–75 age group.

▶ Social trends

Our attitude to dining out, both casually and more formally, has changed over the decades. The hospitality industry has therefore had to adapt in new and exciting ways to meet the demands of its customers. Some of the social trends that affect hospitality are as follow.

Population changes

The population of the UK is estimated at 63.2 million, an increase of 4.1 million (7 per cent) between 2001 and 2011. This is a lot of customers for the hospitality industry. The population aged 65 and over has more than trebled: in 2011 the population was 10.4 million (16 per cent of the UK population) compared to 2.2 million in 1911 (5 per cent of the UK population). Increasing life expectancy in the UK has expanded the 65s and over market for the hospitality industry. (Source: '2011 Census, Population and Household Estimates for the United Kingdom', Office for National Statistics licensed under the Open Government Licence v.1.0.)

Households and families

For many, eating out has become a habit and casual dining is on the rise. Several factors have led to this trend. For example, in many households both parents work full time and young couples have more money to spend. Restaurants, cafés and bars must meet the needs of casual diners, offering an informal eating environment and more exciting foods. Giraffe is a good example of a family-friendly restaurant, offering activities and special menus for children.

Value for money is always important and many customers subscribe to companies that can offer them special deals. More than ever, people want to try restaurants and cafés offering new and unusual foods. They are also looking for a more exciting dining experience, for example, at pop-up restaurants and street cafés.

Education and training

Television shows like *The Great British Bake Off*, *Great British Menu* and *MasterChef* are creating a greater awareness of food and ingredients.

Take it further

Find out more about the trends in the way we choose to spend our money on dining out by visiting the Lost in Catering website. You can access this website by going to www.pearsonhotlinks.co.uk and searching for this title.

Celebrity chefs such as Jamie Oliver, Marcus Wareing and Silvena Rowe have made cooking cool and fun, and hospitality is a popular career choice for school and college leavers. Recognising the need to attract and train new talent, restaurants and awarding bodies are working together to create exciting qualifications.

Labour market

According to People 1st, in 2012, more than a third of hospitality businesses (35 per cent) expect their workforce to increase in the coming year. The events and food and service management areas reported that they were more likely to expect an increase.

Over the last five years, the number of kitchen and catering assistants employed has increased by 7 per cent. Chefs and cooks are the second largest occupational group, followed by waiting staff. These roles have increased by 5 per cent and 21 per cent respectively in the last five years. This reflects the growth in restaurants and dining out, and the trend of pubs becoming increasingly food-led (Source: People 1st, 2013).

It is important to note, however, that the hospitality industry also suffers from high turnover of staff.

Increasing travel for work

More and more people have to commute to work and this adds time to their working day. This is thought to be another reason why more and more people choose to eat out.

▶ Technology trends

Technology can play a vital role in improving the customer experience. For example, in many hospitality businesses customers are able to order room service through smartphones and browse drink lists using iPads. Inamo restaurant, located in London, allows customers to place orders from an illustrated food and drinks menu that is projected on to their table surface. Developments in point of sale checkout systems mean businesses can now keep track of stock levels, as well as process sales and issue receipts.

The internet

New developments allow customers to place their order electronically via a tablet or from a menu projected on to their table.

Customers can now book restaurant tables, hotel rooms or spa days from their computers, tablets or smartphones at any time of the day or night. This makes it increasingly important for businesses to have an online presence. Online reviews are becoming more and more powerful and increasingly customers are using them to make judgement calls about whether to visit a business.

Social media

Businesses must engage with social media. Sites such as Twitter and Facebook allow businesses to communicate directly with customers and to find out what they do and do not like.

In-room technology

Hotels often compete to give their customers the best in-room technology experience. In-room technology can include Wi-Fi access, MP3 docking stations, lighting and climate control, and keyless entry to the hotel room.

Activity 5.7   A room with a view of the future

Carry out your own research to find out more about how hospitality businesses can use technology to benefit their customers. Then, design a hotel room of the future. Think about the types of technology needed to access the room, as well as the technology that will be available within the room. What predictions can you make about the way technology will develop in the next five to ten years?

▶ Environmental trends

As customers become more aware of the impact their behaviour has on the environment, it is increasingly important for the hospitality industry to reduce its carbon footprint. As such, recent years have seen the growth of the 'green hotel'. Environmentally-conscious practice in the industry covers such things as:

- using renewable energy (for example, solar panels)
- installing high performance window glazing
- using low energy lighting
- installing reclaimed flooring
- using water flow systems that recycle water (this is good for washing linens)
- using paint that is low in, or has no, Volatile Organic Compounds (VOCs)
- using recycled paper and items in guest rooms.

▶ Ethical trends

Hospitality businesses must also respond to a range of **ethical** issues that are being questioned by their customers. Figure 5.2 outlines the ethical issues that hospitality businesses must tackle.

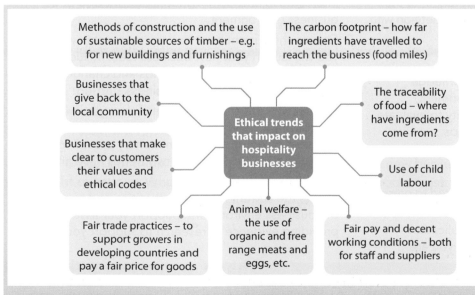

Figure 5.2 Ethical trends that impact on the hospitality industry

↗ Take it further

TripAdvisor has a list of the top ten eco-friendly hotels. Look at this list and note down the different types of environmental initiatives being used by hotels to be 'green'. You can access this list by going to www.pearsonhotlinks.co.uk and searching for this title.

💬 Discussion

Research the Green Tourism Award. What challenges are faced by businesses that want to receive the award?

🔑 Key term

Ethics – the moral principles that should underpin decision-making. Businesses can provide moral and ethical guidelines for how their business affairs are conducted.

◎ Link

Go to Unit 1, Learning aim C, Topic C.1 to find out more about ethical issues and trends.

Take it further

Think of a new product for a hospitality business that meets the needs of today's health conscious and busy customer. Make a presentation outlining the pros and cons of entering this market.

You might want to use a current business that is operating in this market to help you. What products or services do they offer? Are they successful? If so, why do you think this is?

Discussion

How could your college/school restaurant/canteen better meet your needs?

Key term

Mystery shopper – a person employed to visit businesses and report on their experiences of them. They may be employed by the business itself or by a third party.

Businesses must provide products and services that customers want at a price they want to pay. Also, they must persuade customers to buy their products and services rather than those of their competitors. For example, some restaurants have developed their products to take advantage of the trend for buying takeaways and ready meals. Pizza Express now sells their pizzas in supermarkets and JD Wetherspoon have made a commitment to offer healthy dishes – they have a 'menu builder' on their website that allows customers to choose their food based on their dietary requirements.

Identifying new needs

Before starting a new business it is vital to carry out market research into what products and services customers want and who will buy them. A new business idea will need to be financially solid to succeed but it will also need to tap into a new area. Companies can look at social networking sites such as Facebook and Twitter to analyse what people are enjoying now and to identify what their future needs could be.

Continuing to meet established customer needs

Although many customers are very loyal to a brand or business that they know and like, there is no such thing as a customer for life any more. Customers will only remain loyal for as long as hospitality businesses continue to meet their needs. It is, therefore, extremely important that businesses seek feedback from customers continuously. Through customer feedback, businesses are more likely to be able to recognise a gap in their provision and to make improvements.

There are many ways of seeking customer feedback. We can use comment cards, questionnaires or online surveys, hold focus groups, use **mystery shoppers** and gather information from independent online review websites.

Many restaurants now offer gluten-free menus to respond to customer needs. Among others, these restaurants include Prezzo, Zizzi and Pizza Express.

Being entrepreneurial

Our economy needs entrepreneurs to help it grow. They create new products and services, producing new jobs and giving customers more choice and opportunities to spend their money. Entrepreneurs come in all shapes and sizes, however, some common qualities include:

- the ability to use initiative
- having confidence to take calculated risks
- the ability to make decisions
- the desire to carry out thorough planning
- leadership skills
- determination.

Activity 5.10   Being an entrepreneur

Chose an entrepreneur from the list below and decide what it is about their business model that made it so successful. Be prepared to share your ideas with the class.

- Hugh Osmond
- Rose Grimond
- Sir Richard Branson
- Lord Sugar
- Karren Brady
- Jamie Oliver
- Gordon Ramsay

The importance of having a strong vision

A **vision** or **mission** statement is a way of putting the aims of a business into a written statement. It reflects the 'ultimate picture' of a business, including where the business is heading – your ultimate goal.

A vision can help hospitality businesses to make important business decisions and provides a structure against which progress can be measured. The vision is also a key communication tool for customers and staff.

Key terms

Vision – an imaginative description of what an organisation would like to achieve in the mid-term or long-term future.

Mission – a mission statement describes the purpose of a company, organisation or person – its reason for existing.

Constraint – a limitation or restriction on something.

Activity 5.11	Vision or mission statements

Using the internet, examine four different published vision or mission statements.

- What do they have in common?
- What is different about them?
- How do they help a business to plan for the future?

Measures of success

There is little point in running a business or developing a new product if you do not expect it to be successful. Having discovered what customers' needs are, a business then faces the challenge of meeting those needs profitably.

Attracting customers, satisfying them and keeping them should be the primary goals of any hospitality business, since they keep the organisation in business and produce its revenue. However, this must be done within the **constraints** of a budget and it is vital that costs are controlled, so that the business makes a profit.

Hospitality businesses are also concerned with social success. They want to have a reputation as a socially-responsible company. This means being known as a good employer, a company that cares about its customers, that pays a fair price to its suppliers, that adds value to the local community, that is green, and gives to local causes.

Link

- Go to Unit 4: Costing and Controlling Finances in the Hospitality Industry to find more information about financial planning.
- Go to Topic A.4 in this unit, which looks at social and ethical trends and how they influence the way hospitality businesses operate.

Activity 5.12	Investigating new developments in the hospitality industry

Work in small groups to investigate recent developments in the hospitality industry. Each group will work on developments from one of the following areas:

- budget hotels
- fast food
- pubs
- fine dining.

Once you have carried out the research, take part in a whole group discussion of your findings.

To complete the activity, answer the following questions.

1 Identify the key players in your chosen area.
2 Explain what has influenced one company's financial and social success, and its customer satisfaction.

▶ Hospitality business ideas

Introduction

New hospitality products and services are being introduced all the time. Customers' tastes change, and companies are constantly seeking ways to attract new customers. Changes to the business environment mean that companies need to adapt and develop their products and services to survive.

In this section, we will look at the process that businesses follow to assess the feasibility of a new business idea. This will help you to develop your own business idea for your assignment.

In small groups, brainstorm a new business idea for the hospitality industry. Remember, no idea is a bad idea – do not criticise other people's ideas and give everyone a chance to have their say. Use your group's strengths and be careful to consider any potential competitors.

▶ Market research and identifying gaps

Successful hospitality businesses conduct research on an ongoing basis. Market research can identify changing market trends, which bring new opportunities, and help to keep a business competitive. Whether the business is starting out or expanding, research is vital in order to understand the target market and pinpoint gaps and opportunities for new products or services. Figure 5.3 outlines the steps to take when planning and carrying out market research.

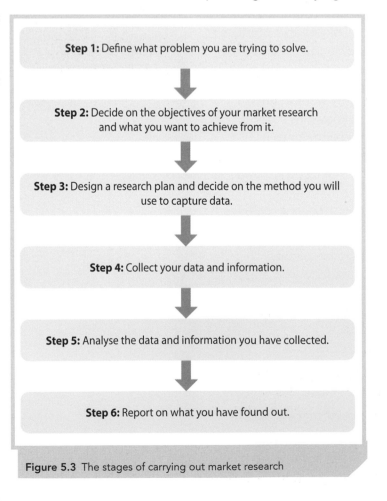

Step 1: Define what problem you are trying to solve.

Step 2: Decide on the objectives of your market research and what you want to achieve from it.

Step 3: Design a research plan and decide on the method you will use to capture data.

Step 4: Collect your data and information.

Step 5: Analyse the data and information you have collected.

Step 6: Report on what you have found out.

Figure 5.3 The stages of carrying out market research

▶ Selecting a product or service

Introducing a new product to the market can be a risky business. Once you have carried out research to help you to develop new products and services, you have to decide which of your ideas is most likely to be successful.

Make sure that you select the right product and that you sell it at the right price, in the right place and using the most suitable promotional techniques.

The product has to have the right features to meet the needs of your customers – for example, it must look good and work well.

The price must be right. No matter how good you think the product is, it will not be successful if customers are not prepared to buy it. Therefore, it must offer value for money.

The product or service must be in 'the right place at the right time'. In other words, there must be a market for the product. For example, there is little point in opening a fine dining restaurant in a motorway service station.

The target market for your product or service needs to be aware of its existence and know about the availability of the product. You must have a way of letting customers know about your products.

▶ Selecting a location

It is vital to choose the right location to sell hospitality products and services or, if the location has already been set, to match the product to the location. You must make sure that there is a ready and waiting market for the product or service. For example, there is little point in opening a fine dining restaurant in an area of town that mainly caters for local university students.

Accessibility

Some hospitality businesses are known as 'destination' restaurants, pubs or hotels. These are the types of business that customers will travel out of their way to. It may be because they have an excellent reputation for food or a wonderful spa. On the other hand, some businesses, for example, a fast food restaurant or a sandwich bar, need to be located where there is a high **footfall** of customers. If you are running a business that customers need to travel to, you will also need to consider how **accessible** it is – does it have parking? Is it easy to get to from a motorway or major road? Is it accessible by public transport?

Style and size of the property

You will also need to think about the property in which you will locate your business – its size, facilities and style.

The style will need to match your vision for the business. A romantic bed and breakfast brings to mind words like 'charming', 'quaint' and 'attractive', but an ultra-modern hotel makes us think of words such as 'contemporary', 'fashionable' and 'modern-day'.

The size of the property will dictate how many people the business can cater for. You will need to make sure you can cater for enough people each day to cover your costs and to achieve your projected income. Size will also affect the furnishings and fittings you can have and, in turn, the style of service you use.

Location

The location will obviously influence the customer footfall to the business but also the cost of running it. In London, it is more expensive to rent a property, whereas other parts of the country are less expensive. You will need to weigh up this initial investment and work out whether you can still make money. You should also consider how close your business will be to direct competitors.

▶ Targeting customers

For any business to succeed, it must have enough customers to buy the product or service it is selling. Businesses must identify their potential customer base, so that they can tailor their marketing efforts, products and services to those customers.

Defining a target customer means pinpointing the specific characteristics of the people who you believe are most likely to buy your products or services. These characteristics are sometimes called a **demographic** profile. Common characteristics used to classify customers are included in Figure 5.4.

Some hospitality businesses will deliberately target a **niche market**. This means they are aiming their products or services at quite a small or specialised group, for example, a café that caters for vegans.

Do you think location might limit the profitability of this business?

Key terms

Footfall – the number of people who go into a business in a particular period of time.

Accessibility – the extent to which a customer or user can obtain a product or service at the time it is needed.

Demographics – studies of a population based on factors such as age, race, sex, economic status, level of education, income level and employment.

Niche market – a product that targets a very specific area of the market, e.g. restaurants that only serve halal meat.

Selecting the most appropriate idea

In Topic A.1, you learned why market research is necessary and how it helps you to assess the suitability of a business idea. All ideas, however good you think they are, need to be assessed, investigated and researched from several viewpoints. Once you have done this, you will be able to say how suitable your business idea truly is.

As well as a SWOT analysis, you could apply a Political, Economic, Social and Technological (PEST) analysis to your idea. A PEST analysis is a business measurement tool. It helps us to understand the growth or decline in a market. It can be used to review:

- the direction a company is taking
- the value of an idea or strategy such as a marketing plan.

Link

Go back to Topic A.3 in this unit to revisit SWOT analysis.

Likelihood of success or failure

One of the reasons we need to assess the suitability of a business idea is to decide if we think it will succeed. Sometimes the market research will lead us to the conclusion that our business idea will not be successful. Your research should help you to establish that:

- you can access your target market
- there is existing demand for the product
- it will be profitable.

When you are estimating your profitability, it is a good idea to think of it from the worst case perspective. This will help you ask yourself the difficult questions that need to be asked.

- If your business launched, which factors could ruin it?
- How likely are these factors?
- If you earned less than your financial projections for the first year, would you still be able to remain in business?
- If the geographical area in which you are thinking of investing suddenly became 'unpopular' with people, would your business be able to keep local customers coming back to you?
- In times of economic hardship, is your business adaptable? Will customers still want to invest in it?

How do you think the location of this juice-bar business will help its survival?

Identifying major barriers for a hospitality business start-up

New businesses often come up against barriers to entry, which they must be able to overcome. Carry out Activity 5.13 to explore what these barriers are.

Activity 5.13 — The barriers facing a start-up hospitality business

In the table below you will see some barriers to entry for a new business. Make a copy of the table and complete it to explain why these things are barriers. The first two have been done for you.

Barrier	Why it is a barrier
A lack of start-up capital	Starting a business often requires a large amount of capital (money). Although it is sometimes possible to raise finance, it can be too expensive to raise the money needed or too difficult to persuade a bank or building society to lend money.
Customer cynicism	Building a reputation takes time. Hospitality businesses work hard to keep their customers loyal, and anyone starting up may need to convince their target market their product or service is better than their competitors'. In other words, they must be able to differentiate their goods and services from those of their competitors.
Licences	
Competitors	
Cash flow	

TOPIC   B.4

Producing an initial plan for a new hospitality business idea

Introduction

You have had an idea for a new hospitality business and you have judged your resources, researched the market, explored how the product will be delivered to the customer, the cost of delivering it, the barriers to starting your business and the potential profit. The idea looks like it will work, but how do you decide whether to go ahead? You will need to produce an initial plan for the business. This section looks at how to produce this plan.

As a class, discuss the information you think will need to be included in a business plan.

Producing a plan

You have the business idea, have carried out your market research and have assessed the suitability of the product. Now what? The next thing you need to do is to organise all of this information and create a business plan for your new idea. Your business plan should include a rationale and supporting evidence.

WorkSpace

▶ Julie Sudiqui

Pastry chef at a country hotel

I have wanted to run my own coffee shop for as long as I can remember. To give myself the best chance of success, I went to catering college after leaving school. I completed a three-year cookery course, specialising in pastry in the final year. I knew when I finished my cookery course that I had skills to prepare and serve food, because I had worked part-time all the way through college. However, I then took a Foundation Degree in Hospitality Management so I could learn more about the skills of running a business.

When I left college I got a job in the kitchen of a really prestigious country house hotel. I worked in every section of the kitchen for the first year and then I moved to the pastry section.

Five years on and I am still at the hotel. I have learned so many new skills. I have to be very organised and detail-oriented. It is amazing how much hard work goes into making sure the things I make look and taste superb. When we are busy, baking can start as early as 3 or 4 a.m. I have to work really long hours and I spend much of my day on my feet – I need a lot of stamina and strength to be a pastry chef.

I love being creative and designing new dishes but I also have to understand the scientific principles behind doing this. I'm using perishable and fragile foods and I need to understand the biology of food safety and the science of combining different food products.

I haven't forgotten my dream to own my own coffee shop and I definitely think I am developing the skills I need to run a business. I'm just waiting for an opportunity. Give me another few years to learn my trade and I'll have the best coffee shop in town.

Think about it

1 Would a job like Julie's appeal to you?

2 Apart from stamina, what other skills might you need to be a pastry chef?

3 What kinds of opportunities will Julie need so she can open her own business?

Learning aim C   TOPIC   C.1

▶ Choice of format

Introduction

To increase your chance of success in business you need to make a number of choices. One of these is the structure or format of your business. This section will examine different business structures.

On your own, come up with a definition for a publicly owned business and a privately owned business. As a group, discuss your definitions and produce an agreed definition for both types of business.

▶ Definitions of business formats

A business can be formed in different ways. The number of people involved in the business's creation, the type of business and how it will operate will inform the business format.

Sole trader

A sole trader is an individual who owns and runs their own business (for example, a restaurant or café). A sole trader has **unlimited liability**. This means that if the business runs up debts, the sole trader must pay them off – even if it means selling their own possessions, like a car or a house. This is a major disadvantage of being a sole trader. On the other hand, it is probably the easiest type of business to set up and the owner is their own boss. A sole trader may or may not employ other staff.

Partnership

A partnership has two or more owners. Responsibility for running the business is shared between the partners. Additional owners mean that more capital can be raised for the business. It is possible that this structure will bring a wider range of talents, skills and business ideas, although this might also bring the disadvantage of partners arguing. Again, this business ownership has unlimited liability. John Lewis is a well-known partnership.

Limited company

Abbreviated to 'Ltd', the owners of a limited company each own a share of the business and are known as shareholders. If the company is successful, the shareholders will receive a financial reward in the form of dividends. Limited companies are often family-run affairs. Hilton Hotels & Resorts is an example of a limited company.

Public limited company (PLC)

In a PLC, shares are usually traded on the stock exchange and can be owned by members of the public. The directors are paid a salary to run the company and may, or may not, own shares. Selling shares to the public means that this company can raise large amounts of money to expand or develop. Whitbread is an example of a PLC.

Link

Go to Unit 1, Learning aim A, Topic A.2 for more information about business ownership.

Key term

Unlimited liability – the owner of the business has a legal obligation to pay any debts/losses made by the business, even if this means selling their own possessions to do so.

Take it further

As a class, name as many different types of businesses in your local high street as you can. Write them down on the whiteboard, grouping all the small businesses on one side and larger businesses on the other. What do all the businesses on the right/left side have in common?

▶ Sources of help and support in developing new hospitality businesses

Introduction

Most people who want to start up a new business need help and support to do so. They may need financial, legal or business advice or they may need a loan of money to help them get started. Fortunately, the government encourages enterprise in this country and there is plenty of support available if you know where to look. This section will examine the help and support available to budding entrepreneurs.

▶ Sources of help

Starting a new business can be a daunting prospect. Fortunately, if you do want to start a business you are not alone, and there is plenty of guidance and support available to help bring your business idea to life.

It may be that you need a loan to get you started or advice on the licences you need to run a business. It could simply be that you would like advice from someone running a business similar to your own or that you need someone to set up a website for you. There are many different avenues of support and advice to help you along the way.

Independent advice

A good starting point is to look at the government service's website. You can access this website by going to www.pearsonhotlinks.co.uk and searching for this title. On the website there is a section called 'Businesses and self-employed' and you will find guidance on a number of areas including:

- business tax
- business premises
- employee benefits
- funding
- licences
- intellectual property.

There are also lots of businesses that can offer you independent advice. The Prince's Trust Enterprise Programme supports unemployed young people aged 18–30 to decide if their business ideas are viable and whether self-employment is right for them. It also offers grants to business start-ups. Regional business development agencies will also be able to provide you with information about opening a business in your area.

Finance and start-up capital

Each high street bank has a business team that specialises in helping new businesses get started. As well as providing you with finance for your business, banks can support you and your idea in lots of other ways as well. For example, they can provide you with a financial adviser, a business mentor, recommendations for business courses to improve your knowledge, advice on creating a business plan and recommendations for network events to build your community of business contacts.

There are also lots of alternative ways to raise finance for your business. A lot of entrepreneurs ask friends and family members to invest in the business (i.e. a cash buy-in) and in return they will receive shares in the business or a percentage of the business's profits. Other entrepreneurs will rely on grants or investment from a venture capital organisation. The television show, *Dragons' Den*, uses this format with entrepreneurs pitching their new business idea to a panel of venture capitalists in order to secure financial investment.

Research – other hospitality businesses

Make sure you talk to hospitality businesses in your local area and those involved with running similar businesses to your own idea. They have been through the process, so they will know all about what you need to do and the ups and downs you might experience along the way.

Take it further

Use the internet to answer the following questions.

- How can a new business obtain start-up capital?
- What is the Start-Up Loans Company?
- What is a Social Enterprise?

You can access useful websites by going to www.pearsonhotlinks.co.uk and searching for this title.

Pitching your business idea to a group can be daunting but it does not have to be if you prepare and listen to advice and guidance.

▶ Support networks

You will need a support system when you start a business and when you are running it. A family member or friend who will listen and with whom you can bounce ideas off is invaluable. You can also get yourself a mentor and you may qualify for a business start-up programme, however, experienced guidance is the best support of all. Some experienced business people become business mentors and spend time with small firms to provide them with experience and tailored help for their business.

Professional bodies

The British Chamber of Commerce (BCC) work with businesses and regional chambers across the UK. Local Chambers of Commerce work with businesses in their area of all sizes and from all sectors. The BCC is a very good networking vehicle as it puts local businesses in touch with each other, as well as with businesses across the rest of the UK. Being able to speak with other hospitality business owners and learn about their experiences of running a business and what is currently happening within the industry is an invaluable aid.

The Institute of Hospitality is the professional body for managers and potential managers in the hospitality industry. It offers qualifications in management and networking opportunities so that members can further their professional and career development.

Trade associations

The British Hospitality Association (BHA) is an organisation that represents hotels, restaurants and food service providers. It is an excellent source of information about current issues and trends in the industry and it lobbies the government, on the industry's behalf, on economic and political issues.

▶ Business model

Introduction

In this section, you will learn about business models. A model is a useful benchmark against which performance can be measured. It can help you to make good business decisions and stop you from making bad ones.

You are applying for a business start-up loan – list the information that the loan company is likely to need before they decide whether you should be given a loan.

▶ Definition of a business model

A business model is the plan of how a company will generate revenue and make a profit from their operations. The model identifies the purpose, function, products and services of the business. It also explains the revenues it is budgeted to make and the costs it will incur. When the bank manager or a potential investor in your business asks about a business model, they really want an answer to the question: 'How do you plan to make money?'

Activity 5.15   What information does an investor need?

A restaurant's business model is to make money by cooking and serving food to hungry customers.

What additional information would an investor need in order to know whether the restaurant will make a profit or a loss?

In pairs, make a list. Then, discuss your ideas as a whole group.

▐▶ Components of a business model

A business model is made up of lots of different elements. Each element is important in its own right and a business model will only be viewed as successful if all of the elements work together.

Market research

The results of your market research must be included in your business model. You need to think about who is reading your business model (it could be someone who knows about business but not about your specialist area of hospitality) and make sure that your research is easy to understand and follow. It should justify your business idea, your vision for the business, the exact nature of the products and the services you will be offering, and the location you will be operating from.

The target market should be identified and your research should show that:

- there are enough customers to buy the goods or services you want to sell
- customers will pay a price that allows you to make a profit
- your business can compete/survive against competitors.

Competitors should be identified along with information on what they charge for their goods or services.

Link

Go back to Topics B.1 and B.2 in this unit to remind yourself of the importance of accurate market research.

Activity 5.16   Have you researched thoroughly?

Check the research you have done for your business start-up idea. Does it give you answers to the following questions?

- Who is your target audience (age; gender; income, etc.)?
- Does your product/company have any competition?
- How much money will you need to set up your business?
- How much do people need your product?
- How are you going to market your product?
- Why will the idea work?

Goods or services?

You need to state what goods and services you will be selling and how you will produce them. When preparing your business model, make sure you can answer the following questions.

- What am I trying to create?
- What will it look like?
- Where will I get it from?
- How much will I charge for it?
- What raw materials do I need to produce it?
- What will be the USP?

Take it further

Use the internet to research the process for opening either a Subway or McDonald's franchise. What is the process? What are the start-up costs?

Means of delivering to the customer

There must be a means of delivering your products and services to the customer. For example, will you distribute your products and services through a franchise? Will you sell directly to another business? Will you sell directly to customers yourself? Or will you be able to sell over the internet?

You need to outline how you plan to deliver your products or services, and explain why you have chosen this option and why it is the best option for your business. Investors will want to see projections for the number of customers you expect to do business with in your first three years.

Business aims

Every business should have a long-term vision or goal. It should identify what you ultimately predict for your business, in terms of growth, values, employees, contribution to society and customer experience. Once you have defined your vision, you can plan how you will move your business towards it. Part of this includes the development of business objectives.

Business objectives

Business objectives are measurable targets to help you achieve the overall aims of your business. An objective is a target that a business sets itself.

To be effective, objectives need to be SMART:

- **Specific** – a precise statement of the desired outcome
- **Measurable** – set in terms of a number value, for example, sales, market share
- **Achievable** – the target can be met
- **Realistic** – the target must be achievable in terms of the resources available
- **Timed** – within a given period of time, for example, 12 months.

Influence of stakeholders

It is important to think about the stakeholders of the business and the influence they may have on it. Stakeholders will include the owners, employees, customers, financiers, suppliers and the local community.

A business is responsible to the different stakeholder groups as follows.

- Shareholders – to generate profits and pay dividends.
- Customers – to provide good-quality products at reasonable prices while operating safely, honestly, decently and truthfully.
- Employees – to provide a healthy and safe workplace, security and fair pay.
- Suppliers – to pay them on time, pay fair rates for the work done and provide an element of security.
- The local community – to provide employment, a safe working environment, to minimise pollution and negative effects of the business activity.
- The government – to abide by the law, pay taxes and abide by regulations.

Finances and costs for start-up

Your business model will need to include details of your finances and the costs required for you to start up. You need to identify what the start-up costs will be and how you will raise the money that you need.

Your start-up costs could include equipment and installation, insurance, premises, fixtures and fittings, initial stock or materials, marketing and advertising materials, legal and professional fees, licences and staff uniforms.

▶ Providing supporting evidence

Your business model will need to include the ongoing costs of running your business, the amount of profit you expect to make and the sources of your income.

You need to make sure you can confidently answer the following questions.

- Why will my idea work? How can I quantify this?
- Where is the opportunity?
- What will the return on investment be? Why, and how?
- The strengths of the business are…?
- The weaknesses of the business are…?
- The opportunities and drivers in the market include…?
- Threats to the business/risks include…?
- I will overcome these risks by…?

Assessment activity 5.3   *English*   2C.P5 | 2C.P6 | 2C.P7 | 2C.M5 | 2C.D3

Your application for the 'Young entrepreneur of the year' competition has been successful! You have been selected as a finalist. The final stage in the competition is to present a business model for your start-up idea to a panel of business people.

Put together your presentation. Make sure it includes the following things.

- An explanation of why you chose your particular business's format – you will need to demonstrate that you considered different options.
- A business model – this should set out clearly all the different components you have learned are in a business model, using sources of help and support

for a business start-up. You will need to explain how your format and model enables the business to carry out its activities, and why your business start-up will be a success because of this. You should explain how your business model has the features to respond to market needs.

- Supporting evidence – you will need to demonstrate that you have researched your business idea thoroughly so that you can explain how your chosen format and research justifies your business idea. You should justify and evaluate the likelihood of success of your idea using evidence you have gathered and comparisons to existing hospitality businesses.

Tip

When presenting your business model, you need to include:

- your research of the market, including potential customers and competitors
- the type of ownership proposed
- whether you will provide goods or services – will you make or buy?
- how you will deliver to the customer

- your business aims
- your business objectives
- your sources of finance and costs for the start-up
- who your stakeholders are and their influence on the business
- a justification of why you think your business will be successful.

Introduction

Eating out has never been so good! There is now a huge choice of cafés, restaurants and bistros, all offering a variety of different foods. Today, people are much more adventurous in their choices of food and there are more healthy eating options available.

Cooking is one of the most important skills you can ever learn. This unit will help you to develop the skills you need to prepare and cook a range of foods. You will learn about different ingredients and cooking methods, and how these contribute to a healthy diet.

This is a practical unit. You need to be very organised to work in a kitchen and you will need to plan what you are going to do before you start to prepare and cook your dishes. You need to demonstrate that you can work safely and hygienically.

Preparing and cooking food is one thing, but presenting your dish is another. You will learn how to make your dish look even more delicious by using garnish and presentation skills. You will learn the value of getting feedback from people and evaluating your own work to help you further develop your skills.

Cooking is fun – let's get started!

Assessment: You will be assessed by a series of assignments set by your teacher/tutor.

Learning aims

In this unit you will:

A understand how to plan a nutritious meal

B be able to prepare food in a safe and hygienic manner

C be able to cook and finish food in a safe and hygienic manner.

I was never really interested in food. Mum did the cooking at home and I didn't care whether meals were healthy or not. This unit has opened up a whole new world to me. I never thought I could work in a kitchen. It was only when I started looking at nutrition and different types of food as part of my BTEC Hospitality course that I asked to do some voluntary work in my local restaurant. I now work there full time and enjoy every minute of it. The best bit? Helping my family plan really fun and healthy meals for the week.

Kate, *18-year-old commis chef*

Planning, Preparing, Cooking and Finishing Food

6

BTEC
Assessment Zone

This table shows what you must do in order to achieve a **Pass**, **Merit** or **Distinction** grade, and where you can find activities to help you.

Assessment criteria			
Level 1	**Level 2 Pass**	**Level 2 Merit**	**Level 2 Distinction**
Learning aim A: Understand how to plan a nutritious meal			
1A.1 Maths Select ingredients for a two-course meal following recipes.	**2A.P1** Maths Plan a nutritious two-course meal that requires different preparation and cooking methods for each course. **See Assessment activity 6.1, page 177**	**2A.M1** Maths Plan a nutritious two-course meal that requires different preparation and cooking methods for each course, justifying the choice of ingredients used in the plan. **See Assessment activity 6.1, page 177**	**2A.D1** Maths Assess the importance of a balanced nutritional content of meals to health. **See Assessment activity 6.1, page 177**
Learning aim B: Be able to prepare food in a safe and hygienic manner			
1B.2 Prepare food items for a two-course meal following recipes, using safe and hygienic working practices with support.	**2B.P2** Demonstrate independent safe and hygienic working practices when preparing different food items for a nutritious two-course meal. **See Assessment activity 6.2, page 188**	**2B.M2** Review the effectiveness of own working practices when preparing different food items for a nutritious two-course meal. **See Assessment activity 6.2, page 188**	**2B.D2** Evaluate the consequences of poor working practices when preparing different food items. **See Assessment activity 6.2, page 188**
Learning aim C: Be able to cook and finish food in a safe and hygienic manner			
1C.3 Maths With guidance, use cooking methods and safe and hygienic working practices when following recipes for a two-course meal.	**2C.P3** Maths Demonstrate independent safe and hygienic working practices when using appropriate methods to cook a nutritious two-course meal. **See Assessment activity 6.3, page 200**	**2C.M3** Justify the methods used to cook and finish a nutritious two-course meal. **See Assessment activity 6.3, page 200**	**2C.D3** English Recommend improvements to the quality of the two-course meal, based on feedback gathered. **See Assessment activity 6.3, page 200**
1C.4 Use finishing methods for a two-course meal following recipes.	**2C.P4** Use appropriate finishing methods for a two-course meal to ensure the meal meets given requirements and specifications. **See Assessment activity 6.3, page 200**		
1C.5 English Gather feedback on the two-course meal.	**2C.P5** English Gather feedback on the two-course meal, using appropriate techniques. **See Assessment activity 6.3, page 200**	**2C.M4** English Use feedback gathered to analyse the quality of the two-course meal. **See Assessment activity 6.3, page 200**	

Maths   Opportunity to practise mathematical skills   English   Opportunity to practise English skills

How you will be assessed

This unit will be assessed by a series of internally assessed tasks. These tasks will be set by your teacher/tutor. You will be expected to show an understanding of the skills needed for proficiency in planning, preparing, cooking and finishing a range of food types. The tasks will require you to produce a nutritious two-course meal using a range of ingredients, preparation and cooking methods. You will need to demonstrate an awareness of safe and hygienic working practices, knowledge of kitchen equipment and what forms a nutritious, balanced diet. Your teacher/tutor will observe you preparing and cooking your meal. You will need to get feedback on the quality of your meal, review it and make recommendations for improvement.

Your assessment could be in the form of:

- diaries and log sheets to show that you understand how to work safely and hygienically
- practical demonstrations to show how you prepare and cook two-course meals safely and hygienically in a kitchen
- teacher/tutor observation records of your practical work
- recipes and notes to show the nutritional value of your meals
- feedback and self-evaluation about the quality of your meals.

Fruits can be classified into five main groups:

- soft fruits – strawberries, raspberries and grapes
- tropical fruits – bananas and pineapples
- stone fruits – plums and peaches
- hard fruits – apples and pears
- citrus fruits – lemons and oranges.

Dairy

Dairy is the general term for milk and products produced from milk, such as butter, cream, yoghurt and crème fraiche. Milk generally comes from cows but goats' milk is growing in popularity, as many people are developing allergies to cows' milk and the products made from it. Dairy products are an important source of calcium, which is essential for healthy bones and teeth. They are also an important source of protein and some vitamins but they should be eaten in moderation as they can be high in fat.

A selection of dairy products

Nuts and seeds

Nuts and seeds are high in fibre and protein, and a great source of healthy oils like omega-3, vitamins and minerals. On their own, nuts and seeds are a healthy alternative to snacks such as chocolate bars and crisps. A sprinkling of single or mixed seeds can add texture and taste to salads or soups. Used in cooking, nuts and seeds are versatile and nutritious, and they can be ground into a powder or paste. Examples are:

- nuts – almond, Brazil, cashew, coconut, pecan, pistachio, walnuts
- seeds – flax, mustard, poppy, pumpkin, sunflower

It is important to note that some people are allergic to nuts and seeds.

Spices and herbs

Spices and herbs come from plants and are used in many different ways in cooking. Different cultures use different spices and herbs to give the dishes their distinguishing taste and flavour.

Herbs come from the leaves of non-woody plants and include basil, chives, coriander, dill, oregano, parsley, peppermint, rosemary, sage and tarragon. Spices come from the roots, flowers, fruits, seeds or bark of plants. Examples include cloves, cinnamon, cumin, ginger, nutmeg, paprika, saffron and vanilla.

Herbs and spices can add unusual depth and flavour to a variety of dishes.

Activity 6.2   Know your foods

Make a copy of the table below. Add an example in every column for each of the seven food classifications: cereals, grains, pulses; vegetables; fruits; nuts and seeds; spices and herbs; meat, poultry and fish; dairy. An example has been provided to get you started.

Food classification	Item	Why eat it?	Recipe you would use it in
Cereals, grains, pulses	Rice	Rice contains carbohydrates, which convert glucose into energy	Chinese/Thai dishes, e.g. steamed rice with stir-fried chicken and vegetables

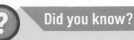

▶ Planning

Preparing and cooking healthy meals does not have to be expensive or complex. Planning can help save money, avoid waste and provide an opportunity to try a range of appealing meals that will excite the taste buds!

When planning a new menu, it is important to consider the following things:

- venue – for example, whether a restaurant, pub, café, school canteen
- types of customers and whether there are any dietary requirements
- budget or cost per head of the menu
- style of food – for example, North American, Asian, oriental, Central or South American, European, vegetarian
- time of year – for example, will you use seasonal produce?
- colour and texture of each dish
- time available to assemble the ingredients and equipment, prepare and cook the meal.

Use these points to think about your own meals.

Selecting recipes for courses

Every restaurant has a menu offering a range of courses – starters, main courses and desserts. The success of the hospitality business relies on good planning to cater for the tastes of its customers, and to provide healthy eating options and value for money.

An average meal should be made up of one-third carbohydrates, one-third fruit and vegetables with the remaining third made up of dairy, protein or some fat.

When choosing recipes for your meal, consider the nutritional value and style of food. You may decide to follow a theme, for example, oriental, South American or vegetarian. Avoid duplicating the main food item in the starter and main course options.

Timings

Important skills to master in the kitchen are being organised and getting the timings right. Some foods take longer to prepare and cook than others. Certain times of the year, such as Christmas, can be particularly busy for restaurants. There will be little time to re-cook meals if something goes wrong, so planning and organisation skills are essential.

The better prepared you are, the easier it is to cook your meal in a safe and hygienic way. Having a recipe and time plan are good ways to prepare. A recipe shows what ingredients and weights or measurements are needed for a particular dish. It also tells you how to prepare, cook and finish the dish. A time plan takes this one step further. It takes account of all stages from **mise en place** to serving the finished dish in order to help you get organised and make sure the meal is served on time.

Do you make sure you are organised by preparing all your ingredients and equipment beforehand?

Figure 6.1 shows an example of a time plan.

Order	Task	Time	Notes
1	Prepare self	10.15	Uniform, personal protective equipment
2	Check recipe and ingredients needed	10.30	Check stocks, dates, quality
3	Organise equipment	10.45	Utensils, equipment, chopping boards, pots, pans, crockery, cutlery, bowls
4	Peel and chop the vegetables	11.00	
5	Clear and clean preparation area	11.15	
6	In a large pan, heat the oil	11.25	Be careful not to splash myself with hot oil
7	Fry the onions until golden brown	11.30	
8	Add the carrots and garlic, and fry together	11.35	Stir continually
9	Add the stock and seasoning	11.45	
10	Bring to the boil, then simmer	11.50	Stir occasionally
11	Finely chop the coriander	12.20	
12	Purée the soup	12.25	
13	Pour the soup into the dishes and sprinkle on the coriander and serve	12.30	
14	Clear and clean	12.35	

Figure 6.1 An example time plan

Practise writing time plans. Here are some ideas to help you get started.

- Allow enough time – tasks may take longer than you initially expect. You will get faster as you get more experience in the kitchen.
- Start with the dishes that need the longest cooking times.
- Some ingredients can be prepared in advance when you have more time. Remember to store them correctly until you use them. Examples include grating cheese or preparing and chopping vegetables.
- Dishes such as omelettes and grilled steaks need to be cooked when they are needed, as they become unpalatable very quickly if left too long before service.

▶ Nutrition

Maintaining a healthy diet and lifestyle is essential. A poor diet can lead to illnesses such as **obesity**, cancer, diabetes and cardiovascular diseases. Some people are overweight or obese, which means they may be eating more than they need to. A balanced diet is the key to getting it right. Healthy foods are those that are: low in saturated fat, low in salt, low in refined sugar, high in fibre, generally fresh and not in a convenience form, without preservatives, artificial colourings and flavourings or other chemical additives.

The eatwell plate

The eatwell plate shows the five different food groups we need to eat and how much of what we eat should come from each food group, in order to have a well-balanced and healthy diet. It is important to think about the best way to cook food so that it retains as much of its nutritional content as possible (for example, opt to steam vegetables where possible).

Table 6.2 shows the main nutrients in food and how the body uses them.

Link

The eatwell plate was designed by the Food Standards Agency (FSA) . Go to Unit 9: How the Hospitality Industry Contributes to Healthy Lifestyles to see a copy of the eatwell plate.

Table 6.2 Nutrients and their uses in the body

Class	Description	Main use in the body
Carbohydrates	There are two groups of carbohydrates: • sugars (dried fruit, milk) • starches (potatoes, cereals, rice, pasta).	A major source of energy.
Fibre	There are two types of fibre: • soluble (oats, carrots, potatoes, apples) • insoluble (wholemeal bread, bran, nuts, seeds, cereals).	Helps the body digest and absorb food. Soluble fibre may reduce cholesterol. Insoluble fibre keeps your bowels healthy and prevents digestive problems.
Fats	There are two main types of fats: • saturated (cheese, sausages, butter, cakes) • unsaturated (oily fish, nuts, seeds, vegetable oils).	Gives the body energy, prevents heat loss and aids absorption of fat-soluble vitamins. If we eat too many fats we consume more energy than we burn and we put on weight.
Proteins	These are made from chains of amino acids (meat, fish, eggs and nuts).	Essential for the growth, repair and replacement of body tissue.
Vitamins	There are two types of vitamins: • fat-soluble vitamins (A, D, E, K) (carrots, spinach, sardines, nuts, broccoli). • water-soluble vitamins (B, C) (liver, eggs, chicken, oranges, kiwi).	Essential for the release of energy from foods fighting infection, the formation of new cells and promoting healthy bones and teeth.
Minerals	These are part of the body's structure and include calcium, iron, potassium and zinc. Minerals are found in milk, cheese, bananas, beef and nuts.	Helps the body grow, develop and stay healthy.
Water	Water is not strictly a nutrient but it is an essential part of any diet.	Essential for the body to function.

Menu design should take account of the guidelines for healthy eating. Dishes with fewer calories in them are usually highlighted so customers can quickly spot them. Some customers cannot eat a 'normal' diet as they may be suffering from medical problems such as diabetes or high blood pressure. This will require them to avoid certain foods. Some people may follow certain diets for religious or ethical reasons and it is important that a variety of options are available.

Portion sizes

Getting the portion size right is a skilful task. This is an important part of the budgeting process in any business to control costs and reduce wastage. Portion size is considered at every stage. Portion size affects the

Did you know?

National statistics for England
• Just over a quarter of adults (24 per cent of men and 26 per cent of women) were classed as obese in 2011.
• Only 24 per cent of men and 29 per cent of women consumed the recommended five or more portions of fruit and vegetables daily in 2011.

Source: Health and Social Care Information Centre (2013) 'Statistics on Obesity, Physical Activity and Diet: England, 2013'.

Link

Go to Learning aim B in this unit for more information about portion control.

Key term

Canapés – small pieces of bread or pastry with a savoury topping.

nutritional value of meals, the amount of each ingredient required when ordering food, the amount of ingredients needed when preparing and cooking food and how much food is plated when food is served to customers. If portions are too small, customers may see their meal as poor value for money and may not return to the business. Too large a portion and customers may leave food which will be thrown away.

▶ Food types

Menus usually offer a range of food items that can be hot or cold. Customers may wish to enjoy an appetiser or starter while their main course is being prepared. Main courses can come in many forms including vegetarian options, meat dishes, pasta and rice dishes or salads. Desserts can be sweet or savoury. During events, **canapés** are sometimes served to wet the appetites of the guests or keep their hunger at bay until they are served their main food.

Table 6.3 shows some example dishes for each course. There are always ways to make dishes healthier and look more attractive. Can you think of ways to improve the dishes in Table 6.3?

Table 6.3 Types of food on a menu

Food type	Example	Notes
Starter	Tomato and basil soup	Suitable for vegetarians. Serve with croutons
	Smoked salmon and melon	Combines fruit and oily fish to provide essential vitamins and minerals
Main course	Chicken korma	Use low-fat yogurt instead of cream for a healthier option
	Mushroom risotto	Serve with vegetables or salad as an optional accompaniment
	Stir-fried teriyaki steak salad	A healthy Asian-type meal
	Tiger prawn, tomato and basil tagliatelle	Serve with fresh basil leaves
	Black bean and vegetable pasta	May be suitable for vegans
	Venison sausages with mash	Serve with green vegetables and thyme gravy
Desserts	Summer fruit salad	Add orange juice and apple juice. Offer ice cream, whipped cream or yoghurt
	Bread and butter pudding	Sultanas can be added
	Cheese and biscuits	Serve with grapes

You may wish to come up with your own ideas. Experiment by choosing a theme for your menu and think of alternative dishes, for example, Italian.

Assessment activity 6.1   *Maths*   2A.P1 | 2A.M1 | 2A.D1

Your school's head teacher is hosting an all-day meeting with the board of governors. She has asked you to plan, prepare and cook a two-course meal to be served at lunchtime. The governors are very keen to see evidence of healthy eating in the school, so you will need to demonstrate an understanding of the nutritional value of different ingredients within your menu.

1 Research a range of nutritionally balanced menu options and the ingredients you would use. Explain and assess why it is important for your health to eat meals that are nutritionally balanced.

2 Decide on a two-course meal – the main food items in both courses should not be repeated. Explain how each course is nutritionally balanced and justify why you chose those ingredients.

3 Prepare the recipe for your two-course meal. Include a list of ingredients needed; a description of the methods you will use to prepare and cook the meal; the equipment you need to prepare, cook and finish the meal; the timings for assembling ingredients and equipment, preparation, cooking and finishing the meal; and key hygiene and safety points.

Tips

- Use actual news articles to compare the effects of poor dietary choices against the effects of eating healthy food.
- Speak to staff working in different hospitality venues to gain a better understanding of catering for the needs of different people (including cultural and special dietary requirements).

Learning aim B   **TOPIC**   **B.1**

▶ Preparing different types of food items

Introduction

This section will help you to consider a range of food preparation methods. You will also learn about the tools and equipment you will need to prepare different foods.

Look at the design of a commercial kitchen. What happens in each area of the kitchen? Why is the kitchen laid out like this?

Everyone working in a kitchen has a responsibility for preparing food in a safe and hygienic manner. Figure 6.2 explains the different responsibilities of people working in a professional kitchen.

Head chef:
- in charge of the whole kitchen
- supervises staff and all aspects of the kitchen
- orders raw ingredients
- maintains hygiene standards.

Sous chef:
- responsible for food production
- responsible for the smoothday-to-day running of food preparations
- makes sure food goes out to customers at the highest standards.

Chef de partie:
- responsible for one area of the kitchen.

Commis chef:
- works in different areas of the kitchen, learning about all aspects of cooking in each area.

Kitchen porter/assistant:
- carries out duties such as clearing and cleaning, washing up, basic food preparation and putting away food deliveries.

Figure 6.2 Who does what in a professional kitchen?

Food preparation methods

Preparing food before it is cooked is a technical activity that requires care and attention. It is important to use the correct equipment and most suitable method to prepare each food item. For example, you might use the claw cutting technique to prepare onions and the bridge cutting technique to prepare vegetables such as leeks. With practice, kitchen staff work efficiently, safely and become proficient in knife skills. Remember, any food that is not being used immediately should be stored correctly.

Table 6.4 shows the most common methods of preparing food.

The claw cutting technique

The bridge cutting technique

The creaming technique

The rubbing-in technique

Table 6.4 Food preparation methods

Technique	Function
Beating	To rapidly mix ingredients together and incorporate air, e.g. beating egg yolks with sugar until light and fluffy
Chopping	To cut food into cubes
Creaming	To soften ingredients such as butter and sugar to make them smooth and fluffy
Cutting	General term for dividing food into smaller pieces (terms may include dice, slice, julienne, brunoise, baton, batonette, paysane, chiffonade)
Dicing	To cut food into small cubes
Folding	To gently mix ingredients where one item is heavier than the other, e.g. when baking to allow the goods to rise (it preserves the texture of each ingredient)
Grating	To reduce food item into small pieces by rubbing it against the sharpened and raised edges of small holes
Mixing	To combine two or more ingredients into one
Peeling	To remove outer skin or layers from fruit and vegetables such as potatoes and apples
Rubbing in	To mix flour and fat together in baking, e.g. bread, crumble mix
Shredding	To cut, slice or tear into thin pieces such as lettuce, cabbage
Stirring	To move ingredients around in a circular motion – a gentle form of beating

Weighing, portioning and measuring

Chefs should understand basic weights and measures so they can follow the instructions in recipes correctly. Food is expensive to buy and it is ordered according to a menu and budget. If chefs do not weigh and measure ingredients correctly, food will be wasted and money lost.

When cooking, it is important to use only the quantities of ingredients needed and to serve dishes according to an allocated number of portions. That way, customers will get the same amounts and the business will keep within its budget.

Some recipes and equipment use metric measurements, whereas others use imperial measurements. These are compared in Tables 6.5 and 6.6.

Table 6.5 Weights and measures

Units	Metric	Imperial (approximate)
Capacity:	55 ml	2 fl oz
• millilitre (ml)	75 ml	3 fl oz
• fluid ounce (fl oz)	150 ml	5 fl oz (¼ pint)
	275 ml	10 fl oz (½ pint)
	570 ml	20 fl oz (1 pint)
Weights:	25 g	1 oz
• gram (g)	50 g	2 oz
• ounce (oz)	150 g	5 oz
• pound (lb)	200 g	7 oz
• kilogram (kg)	450 g	16 oz (1 lb)
	1000 g (1 kg)	36 oz (2 ¼ lb)

Table 6.6 Oven temperatures

Celsius (°C)	Fahrenheit (°F)	Gas mark	Description
120	250	½	Very cool
140	275	1	Cool
150	300	2	Cool
170	325	3	Warm
180	350	4	Moderate
190	375	5	Moderately hot
200	400	6	Fairly hot
220	425	7	Hot
230	450	8	Very hot
240	475	9	Very hot

If you use a fan-assisted oven, you will need to make a further adjustment for the temperature. These ovens are more efficient and should be set at a lower temperature than ovens that are not fan-assisted.

▶ Tools and equipment used to prepare food

Introduction

Preparing and creating good food requires the right equipment and tools, and knowing how to use them. In this section, we will look at standard kitchen tools as well as small- and large-scale equipment.

In small groups, look at some different recipes. What tools and equipment do you need to prepare the ingredients? What safety factors would you need to consider when using and cleaning them?

Utensils and equipment are the tools of a chef's trade and must be clean, safe and in good working order. We will look at a range of items in a typical kitchen.

▶ Tools

Tools should be easily accessible and stored safely. Tools should be checked at the beginning and end of a shift to make sure they are in good working order. They should be checked again immediately before use. Always follow the manufacturer's instructions when using preparation equipment. Staff should also be trained so that they use the equipment correctly and safely.

It is important to be familiar with the layout of the kitchen so that utensils and equipment can be located quickly. Experience will make sure you become skilled in the use of tools.

Examples of small-scale kitchen tools used in a typical kitchen to prepare food include:

- apple corers
- colanders (for washing and draining)
- hand or bench food processors
- hand graters and zesters

- kitchen scissors
- knives
- peelers and slicers
- spatulas and spoons.

You should know what each item can be used for. Table 6.7 shows some examples of large-scale kitchen equipment.

Table 6.7 Common large-scale kitchen equipment used to prepare food

Equipment	Definition
Blender	High-speed equipment used to blend foods such as soups, fruit juices, purées, batters. Take care when blending hot foods and make sure the top is secure before using.
Bratt pan	Large versatile piece of equipment used to cook food in a variety of ways such as boiling, braising, frying, poaching, steaming and stewing.
Bread mould	Pans to hold dough in shape while it bakes. Commercial moulds are heavy duty and available in different shapes and sizes.

continued

Table 6.7 *(continued)*

Equipment	Definition
Microwave	An electric oven used to cook food or heat liquids very quickly. It converts electricity into high-powered radio waves. The microwaves bounce back and forth off the reflective metal walls inside as food spins slowly on the turntable, allowing the food to cook evenly. Metal cannot be used in microwaves and food may still be cooking after it has been taken out of the oven.
Mixers	Bench mixers are used for mixing smaller or low volume foods together. Floor-standing mixers are used for larger volumes of food. If fitted with a guard, make sure this is in place.
Oven	Appliance used for cooking food. Ovens can be fuelled by gas, electricity, oil or solid fuel. Combi ovens allow a variety of cooking methods including steaming and baking and can cook large amounts of food. When using large ovens, protective sleeves may be needed to avoid burning yourself.
Pastry break	Metal pastry cutters come in different shapes and sizes. They can be used for cutting out other food items such as cookies. Pastry wheels are available as single items to create waved edges or as multiple wheels for preparing larger volumes of pastry.
Racks	Metal storage to place food in the oven or leave food to cool afterwards in a safe place. Use protective gloves or sleeves to avoid burns. They can be single racks or multiple racks, usually wheeled straight into a commercial combi oven.
Scales	Equipment for weighing food items. Scales can be digital or mechanical.
Steamer	Equipment used for steaming foods such as fish, vegetables and some puddings. It is considered a healthy method of cooking.

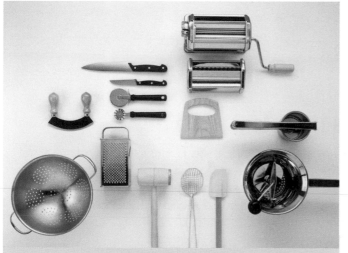

Are you familiar with these items of small-scale preparation equipment?

How can large mechanical devices help reduce preparation time?

▶ Importance of quality of food

Introduction

In this section, you will consider the importance of using good-quality ingredients and products when preparing and cooking food. You will also think about the impact for customers and for the business if problems arise with the quality of food items.

In small groups, look at a range of food items and ingredients. What are the quality points to consider for fresh ingredients, tinned goods, packaged food, chilled and frozen goods? What should you do if the quality is below standard?

▶ Quality issues

Food must be checked at all stages of its life in the kitchen – on delivery, before preparing and cooking it, and before presenting it to customers. By doing this, the kitchen staff will have done all they can to make sure the food is fit to eat. Use your eyes, nose and hands to check the quality of food. Table 6.8 shows the quality points you should consider.

Table 6.8 Quality aspects of food

Quality point	Points to check	
General appearance	• Is the packaging damaged or the tins badly dented? • Is the cling film torn? • Is there any freezer burn? • Are the tops secure on bottles and jars?	• Is there any mould growing? • Is there a layer of slime on the surface (except on fish)? • Has the food been labelled correctly?
Colour	• Is the food the correct colour for that item?	• Does brightly coloured food appear pale?
Smell	• Is there something unusual about the smell?	• Does it smell like sulphur or ammonia?
Texture	• Are vegetable items soft and limp instead of crisp?	• Is raw meat sticky? • Is fruit soggy and bruised?
Dates	• Is it within its use-by or best-before date?	

▶ Why food quality is important

The quality of food is important to any successful hospitality business. Customers will not return if the food served is not as expected. A business's good reputation can easily be lost if customers see or hear negative reports or if the restaurant receives bad publicity. Social media has the ability to quickly spread positive and negative views about businesses and review websites such as TripAdvisor can either make or break hospitality businesses.

The quality of food can be improved by using locally sourced ingredients as these will be as fresh as possible and are often cheaper too. Fruit and vegetables naturally grow in cycles and ripen during certain seasons each year. The ripening process allows the food to develop all of its nutrients and flavours.

It is important to monitor stock to make sure that food items and ingredients are stored correctly, are at the correct temperature and are not used past their use-by date.

You should look out for food spoilage and pests. If food has to be thrown away, this is usually recorded so that wastage can be monitored. Wasting food eats into a business's profits. You should report any problems with food to your supervisor.

In the workplace, the service staff will be the first to find out if customers feel there is a problem with the quality of the food. They often use questionnaires to find out what their customers think. This is important to make sure customers return and, hopefully, bring along other people!

TOPIC B.4

▶ Working in a safe and hygienic manner and storing food items

Introduction

In this section, you will learn about the importance of working safely and hygienically. All equipment used in the preparation must be clean, safe and in good working order. You must also make sure that you have a smart personal appearance, wear the correct clothes and use good hand-washing techniques.

Think about your school or college canteen – what safe and hygienic practices can you see being carried out? Can you think of other ways to make sure food is prepared and cooked safely?

▶ Personal responsibilities

Under the Health and Safety at Work etc. Act 1974 (HASAWA), employees and employers have responsibilities to carry out their duties in a safe and healthy manner. When working, employees must:

- comply with the law and workplace rules
- take reasonable care of themselves, their own safety and that of others
- undertake training, as requested, and use only the equipment they have been trained on
- report anything that may be unsafe or could cause an accident.

▶ Personal hygiene

The human body can be a breeding ground for bacteria. Bacteria can be passed on to food and in turn passed on to customers if you do not keep yourself clean. A high standard of personal hygiene is a requirement for anyone working in a kitchen. Follow these basic principles.

- Bath or shower daily, wash your hair regularly and use non-perfumed deodorant.
- Keep your hair out of food – tie back longer hair.
- Keep your nails short and clean – do not wear nail varnish, as this can chip off and fall into food.
- Avoid wearing strong perfume or aftershave, as this can taint food.

Link

Go to Unit 3: Food Safety and Health and Safety in Hospitality for more information about basic safety legislation and regulations.

Link

Go to Unit 3: Food Safety and Health and Safety in Hospitality for more information about personal hygiene.

- Do not wear jewellery, as this can harbour bacteria and parts can become loose and fall into food.
- Do not smoke, drink, eat or chew gum while working.
- Cover cuts and sores with waterproof dressings to prevent harmful bacteria spreading to food.
- Wash your hands regularly to avoid contaminating food. Figure 6.3 shows the correct procedure for washing your hands.
- Avoid unhygienic habits – do not lick your fingers, pick your nose, ears or teeth and do not scratch your hair.

Remember

You should wash your hands:

- on entering a food area
- before starting work
- between each task
- between handling raw and cooked food
- after any cleaning activity
- after dealing with food waste or rubbish
- after touching your face, hair or other part of your body
- after coughing, sneezing or blowing your nose
- after going to the toilet.

1 Find a hand washbasin and wet your hands with hand-hot water.

2 Use antibacterial liquid soap or gel to wash and clean hands and under nails.

3 Rinse hands thoroughly with clean water.

4 Dry hands with a paper towel.

Figure 6.3 It is essential to follow the correct procedure when you are washing your hands.

▶ Correct work attire

Kitchens can be hot and busy areas, so it is important that you are dressed correctly at work.

Clothing

Your uniform should fit correctly and be comfortable to wear. You may be asked to wear an apron, tie back long hair or wear protective headgear (for example, a skull cap) to prevent any hair falling into food. This also stops hair from falling into your face when preparing and cooking food.

Shoes

Full shoes will help to protect your feet in the event of an accident, for example, if you spill a hot liquid or drop a pan or sharp knife. They should be flat to prevent accidents.

Gloves

You should wear protective gloves when you are using chemicals, washing equipment or preparing large quantities of raw food items.

▶ Reporting accidents and near accidents

Many **accidents** can be avoided if staff are vigilant and report anything they see that could cause harm. All accidents should be reported as soon as possible, so that injured people can get the help they need and hazards can be dealt with. Accident report forms are used to record the details of all accidents (see Figure 6.4 for an example). The main information that should be recorded is:

- date and time of the incident
- name, job title and address of the injured person
- location of the accident
- cause and nature of the injury
- name and job title of the person recording the details.

Determining the cause of an accident is extremely important. It is essential that minor or **near accidents** are reported and investigated to identify their cause. Measures can then be put in place to prevent them happening again.

▶ Identifying potential hazards

In Unit 3 we looked at potential food **hazards**. In the hospitality industry there are many general and common hazards in a kitchen environment. These include:

- hot ovens
- hot liquids – including food and oil
- faulty electrical equipment.
- busy staff moving from one place to another
- wet floors

Potential hazards need to be made safe. Staff should only do this if their own safety is not at risk. Hazards should be reported as soon as possible to maintain a healthy and safe working environment. **Hazard Analysis and Critical Control Points (HACCP)** is a system used by businesses to make sure there are adequate controls in place for food safety management.

> **Key terms**
>
> **Accident** – an unplanned event that may include injury or property damage.
>
> **Near accident** – an event that could have caused harm but did not.
>
> **Hazard** – something with the potential to cause harm.
>
> **Hazard Analysis and Critical Control Point (HACCP)** – a system used by food businesses to look at how they handle food, to help them put in place procedures to prevent food safety hazards and to make sure the food they produce is safe to eat.

Report of an Accident, Dangerous Occurrence or Near Miss

Date of incident _____   Time of incident _____
Location of incident _____
Details of person involved in incident
Name _____   Date of birth _____   Sex _____
Address _____
_____   Occupation _____
Date off work (if applicable) _____   Date returning to work _____
Nature of injury _____
Management of injury   ☐ First Aid only   ☐ Advised to see doctor
                        ☐ Sent to casualty   ☐ Admitted to hospital
Account of accident, dangerous occurrence or near miss
(Continue on separate sheet if necessary)

Witnesses to the incident
(Names, addresses and occupations)

Was the injured person wearing PPE? If yes, what PPE? _____

Signature of person completing form _____
Occupation _____   Date _____

Figure 6.4 A typical accident reporting form

Discussion

- Discuss the difference between use-by dates and best-before dates.
- What are high risk foods? Find examples in a kitchen.

Key terms

Cross-contamination – can occur when bacteria that may cause disease are transferred to food, for example from hands, kitchen equipment or from other foodstuffs (e.g. blood dripping from raw meat onto a trifle that has been stored below it in the refrigerator).

Bacterial growth – growth of germs. Some bacteria are harmful and can cause food poisoning. Bacteria need food, time, temperature (between 5–63°C) and moisture to grow.

Spoilage – food that is no longer safe to eat. It will look, smell, feel and/or taste wrong.

Freezer burn – occurs when frozen food has been damaged due to air reaching the food. On meat it shows as a greyish brown discolouration. It generally occurs when food is not wrapped in air-tight packaging. Although unsightly, freezer burn is not a food safety risk, but it does affect the food's quality and taste.

Stock rotation – a process of making sure that items of stock with the shortest expiry date are used before ones with a longer expiry date. Products that need to be used first are stored at the front of the storage area.

Correct food storage

All food should be stored correctly to make sure that **cross-contamination** does not occur and to stop **bacterial growth**. This keeps food safe for customers to eat. Food items stored in kitchens can generally be found in freezers, refrigerators and dry storage. It is important to store raw and cooked food separately. Large kitchens have separate fridges and freezers for raw and cooked items to avoid cross-contamination.

Freezer storage

Preparing large quantities of food can be cost-effective and freezing helps to preserve food items so they can be used at a later date. The temperature of a freezer must be at −18°C or below. Some freezers have digital temperature displays but it is common practice to use a thermometer or temperature probe to check the temperature manually before, during and at the end of every shift.

Chilled storage

Food should be stored safely in fridges (refrigerators) to prevent food poisoning. Chilled food must be stored at 8°C or below. Ideally, the temperature of a fridge should be between 0–5°C. In a busy kitchen, the temperature may be higher as staff will constantly be using the fridge, but they should remember to keep the door closed as much as possible. It is essential that staff record the temperature of the fridge on a regular basis to keep food safe. Some fridges have digital temperature displays but it is common practice to use a thermometer or temperature probe to check the temperature manually before, during and at the end of every shift.

Table 6.9 explores how to store food safely in fridges and freezers.

Table 6.9 How to store food in refrigerators and freezers

What should I do?	Why I should do this?
Check the quality of the food.	To avoid spreading bacteria to other food.
Wrap the food well – wrap in cling film or place food items in plastic containers.	To avoid **spoilage** and **freezer burn**.
Clearly label the food – record the food item and date of storage.	To identify the food item and how long it has been stored.
Check the temperature of the equipment – read the digital display and use a temperature probe.	To keep food safe and at the correct and legal temperature.
Store food away from the cooling unit.	To allow air to circulate throughout.
Rotate food – use food with the earliest date first.	To avoid food spoilage and prevent food poisoning.
Follow the manufacturer's instructions.	To keep food safe and avoid damage to equipment.
Do not overstock fridges or freezers.	To make sure air vents are not blocked and to prevent food getting too warm.

Activity 6.4   Where to put me?

Look at the images of food items below. Which shelf in the refrigerator should they be stored on? For each food item, say what the shelf number should be.

Dry storage

Dry foods, such as flour and rice, should be stored in areas that are clean, dry and well ventilated. Food should be kept off the floor to avoid damage and placed in covered containers. Dry foods should be clearly labelled and stock rotated regularly. Effective **stock rotation** and control plays an essential part of managing food safety. It makes sure that items with the shortest expiry date are used before ones with a longer expiry date. Monitoring allows staff to order supplies in good time before they run out.

▶ Consequences of unsafe practices

Successful hospitality businesses have in place controls and monitoring systems, which are designed to keep a workplace safe and healthy with high standards of hygiene. Staff should be trained in the correct procedures for safe working.

When things go wrong, it can be a devastating blow not only to a business and its staff but also to customers. Consequences of unsafe practices can include:

- accidents and near misses
- unhappy staff
- food poisoning
- customer complaints
- negative publicity
- poor reputation
- loss of hygiene ratings and awards
- investigations
- improvement and prohibition notices
- fines
- imprisonment
- closure.

Discussion

Interview representatives from hospitality businesses to obtain their views on the consequences of poor working practices when selecting and preparing different food items. What are their experiences? What advice can they give to you? Discuss your findings with your group.

? Did you know?

If an employer can show that they have taken every reasonable precaution to ensure the safety of food, then this is called due diligence. This may include putting into place systems to minimise risks, staff training, cleaning schedules, record keeping and personal hygiene systems.

▐▶ Good practices for preparing food

Food must be kept safe during its time in the kitchen. This means keeping up safe and hygienic practices at all times. Table 6.10 shows things you can do to keep food safe.

Table 6.10 How to prepare food safely

What should I do?	What should I not do?
• Maintain good personal hygiene and keep uniform clean.	• Wear jewellery, nail polish or heavy make-up.
• Wear correct uniform and protective equipment.	• Eat or chew gum.
• Behave sensibly and professionally.	• Smoke.
• Use the correct equipment, such as knives.	• Lick fingers.
• Use the correct colour-coded chopping boards.	• Touch and scratch face and body.
• Check the temperature of the food.	• Pick nose.
• Check the date and quality of the food.	• Touch or comb hair.
• Wash hands regularly.	• Misuse equipment or use faulty equipment.
• Keep raw and ready-to-eat foods separate.	• Misbehave.
• Follow all food safety training and kitchen rules.	• Place raw food above cooked or ready-to-eat food.
• Report faulty equipment and signs of pests.	• Place hot food in the fridge.
• Store food correctly and at the correct temperature.	
• Ask if I need help.	

▐▶ Legislation

Link

Go to Unit 3, Learning aim B, Topic B.1 for more information about food safety legislation.

Legislation and regulations have been introduced to make sure that staff and customers are safe. The Food Safety Act 1990 is one of the main pieces of legislation that governs the preparing and cooking of food, and it applies to all food businesses. The legislation stops businesses treating food in any way that would be damaging to the health of people eating it. It stipulates that food should be of good quality and that it should be labelled and advertised in a way that is not misleading or false.

In 2006, the Food Hygiene (England) Regulations were passed. These require food operators to put in place control measures to confirm that all reasonable precautions are taken to maintain food safety. Food hygiene rating schemes have also been introduced.

Assessment activity 6.2   2B.P2 | 2B.M2 | 2B.D2

The governors are delighted that you are cooking their two-course lunch. They are keen to know more about the processes involved in preparing your dishes, including selecting ingredients, measuring the quantities correctly and your preparation methods. They also want to know about safe and hygienic practices.

Create a log or diary for the governors, recording information while you prepare the meal. You should include the following information.

1 A demonstration that you have used safe and hygienic working practices when preparing the food items and that you have used the correct measurements and preparation methods.

2 A review of the effectiveness of your own working practices when preparing different food items – how well did you prepare the food items using safe and hygienic working practices?

3 An evaluation of the consequences of poor working practices when selecting and preparing different food items – you could include examples of good and poor practice.

Tips
- To gain a better understanding of preparing food safely and hygienically you could speak to staff working in different hospitality venues.
- Use images in your log or diary to show how you prepared food safely and hygienically using a variety of methods and ingredients.
- Use real news articles or industry examples of breaches of legislation and protocols.

▶ Cooking and finishing food

Introduction

In this section you will learn how to finish and present dishes to make them attractive to customers. You will also learn techniques to collect information about the preparation, cooking and finishing of food to help improve aspects of your work.

In small groups, discuss different ways in which eggs, potatoes and chicken can be cooked. What is the healthiest cooking method for each item? Provide an example recipe for each food item using this method.

▶ Food cooking methods

Being able to cook food is a basic but essential skill. Food has to be cooked:

- because it cannot be eaten raw
- to destroy any harmful bacteria and microorganisms that could damage your health
- to develop or improve its flavour
- to aid digestion
- to allow essential nutrients to be more easily absorbed by the human body
- to extend the life of **perishable** items.

By using different cooking methods, chefs can achieve different textures and results. There are two general cooking methods: dry heat cooking and moist (or wet) heat cooking.

Dry heat cooking

Dry heat is cooking using air or fat and, generally, foods have a rich flavour caused by browning. Dry heat cooking uses heat transferred to the food item without using moisture. This method typically involves high heat and temperatures.

This method of cooking can be fairly quick. It allows meat to be well seared on the outside but rare on the inside, which is favoured by some customers. It is a healthy way to cook food as fat is extracted and left behind, reducing dietary fat intake. Cooking by dry heat also preserves the vitamin content better than moist heat methods. However, if food is not cooked correctly it can dry out and result in tough, chewy meat.

Moist/wet heat cooking

Moist heat cooking involves any technique that uses moisture. This includes cooking with water, steam, stock, wine or some other liquid. It is used to emphasise the natural flavours of food. Cheaper and tougher cuts of meat (such as beef brisket) can be cooked for a longer period of time using low heat and plenty of moisture, which leaves it tender.

Did you know?

The browning of meat when seared is called the Maillard reaction. Research what causes this reaction to occur.

Key term

Perishable – food that can spoil or go off very easily.

Mushrooms being sautéed – a dry heat cooking method

Table 6.11 lists some dry and wet heat cooking methods.

Table 6.11 Dry and wet heat cooking methods

Cooking method	Wet	Dry	Definition/explanation	Food types that can be cooked using method
Baking		✔	This is a healthy cooking method. Food is cooked in an oven. The temperature and time taken to bake the item will vary depending on the type of food or dish being cooked.	Fish pie, shepherd's pie, potatoes, squash, fruit pies, tarts, cakes
Boiling	✔		This is a healthy cooking method. Foods are submerged in cold or boiling water depending on the item and cooked at 100°C for a very short time. Use as little water as possible to avoid overcooking, so all the vitamins and flavour are retained. Nutrients can be lost into the boiling water but this can be used to make other foods such as gravy.	Eggs, rice, pasta, potatoes, broccoli
Braising	✔	✔	Braising uses both wet and dry heat. Typically, the food is first seared at a high temperature then gently simmered in water or stock until cooked. Trim the fat from meat before cooking for a healthy option.	Lamb shanks, beef, chicken, parsnips, potatoes, fennel
Deep frying		✔	Food cooked by being submerged in pre-heated oil or fat, using a deep fryer or chip pan. Food is often covered in batter or breadcrumbs to protect it from the heat and to help seal in some of the nutritional content.	Haddock, potatoes, doughnuts
Grilling		✔	Cooking of food above or below a heat source using a grill, grill pan or griddle, or a combination of the two heat sources using a toaster. This is a healthy option as grilled foods have a lower calorie content than fried foods – the fat drips off as the food cooks.	Salmon, steak, peppers
Microwaving		✔	This is a healthy cooking method. Heating foods quickly and efficiently in a microwave oven, which uses high-frequency power waves. It does not brown food and no metal objects can be placed in the oven.	Fish, meat, poultry, vegetables, soups, sauces, desserts
Poaching	✔		The process of gently cooking food in liquid. Food is normally added to boiling water and then held at a simmering temperature of 90°C until cooked. Food often retains its flavour and juices, keeping it tender.	Trout, salmon, eggs
Pot roasting	✔		This is a slow method of cooking food in liquid on a bed of root vegetables in a covered pan. Meat can be seared before cooking.	Beef, lamb tagine, chicken

continued

Table 6.11 *(continued)*

Cooking method	Wet	Dry	Definition/explanation	Food types that can be cooked using method
Roasting		✔	Cooking food in dry heat which can be from an open flame, oven or other heat source such as a spit. Food is placed in a rack, roasting pan or rotisserie with oil or fat added to keep it moist. Roasting meat or vegetables causes natural sugars to caramelise creating a crisp outer coating and tender centre.	Chicken, lamb, potatoes, root vegetables, beetroot, fennel
Sautéing		✔	Cooking food quickly in a minimal amount of fat over relatively high heat. This method can be used to brown food and add texture. The pan must be large enough to hold all the food in one layer.	Potatoes, mushrooms, onions
Searing		✔	Technique used in grilling, baking, braising, roasting, sautéing in which the surface of the food (usually meat) is cooked at high temperature so that a caramelised crust forms. This helps to retain the juices of the meat and adds colour and surface texture to the finished product.	Lamb, beef, pork
Shallow frying		✔	Food is cooked quickly in a pan or metal griddle plate using a small amount of pre-heated cooking oil or fat. Use low-fat oil and a non-stick pan for a healthier option.	Plaice, beef steak, turkey escalope
Simmering	✔		Food is usually placed in boiling water and then brought back to the boil, after which time the heat is reduced. This method helps to prevent damage to the texture and colour of the food.	Rice, pasta
Steaming	✔		Foods cooked in the steam from boiling water. This is a healthy option as it requires no fat to be added and helps to lock in the nutrients in the food. It makes some foods lighter and easier to digest. When cooking with steam, work safely to avoid accidents.	Rice, kale, purple sprouting broccoli
Stewing	✔	✔	Small pieces of meat cooked slowly in liquid, often with added flavourings such as vegetables and herbs. The resultant liquid forms part of the finished dish. Meat is usually seared before stewing. Skim the fat from the surface for a healthier stew.	Lamb, beef, veal
Stir frying		✔	Frying quickly over high heat using a small amount of oil, usually in a wok or frying pan. This method uses little oil and cooks vegetables quickly to retain texture and taste. Use a non-stick pan to reduce the amount of oil needed and keep the food moving so it does not burn.	Slivers of chicken breast, carrots, bamboo shoots

Seasoning and tasting food

Seasonings are added to food during cooking to replace essential nutrients lost in the cooking process or to improve the flavour. They are designed to complement food, not overpower it. Traditional seasonings are:

- salt (table salt or sea salt)
- pepper (ground white or black pepper, peppercorns).

These can also be added during preparation or after cooking. Other seasonings or spices such as garlic, mustard, cumin, ginger and chilli peppers and herbs such as basil, coriander leaf and parsley.

Marinades can be used before cooking to soften and flavour foods such as fish, meat and chicken.

Tasting food is an important part of the cooking process, which takes time and experience. Tasting food is important to check that it is fully cooked, the level of seasoning is correct, the consistency and texture of food are right and that the flavours have developed as they should. Use a different spoon to check each time you taste food to avoid cross contamination.

Following recipes

A recipe is a set of instructions that tell you how to prepare and cook a dish from a list of ingredients and their weights or measurements. It will also include relevant temperatures (such as pre-heating the oven to 180°C) and timings (such as boiling for 10 minutes).

By using recipes, accurate food orders can be placed and the exact number of portions calculated. This is helpful when pricing menu items and calculating costs. It is also helpful for the chef as they know how much they need of a particular ingredient and what the required cooking stages are.

Link

Go to Unit 4, Learning aim B, Topic B.2 for more information on how to price dishes.

A recipe for an Indonesian salad

Correct temperatures

Different food items have different cooking requirements. The same food item may also have different requirements if you use different cooking methods. Some foods only need a short cooking time whereas others need longer cooking times. It is important to check the temperature and timings in the recipe at the planning stage, so you can organise yourself, preheat the oven if necessary and make sure the meal is cooked and served at the correct temperature, and on time. You may need to hold the food before serving (at 63°C or above). This needs to be factored in to avoid overcooking the food.

It is a legal requirement that controls are put in place to record temperatures taken in the kitchen. Make sure that temperature documents are available when cooking, so that you can record the **core temperatures** as you go along. Table 6.12 shows the minimum acceptable core temperatures and timings.

Key terms

Core temperature – the temperature at the centre or thickest part of food. When probing, be careful not to spear through the food and touch the pan or pot with the probe as this will give a false reading.

Coeliac disease – hypersensitivity to wheat gluten, which leads to a failure to digest food.

Table 6.12 Cooking temperatures and times

Description	Temperature	Notes
Cooking	75°C or 70°C for 2 minutes	Core temperature
Reheating	75°C	Reheat food only once
Hot holding	63°C	Measure the temperature during service and every two hours

Remember too that cooking times should be gauged to preserve the nutritional value of the food. By overcooking, nutrients can be lost, for example, vegetables that are boiled for too long will lose vitamins and minerals.

Activity 6.5 — Key temperatures

Look at the thermometer in Figure 6.5. What happens at the following key temperatures?

- 100°C
- 82°C
- 75°C
- 63°C
- Between 8°C and 63°C
- Below 8°C
- Below 5°C
- 0°C
- −18°C or below

Healthy eating considerations

Preparing a balanced meal helps us to stay healthy. In the process of cooking, heat affects the nutrients in food. When preparing menus and dishes, chefs will consider the guidelines for healthy eating and also the method of cooking. Menus often signpost readers to healthy options by stating the numbers of calories per portion or whether it is a low-fat or low-sugar option. Symbols can also indicate whether dishes are suitable for vegetarians, vegans, diabetics or those with **coeliac disease**.

Very often, the main ingredient of a dish can be cooked in a variety of ways and it is useful to consider this when preparing the menu. By using different cooking methods, the menu will appeal to a range of customers. Look again at Table 6.11 to remind yourself of the range of cooking methods you can use.

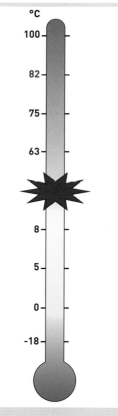

Figure 6.5 Temperatures are essential to food preparation and cooking.

Link

Look back at Topic A.1 in this unit and the section on nutrition.

Minimising food waste

Food waste costs money. Following recipes and workplace instructions will help to reduce the amount of wastage in the kitchen. When receiving a delivery, or preparing or cooking meals, check the date and quality of all food items to make sure that the food is fit for purpose. Perishable food should always be stored correctly in the freezer or fridge to prolong its shelf life. Regular monitoring of stock will also identify food that is nearing its use-by date. Food should always meet workplace standards at all stages of its storage, preparation and cooking.

Planning meals in advance helps to reduce the amount of food wasted. Buying in bulk can help provide cost-effective ingredients that are regularly used in different dishes.

Tools and equipment for cooking food

Introduction

Cooking requires patience, practice and the right tools and equipment. This section will introduce you to the types of small and large pieces of equipment used to cook and finish food in a typical kitchen.

In groups, discuss some of the safety aspects you should consider when using tools and equipment to cook food in the kitchen.

Tools and equipment

A variety of utensils and equipment can be used for cooking and it is important that you have the correct equipment to hand. Generally, the more expensive the equipment, the better its quality. With cheaper products, parts may become loose or not fit well. All items should be fit for purpose and any faulty equipment should be reported. Staff should always be trained before using any type of equipment, particularly large-scale equipment.

Examples of a chef's cooking utensils and tools are shown in Table 6.13.

Table 6.13 Small cooking utensils and tools

Utensils	Small tools/equipment	
Fish slice	Baking trays	Moulds – for jellies, mousses and custard-based desserts
Knives	Can opener	Ovenproof dishes
Masher	Colander/sieve	Pans – saucepan, frying pan, sauté pan
Palette knife	Colour-coded chopping boards	Protective gloves
Spatulas, ladles and spoons	Cooling racks	Roasting rack
Tongs	Funnel	Scales
Whisk	Foil and greaseproof paper	Tab grabbers – food order holders
	Measuring jug	Thermometer/probe

Table 6.14 lists the types of larger pieces of equipment a chef may need.

Table 6.14 Large-scale cooking equipment

Name	Description
Bain-marie	An appliance that uses hot water to keep food hot during service without burning food items.
Baking trays	Flat rectangular metal sheets with low sides used for baking food such as cookies. Other examples of baking trays are moulded to bake muffins and pies.
Deep-fat fryers	An appliance for frying food. Items are usually fully immersed using wire baskets. Care must be taken when using and cleaning these items.
Frying pans	A pan with no lid and sloping sides that help to prevent a build-up of steam in the pan.
Greaseproof paper	Used to absorb fat or oil and to prevent food items sticking to the tin or tray.
Grills	An appliance that heats from above or below, or both (as in a toaster). Flare grills can be used to cook steaks. The bars give a striped appearance to cooked meats.
Ovenproof dishes	Dishes made from heatproof material that will not break or crack when placed in hot ovens. They are available in different shapes and sizes.
Ovens	Appliance used for cooking food. Ovens can be fuelled by gas, electricity, oil or solid fuel. Combi ovens allow a variety of methods of cooking, including steaming and baking, and can cook large volumes of food. When using large ovens protective sleeves may be needed to avoid burning yourself.
Protective gloves	An item of personal protective equipment that can withstand heat. Used to protect hands when taking food out of hot ovens or grills.
Salamanders	A type of grill that can be heated to high temperatures and used for glazing, browning or caramelising savoury or sweet dishes.
Salmon kettles	A long oblong metal pan with round ends used to poach fish. It is usually made of stainless steel, aluminium or copper. The kettle has a basket with two handles used to lift the fish in and out.
Saucepans	A deep cooking pan with straight sides and a flat bottom, usually made from metal, with a long handle and a lid. It has a variety of uses which include boiling food and making sauces and soups.
Sauté pans	A pan with a wide, flat bottom so food is not too crowded in the pan. It has straight sides so food does not overspill when shaking it, a long handle and a lid. It is used to sauté vegetables and meat.
Shallow fryers	A type of pan or metal surface used to cook food using a small amount of fat or oil at a high temperature. It requires constant care and attention. Includes items such as a wok, omelette pan, crêpe pan, flambé pan and sauté pan.
Steamers	Equipment for steaming foods such as fish, vegetables and some puddings. Multi-layered steamers provide an efficient way to cook several food items at the same time.

▶ Finishing food

Introduction

Good presentation of food is an important part of the meal experience. Customers 'eat with their eyes'. If the food looks unattractive on the plate, they will quickly turn off and begin to look for faults in the cooking.

Think of your favourite starter, main course and dessert. What would you use to present each of these dishes? Would you need any garnishes or accompaniments?

▶ Finishing dishes

Adding the finishing touches before a meal is served to a customer is an important stage in food preparation. The dish should be finished according to given specifications and customer requirements to meet business standards. For example, customers may have allergies and ask for certain ingredients be removed from a dish to avoid harming them. The chef will have considered this request at all stages in the preparation, cooking and finishing stages.

When recipes are followed correctly, chefs should use the same ingredients, portion sizes and seasoning. Completed dishes should, therefore, have the same appearance, colour, texture and flavour regardless of which chef has cooked the dish.

▶ Garnishes

Garnishes must be edible and should contribute to the food or dish by adding form, colour and texture. They should complement the food and lift the presentation to make the finished dish appear more appetising. They should not distract from the main part of the dish.

Some examples of garnishes include:
- lemon wedges – usually served with fish
- oranges, lemons and limes – sliced with the skin scored to make a cartwheel effect
- gherkins and olives
- parsley in small 'picks' or finely chopped
- radishes cut into roses
- croutons cubed and seasoned pieces of baked or sautéed bread
- dressings drizzled over food – such as Caesar, French, olive oil, balsamic.

▶ Accompaniments

The purpose of an accompaniment is to improve the flavour of a dish or to counteract its richness or texture. It makes the dish extra special. Let's explore some foods and their most common accompaniments in Table 6.15.

The accompaniments should always be checked before service to make sure it is the correct one to serve with the dish.

Table 6.15 Food accompaniments

Food	Accompaniment
Hors d'oeuvres	Oil and vinegar
Prawn cocktail	Bread and butter
Fish	Horseradish, tartar or hollandaise sauce, bread and butter
Beef	Horseradish sauce
Deep-fried fish in batter	Brown or tomato sauce, bread and butter
Vegetables	Butter
Pasta	Grated parmesan cheese
Steak	English or French mustard
Venison	Redcurrant jelly
Lamb	Mint sauce/jelly
Pork	Apple sauce
Turkey	Cranberry sauce
Cheese	Grapes, chutney, biscuits
Curry	Mango chutney, poppadoms, chapattis
Desserts	Fresh cream, ice cream, custard

Key term

Hors d'oeuvres – small and savoury appetisers served hot or cold.

Presentation equipment

The presentation of food is an art. The best chefs and caterers show individuality, flair and imagination in the presentation of their food, and display creative talent. Think of a plate of food like a picture, with the rim of the plate being the frame.

There is a wide range of plates in different shapes, designs, sizes, patterns and colours. The plates should reflect the style and quality of the food, as well as the character of the business. They can be made from bone china, slate or even wood to accommodate different meals and courses. Some dishes come with lids that help to keep the food hot, which may be useful when customers sit some way from the kitchen, such as an outside terrace or patio. Other dishes are ovenproof to enable the food to be cooked in a container that may in turn be served directly to the customer. This enables quick service to be achieved, as the food does not need to be portioned.

Thought must also be given to the containers used to serve gravy, sauces and accompaniments. These can be made of china, stainless steel or silver and should be served at the same time as the dish. Suitable spoons or ladles should also be available for service.

Platters and silver salvers can be used to present larger amounts of food, for example, during functions, weddings or banquets.

Would you be impressed if you were served this plate of food? The appearance and portion size of each plate is the same

▶ Reviewing food preparation, cooking and finishing practices and methods

Introduction

This section will help you to understand the importance of reviewing your skills in food preparation, cooking and finishing dishes. You need to know what went well and what your customers enjoyed about the meal. You also need to know what did not go to plan, and why. This will help you to improve your skills.

Think about three dishes that you do not normally eat. Give reasons why you do not usually eat them based on the appearance, smell, taste, colour and texture of each dish. Discuss your thoughts with your group and produce a vocabulary poster with useful words for describing food.

In order to assess what works well, or not so well, you need to be able to review the dishes you produce. The best way to do that is to gather feedback from both your customers and your colleagues.

Link

Go to Unit 7: Food and Beverage Service in the Hospitality Industry for more information about review techniques.

▶ Review techniques

To help improve standards of work and the quality of dishes, it is important to get feedback. There are a number of ways in which this can be done.

First, ask the customers. Simply asking if they are enjoying the food gives instant feedback and provides an opportunity to turn an unhappy customer into a happy one. More formal and structured information can be obtained by using comments cards or questionnaires.

Second, ask the staff. Those preparing food items can provide feedback about the quality of the ingredients, equipment used, methods of preparation and the time it takes to prepare the ingredients. Chefs can provide valuable information about the cooking methods and equipment, the time it takes to cook the meal from taking the order, the quality of the final dish and service time. Service staff may provide a valuable insight into customer expectations and preferences.

The success of any business relies on its ability to act on the outcome of feedback – to further develop staff where necessary and to improve the quality and presentation of their dishes.

Activity 6.6   Customer questions

In pairs, think up a list of questions you would ask customers of a restaurant in your local area if you wanted to find out whether they liked the restaurant and what, if anything, they would change or improve.

Reviewing preparation, cooking and finishing

Reviewing performance is essential to the development of an individual's knowledge and skills. It helps to identify what went well and areas for further development. When reviewing the food preparation, cooking and finishing stages, it is useful to consider all working practices and cooking methods. Giving one another feedback allows individuals to compare their knowledge and skills, and to learn from others.

Table 6.16 shows a checklist to help you review your own performance.

Table 6.16 Reviewing performance

Performance	How well did you...
Planning	• Consider the menu items • Achieve a nutritional balance for healthy eating • Check the availability of all ingredients • Check the freshness of ingredients • Meet the budget • Identify the correct utensils, equipment and serving plates/dishes • Consider safety factors for utensils and equipment to be used
Timing	• Plan each stage • Allow time to heat appliances (e.g. the oven) if necessary • Allow time to assemble and check the utensils and equipment • Allow time to assemble the ingredients and check the use-by or best-before dates • Check when you needed to start preparing and cooking each course • Allow time for finishing dishes
Working method	• Clear and clean as you worked • Use the correct utensils and equipment • Work safely and hygienically • Follow the recipe • Use the correct preparation methods • Use the correct cooking methods
Quality, appearance, taste, colour and texture of food	• Maintain the quality of food throughout preparation and cooking • Produce the correct consistency for the food item (e.g. thickness of a soup or sauce) • Produce a varied and correct texture (crunch, soft, crisp) of food item and accompaniment • Consider the taste (sweet, sour, salty, bitter, well seasoned, undercooked or overcooked) • Consider the colour (correct for the food item and cooking method) • Consider the overall presentation of the finished dishes • Ensure the food looks appetising

It is also important to consider how you would make improvements. Answer the questions in Table 6.17.

Table 6.17 Reflective questions

Performance	Questions to reflect on
Recommendations for improvement	• What did I do well? • Did I use the correct ingredients and measurements? • Were my preparation and cooking techniques correct? • Did I follow safe and hygienic practices? • What feedback did I receive? • What can I do better next time?

Assessment activity 6.3   *English, Maths*   2C.P3 | 2C.P4 | 2C.P5 | 2C.M3 | 2C.M4 | 2C.D3

The governors are delighted that you are cooking their two-course lunch. They are keen to know more about the processes involved in cooking your dishes and how you worked safely and hygienically. They also want to know about the process involved in finishing and presenting your dish.

Create a log or diary for the governors, recording information while you cook and finish the meal. You should include the following information.

1 A demonstration that you have used the required cooking methods safely and hygienically.

2 A demonstration that you have used appropriate finishing methods so that the meal is presented attractively.

3 A justification of why you used the methods you did to cook and finish your meal.

The head teacher is considering introducing healthy alternatives to the school's current menu. To help her do this she would like you to find out what the governors thought about your two-course meal by gathering feedback using review techniques. She would like you to analyse the quality of your meal using their feedback and then make recommendations to improve the quality.

Tips

• To gain a better understanding of nutritional values when cooking and how to present food, you could speak to staff working in different hospitality venues. You could find out how they get customer feedback on their products.

• Use images in your log or diary to show how you cooked and finished food safely and hygienically.

WorkSpace

▶ Alexander Ellis

Head chef in a hotel restaurant

I have worked at The Coach House for over two years now. The hotel has a reputation for the excellent standard of the food and service provided. The restaurant was refurbished recently and has just been awarded its first Michelin star. As head chef, I'm proud of what has been achieved.

After completing my Hospitality Apprenticeship, I moved to London and worked in some top restaurants, mentored by some of the best chefs in the world. It was there that I learned how to do things right first time and to work under pressure. I specialised in patisserie before being promoted to sous-chef. I joined this hotel as the head chef. The owners wanted a successful and profitable restaurant. They had a high turnover of staff and a poor reputation for the quality of food. I was up for the challenge!

Since I joined, I have helped to put a business case together for the refurbishment of the kitchen and its equipment. I have improved levels of safety and food hygiene, and developed a training programme, making sure all staff held a food safety qualification. I worked with the owners to design a menu, which changes every season. I also work with local suppliers to find the best quality food, delivered fresh each day. I'm responsible for stock control, portion sizes and final dishes.

The hotel teams now have to work together to maintain their standards and increase turnover to pay for the improvements that have been made. I'm really excited about the next few months. We have a number of important functions coming up and working with the clients helps me to explore my creative talents to ensure they enjoy the best dining experience possible.

If you are passionate about food, love to cook and have good organisational skills, then this could be the job for you. The path isn't always easy as it involves long and often unsocial hours and you are expected to work in busy and competitive environments. The reward, however, is the opportunity to make a difference!

Think about it

1 Why is it essential to have good organisational skills when working in a kitchen?

2 Can you identify the accolades and awards which are available in the hospitality industry? Why are these important to businesses?

3 What are the different types of speciality chefs working in the hospitality industry? What would be your chosen route and what further courses and qualifications can you undertake to achieve this?

Introduction

This unit will give you an understanding of what it would be like to work within the food and beverage area of the hospitality industry. You will gain an understanding of the importance of providing food and beverage service with passion and excellence. This means taking pride in the service you provide and making sure that the customer leaves with a memorable experience of both the service and the business.

This unit will help you to develop the skills and practices needed to work in food and beverage service. You will gain an understanding of how to set up a work area using professional and personal presentation skills, safe and hygienic practices, as well as the correct equipment for the service style you are using. You will understand the importance of using professional and personal presentation skills, as well as the consequences of not doing so.

You will also be able to practise providing food service to customers and be able to gain feedback about the service that you have provided. You will then need to review and reflect on your own skills and performance, and suggest any areas that need improvement.

Assessment: You will be assessed by a series of assignments set by your teacher/tutor.

Learning aims

In this unit you will:

A understand how to use professional, safe and hygienic practices when preparing the food and beverage service area

B provide food and beverage service to customers professionally, safely and hygienically.

> When I realised that I would have to serve real customers in a restaurant I was absolutely petrified. Studying this unit gave me the confidence to work in the restaurant and deal with customers. I prefer the kitchen environment but I'm no longer scared of talking to customers. This unit has helped me to improve my approach and understanding of serving food and beverages.
>
> James, *BTEC Level 2 First in Hospitality student*

Food and Beverage Service in the Hospitality Industry

7

BTEC Assessment Zone

This table shows what you must do in order to achieve a **Pass**, **Merit** or **Distinction** grade, and where you can find activities to help you.

Assessment criteria			
Level 1	Level 2 **Pass**	Level 2 **Merit**	Level 2 **Distinction**
Learning aim A: Understand how to use professional, safe and hygienic practices when preparing the food and beverage service area			
1A.1 Identify professional, safe and hygienic practices that should be followed when preparing a food and beverage service area.	**2A.P1** Describe professional, safe and hygienic practices that should be followed when preparing a food and beverage service area. **See Assessment activity 7.1, page 220**	**2A.M1** Review the effectiveness of own professional, safe and hygienic practices when preparing a food and beverage service area. **See Assessment activity 7.1, page 220**	**2A.D1** Evaluate own performance when demonstrating professional, safe and hygienic practices for preparing a food and beverage service area. **See Assessment activity 7.1, page 220**
1A.2 Use professional, safe and hygienic practices when preparing a food and beverage service area, with guidance.	**2A.P2** Demonstrate independent professional, safe and hygienic practices when effectively preparing a food and beverage service area. **See Assessment activity 7.1, page 220**		
Learning aim B: Provide food and beverage service to customers professionally, safely and hygienically			
1B.3 Use an appropriate service style when providing food and beverage service to customers.	**2B.P3** Demonstrate effective use of two different service styles when providing food and beverage service to customers. **See Assessment activity 7.2, page 231**	**2B.M2** Demonstrate effective use of two different service styles when providing food and beverage service to customers, dealing with special requirements and requests. **See Assessment activity 7.2, page 231**	**2B.D2** Demonstrate confident and effective use of customer service skills in two different service styles when providing food and beverage service to customers, dealing with special requirements and requests. **See Assessment activity 7.2, page 231**
1B.4 English Gather feedback on own food and beverage service skills.	**2B.P4** English Gather feedback on effectiveness of own food and beverage service skills, using appropriate techniques. **See Assessment activity 7.2, page 231**	**2B.M3** English Use feedback gathered to analyse the effectiveness of own food and service skills. **See Assessment activity 7.2, page 231**	**2B.D3** English Recommend improvements to own food and beverage service skills, based on feedback gathered. **See Assessment activity 7.2, page 231**

English   Opportunity to practise English skills

How you will be assessed

This unit will be assessed by a series of internally assessed tasks. These tasks will be set by your teacher/tutor. You will need to show that you have gained an understanding of food and beverage service and that you can demonstrate how to provide this service to customers professionally, safely and hygienically. You also need to demonstrate the ability to prepare, maintain and clean down the service area.

Your assessment could be in the form of:

- assignment work
- completing a personal statement (for example, in a log or diary) during assignment work
- completion of practical tasks
- observation and witness statements.

▶ Professional, safe and hygienic practices

Introduction

The hospitality and catering industry, and in particular the area of food and beverage service, relies on employees to adopt and carry out professional, safe and hygienic practices at all times. In this section, you will learn about the standards needed for a successful food and beverage service.

Think about a time when you were a customer in a food service environment. Identify the good and bad practices that you observed. Think about how this experience has influenced your views of food and beverage service in general as well as the business you visited.

Hospitality businesses, large and small, need to make sure that the quality of their products and the service they offer is consistent and reliable. A well-presented hospitality business and professional-looking staff help to give a customer confidence that they are going to be served well and with a high-quality product or service. For example, if you go into a café where sandwiches are made to order, and you see staff handle food with no gloves on and use the same knife to spread both butter and **condiments** onto the bread, you would not feel confident that basic hygiene standards were being met. You might even decide to go elsewhere. If you go to a restaurant and are served your drink in a dirty glass, or if your **cutlery** has not been washed properly, you could worry that you might go home with food poisoning. Presenting a quality product or service in a professional manner is essential if you want customers to return.

Key terms

Condiment – used to add flavour to food, e.g. sauce, relish, pickle.

Cutlery – the tools or equipment that we use to eat with.

▶ Professional practices

Every business should have a set of standards that reflect the business's core values and adhere to professional practices. All members of staff should be aware of, and follow, the standards that are expected of them.

Behaviour and attitude

Providing a professional, positive and happy customer experience is at the heart of good customer service. How you behave can affect a customer's experience. For example, if a restaurant diner feels that staff have been rude and inattentive, or sees a messy chef working in what looks like a disorganised kitchen, they are unlikely to return to the restaurant or suggest it to friends. Every member of staff has a responsibility to provide a service that is of the highest standard – a positive attitude lets customers know that you care. This might include having an upbeat and helpful attitude, standing tall, smiling when a customer enters the premises and saying thank you when they leave.

Communication skills

If you are responsible for delivering customer service, you may be the only person who has contact with a customer. Therefore, it is essential that customer-facing staff have good written and verbal communication skills in order to serve customers professionally.

A customer's experience of food and beverage service can often affect their impression of your business. Good communication skills are essential and must fit the situation at all times throughout the service period. It is important to understand that communication is key to your role in the following ways.

- **Listening skills** – if you do not listen to a customer's requests you cannot guarantee to give them the right products. This can have serious consequences. For example, if a customer tells you that they have a nut allergy, and they order a dish that you know contains traces of nuts, but you do not tell them because you have not really been paying attention, they could suffer from a severe allergic reaction. If you had listened properly, you could have shown them alternative dishes that were nut-free and avoided a dangerous situation. Appear attentive and ask relevant questions.

- **Speaking** – speak clearly to customers so that you can be heard and understood and vary your pitch and tone to show that you are interested in the customer. You might serve customers who do not have English as a first language or who have specific needs such as hearing difficulties. They will rely on you to speak clearly so that they can understand you; in some circumstances they may lip-read and so they will need to watch closely and interpret what you are saying. It is, therefore, important that you do not use slang or specialist terms. You might also need to tell customers about special dishes of the day that are not on the menu. If customers cannot hear or understand what you are saying, they might miss the opportunity to order a dish that they would have preferred.

- **Relaying messages and orders accurately and promptly** – this is particularly important to make sure the customer gets what they order and within a reasonable amount of time. When you take an order at a table it is a good idea to repeat the order back to the customer to make sure that what you have written down or memorised is accurate and to avoid mistakes during service. Mistakes can irritate and annoy customers. You will also need to pass on the order to people preparing the food and make sure they have understood what the customer wants. For example, if a customer says they would rather have chips than rice with their meal, you need to write this down and tell the kitchen staff. If you take down the order incorrectly, the kitchen staff will need to carry out extra work to fix your mistake and food will have been wasted, causing a loss to the business.

- **Body language** – we do not just communicate using speech – our body language also helps us convey what we want to say. Body language is non-verbal communication and it is vital to the role of food service staff. Our body language is conveyed through our eye contact, facial expressions, posture, movement and gestures. It is important to make sure that your body language gives a positive image. A good understanding of how you come across to customers will help with this. It is important that you appear welcoming and confident rather than scatty and bored. Positive body language will give customers confidence that they are going to receive a high-quality product or service.

Take it further

Discuss with a partner the ways that body language can signal how a person is feeling or what they are communicating in a non-verbal way. List five positive and five negative examples of body language.

Figure 7.1 shows various examples of different body language. Which example do you think is the most effective?

Figure 7.1 Which illustration do you think shows the best level of customer service?

Activity 7.1   Communicating effectively

In small groups, think about the communication chain between a customer, a cashier and kitchen staff working at a drive-through fast food restaurant. Role play a situation where an order is being placed at the drive through and identify areas where information could be miscommunicated. It is lunchtime in the fast food restaurant and orders are coming in quickly and in high numbers, both from inside the restaurant and the drive through.

What measures do you think are necessary to make sure all of the information from the customer is communicated correctly and efficiently?

Teamwork

No matter which area of hospitality you work in, you will need to work as part of a team. A team is a group of people who are working to achieve the same goal or task. For example, you may be part of a team of waiters and waitresses working a lunch shift at a restaurant. Everybody in the team has a role to play and will need to contribute to delivering safe, hygienic and professional practices during the service period. To work together as a team and be effective you will need to show that you can:

- carry out your role and assist with other people's roles as needed to meet the tasks or goals set by your manager
- follow written and verbal instructions given to you by others
- communicate effectively with team members to make sure everyone is well informed and aware of what is happening
- provide help to others as and when required
- work together and/or use your own initiative to solve problems.

Take it further

List the possible consequences of not working as a team in a food and beverage service environment.

Each member of staff needs to play their part, from the kitchen staff preparing and cooking food safely and providing clean dishes, cutlery and glassware, to the food servers making sure that tables are well presented and hygienic, and that their own appearance is clean and tidy. If this is achieved, customers will feel confident that they are going to receive a quality product or service.

Complying with codes of practice

Codes of practice are usually set out for a business by senior management. It is important that all staff are aware of, and work within, the different codes of practice that relate to their role. Codes of practice make sure that a business runs smoothly, that standards are kept to, that customers enjoy their experience and that employees and customers are safe. The senior management team might use legislation that governs the hospitality industry to help them write their codes of practice.

Staff should know about codes of practice in the workplace covering:

- customer service
- safety and hygiene
- protection against disability discrimination
- equality and diversity
- data protection.

The customer service policy sets out rules for the service customers receive. The customer service policy will help to:

- identify the expectations of staff
- improve customer satisfaction
- set the standard for the business and service
- set standards in relation to the behaviour and conduct of staff
- identify procedures for dealing with customers and customer complaints.

Activity 7.2   Legislation

Research three pieces of legislation related to the hospitality industry that might inform a business's codes of practice. If you were writing a code of practice, what points would you pull out from the legislation to cover in your code of practice?

Personal presentation

A customer's opinion of you and the business you work for will be formed within a few minutes of meeting you. Staff who are untidy, scruffy or who have poor personal hygiene will convey a very poor image of themselves and the business they work for. Staff who are tidy, presentable and who take pride in their appearance will convey a smart, professional image.

Staff must pay particular attention to their personal hygiene. You should:

- wash or shower daily and use a lightly-perfumed deodorant, perfume or aftershave (nothing too overpowering)
- keep your hair neat, tidy and clean (and tie long hair back so that it does not fall into food and drinks)

Take it further

Get a copy of a customer service policy from a hospitality business. Find out how the business trains staff to understand how to deal with discrimination, equality and data protection issues. You could choose a large business chain as it will probably publish its policies on its website.

Link

For more information on safety legislation and regulations that control safe working practices in the hospitality industry, go to Unit 3, Learning aim B, Topics B.1 and B.2.

If your appearance is smart and clean, the customer will feel confident that they are going to receive a professional and hygienic service.

- keep your fingernails short and do not wear nail varnish as it can flake off and enter the food being served
- brush your teeth well and make sure you have fresh breath
- avoid wearing too much make-up
- keep jewellery to the minimum – this can get in the way and may also be dangerous
- keep your uniform clean and in good repair
- wear clean, suitable footwear (the more comfortable the better – you could be standing for long periods of time)
- cover all cuts and wounds with suitable, clean and waterproof dressings
- avoid unhygienic habits such as coughing and sneezing over food, picking your nose and ears, scratching your hair and licking your fingers – these can put off customers and transfer bacteria onto your hands and to the food and drink you are serving.

Safety and hygiene considerations

The Health and Safety at Work etc. Act 1974 (HASAWA) applies to all businesses. It states that all employers have a responsibility to ensure the health, safety, wellbeing and security of their employees and customers. The law also states that an employee is responsible for ensuring the safety and wellbeing of others.

General safety

Restaurants, bars, pubs and kitchen areas can be dangerous places. Staff are often busy and concentrating on giving customers efficient and timely service. You should always be on the lookout for potential hazards and report anything to your supervisor that might be a safety problem.

There are many things that you can do to try to prevent accidents.

- Take care when opening doors between staff areas and customer areas. People might be standing close to the door on either side of it! Professional kitchens normally have one door for staff to enter the kitchen and a separate door for them to leave the kitchen. This simple practice makes sure that people do not get hit by swinging doors, and it also reduces delays to service. If there is only one door it is a good idea to have a glass panel in it so that staff can see if anyone is behind it.
- Cellars are often below ground and deliveries are made by lowering barrels and other products through a door in the street above. It is essential that only trained staff using the correct safety equipment accept deliveries.
- If you are serving a very hot dish, use a service cloth to protect you from burning your hands. Warn the customer that the dish is hot before they touch it.
- Food service staff should always use trays to carry equipment. This helps to support the weight and reduce the workload.

When carrying trays you should follow these simple rules.

✓ Do not overload the tray.

✓ Use the right tray for the job.

✓ Place the load on the tray so that the weight is evenly spread.

✓ Do not pile things too high.

✓ Always pick up a large tray using two hands.

Dealing with spillages and breakages

Due to the nature of the hospitality industry it is inevitable that spillages and breakages may happen, even when staff are being careful to prevent them. Customers may also cause spillages or breakages, for example, by tipping liquid from a glass while carrying it back from the bar to their table. You should deal with spillages and breakages immediately as customers or other members of staff could slip or trip on them. Here are some tips for dealing with spillages and breakages.

✓ Always clear up spillages and breakages immediately, taking care to prevent further harm to staff and customers.

✓ Use the correct warning or safety signs to inform others of the risk.

✓ Correctly dispose of any broken items. Broken glass or **crockery** usually need to be placed in a special bin so that an unsuspecting member of staff is not harmed when disposing of the rubbish bin.

✓ Never clear up broken glass or crockery with your bare hand. Use a dustpan and brush.

✓ Report all breakages to your supervisor, especially if it has affected the customer. You may have a book for recording breakages or faults.

Remember, you can try to prevent spillages and breakages by not stacking crockery and glasses too high on trays and being aware of your surroundings.

Prevent accidents happening by using the correct warning signs.

Hand hygiene

Keeping your hands clean and washing them at the right times during the service period will prevent the risk of contaminating food. Hands should be washed regularly, including:

● at the start of a shift

● after using the toilet

● after smoking/eating

● after using cleaning materials

● at key stages during food preparation, for example, after preparing meat or fish, and before touching, or after working on, other food products.

Link

For more information on safety signs, go to Unit 3, Learning aim B, Topic B.2.

Key term

Crockery – the china that you use to serve dishes to customers at their table, e.g. plates and bowls.

Link

Go to Unit 3, Learning aim A, Topic A.1 for more information about how to wash your hands thoroughly.

Link

- Go to Unit 3: Food Safety and Health and Safety in Hospitality and Unit 6: Planning, Preparing, Cooking and Finishing Food to learn more about how to prepare food safely.

- To learn more about hazards, and also how to lift and handle items safely, go to Unit 3, Learning aim B, Topic B.2.

Handling food and beverages safely

Customers are at risk of becoming ill if the food and drink they consume is not handled safely or is dirty. Handling food in a safe and correct manner is, therefore, vital to the prevention and control of food poisoning and food-borne illness. Staff working with food should receive and follow food safety training and should follow codes of practice about the safe handling of food and drink. It is the responsibility of the food handler to provide food that is safe to eat and free from anything that may cause the customer harm.

Hazard spotting

In order to make sure the workplace is safe for both staff and customers it is a good idea to complete hazard spotting activities. For example, a nominated employee could complete a safety checklist throughout the day. The checklist could include checks such as making sure spillages have been cleaned up immediately, that warning signs have been used and that the service area is tidy and walkways are clear. You should also make sure that you report hazards to a supervisor immediately. Trailing wires and wet floors are both examples of common hazards that may be found in a food service area. Figure 7.2 shows some of the hazards you might find in a restaurant.

Figure 7.2 Can you spot the hazards in this restaurant?

Safe storage of items

Equipment is often stored and stacked away for future use in the food service area and it is important to make sure this has been done safely and securely. Here are some simple tips for storage.

- Do not over stack equipment – make sure piles of items, for example, plates or chairs, are not too high as this may cause them to topple.
- Never store equipment in public areas or in areas that are visible to the public eye.
- Unplug and wind up the cables of electrical items that are not in use.
- Store crockery or glasses that are not being used safely and securely in packaging to prevent breakages, chips and cracks.
- Store cutlery in a specially designed container or drawer which separates out the individual items. This will stop cutlery being damaged.
- Store heavy items near to the ground to reduce lifting, but not too near that items become dirty.
- When moving items to store them away, use a trolley to support and carry the weight.

Maintaining a clean work area

Work areas are often on view to customers, so it is important to keep them clean and tidy. You can contribute to keeping a clean work area by cleaning regularly and disposing of waste. Dirty work areas are also a health risk.

Here are some tips for maintaining a clean work area.

- Dispose of waste regularly, including recyclable materials.
- Take used glasses, crockery and cutlery to the washing-up area. Do not leave them where they were used or where customers can see them.
- Store correctly, and out of sight of customers, any equipment and products used for cleaning.
- Wipe down tables and surfaces using clean cloths and an approved sanitiser or disinfectant. Make sure cloths are cleaned ready for the next session.

It is also important to clear down service areas at the end of a service period or session. This prevents the spread of bacteria and leaves a pleasant environment for staff working during the next session.

Complying with food hygiene regulations

In order to provide a professional, safe and hygienic service, employees need to understand the regulations that govern food hygiene. They also need to know why hygienic working practices are important. Staff should be trained on how to carry out these practices and have an awareness of the consequences of non-compliance.

Discussion

Surveys show that most customers believe strongly there is a link between good hygiene and cleanliness, and good quality. Most customers feel that excellent hygiene standards are just as important as good food and service. If a customer visits a café toilet and finds that it is dirty, what are they likely to think? What assumptions might they make?

Link

Go to Unit 3: Food Safety and Health and Safety in Hospitality for more information about food safety legislation, regulations and procedures.

▶ Preparing for food and beverage service

Introduction

Food and beverage staff have a lot to do in order to set up the service area ready. The amount of set-up required will vary due to the type of business and the style of service.

Think about five different businesses in your local area that serve food and beverages. Record the name of the business, the type of service it offers and a selection of the items on their menu. Suggest different styles of service that each business could use.

▶ Types of businesses providing food and beverage service

There are many businesses within the hospitality industry where food and beverage service is offered. The businesses will vary due to size, location, service style and customer. Examples of business types where food and beverage service is on offer include:

- hotels
- restaurants
- pubs
- bars and nightclubs
- cafés, coffee lounges
- contract food service providers
- hospitality services
- membership clubs
- events.

Activity 7.3   Types of hospitality businesses

Look at the photos on this page. Identify at least one business in your local area that fits into each business category. What type of hospitality services does each business offer?

▶ Preparing the food and beverage service area

A customer's first impressions on entering a hospitality business are very important. Preparing the food and beverage service area properly is, therefore, of great importance. Think of a local restaurant or café you have been to recently. Did the premises smell fresh? Was the area visually clean and appealing?

Can you identify the different types of hospitality businesses shown in these photos?

Preparing the food service area will involve:

- cleaning the food service area
- organising the area
- arranging, laying and presenting tables.

Cleaning and organising service areas

All businesses will probably employ cleaning staff. However, food service staff will be expected to know how to clean work-related areas and make sure they are presentable. A clean working area sends a strong message to customers about the quality of care taken by staff and the business. A clean service area requires staff to:

- clean and dust the furniture
- arrange the furniture
- hoover furniture, carpets and other floor areas
- polish tables and other surfaces
- clean and maintain all areas used to provide the service of food and beverages – remember to always use clean cloths, dusters, mops, etc., and to store cleaning equipment out of view of customers.

It is important to clean the room before laying tables.

Table layout and set-up

The layout of tables will vary depending on the business and the type of service being provided. Different businesses have different tables and these will be of different shapes and sizes – round, rectangular or square. Round tables allow all of the guests at the table to be able to talk to, and see, each other. Rectangular and square tables take up less space than round tables and can be joined together to make bigger tables for larger groups. However, in some businesses, such as canteens, tables and benches are fixed to the floor. Restaurants tend to use tables that can be moved between services to allow the business to accommodate varying party numbers/**covers**.

A hospitality business can also set its own tone, atmosphere and style by deliberately choosing a specific type of table and chair. For example, you might have been to a Japanese noodle bar where they have fixed tables and benches to allow for larger parties of people to share tables and to create an informal dining experience.

Remember

Always handle cutlery to a minimum. When doing so, make sure that you only touch the handle and not the part that customers put into their mouths.

Key term

Cover – a place setting at a table in a restaurant.

A static restaurant set-up – these tables and benches are fixed and would suit a more informal style of dining

Discussion

Choose four different businesses that serve food and beverages (e.g. a café, takeaway business, mid-range restaurant and high-end restaurant). How have the tables and chairs been arranged? What vibe and atmosphere does this set?

Key term

Cruet – salt and pepper pots.

Once the tables are in place, they should be checked to make sure they are evenly balanced and clean. Where needed, a tablecloth can be put on the table. In some businesses, table mats will be used and in others, cutlery will be placed directly on the table. It is good practice to polish cutlery before placing it on the table. In many pub-style restaurants, the table is bare and the customer has to collect their own cutlery, condiments and sauces.

Where cutlery is part of the set-up, it should be laid around a large plate to make sure there is enough space. Cutlery should be placed directly in front of where the customer will be sitting. Once you have laid the cutlery (and removed the plate if preferred), place the glasses (usually to the top of the knife), then the **cruet,** and finally any flowers that may decorate the table.

Carry out a final check of the table to make sure that all of the equipment is clean and correct before the arrival of customers; this is essential for a smooth and efficient food service.

Reporting any problems affecting service

Now and then problems may occur that have an effect on the food and beverage service. All food service staff need to make sure that any problems are reported immediately to a supervisor or manager.

Typical problems may be about:

- food
- beverages
- service equipment.

When problems are ignored or not reported this can lead to unhappy customers, complaints, a poor business reputation and loss of business if customers are put off returning. In some circumstances, problems can also lead to accidents. For example, if a customer is selecting their own food items from a hot food buffet which has a faulty lead, they may have an electric shock, or if a cable is trailing across the floor to its socket, customers are at risk of trips and falls.

Activity 7.4   Food, beverage and service problems

Imagine you work in a self-service café where customers order and pay for their items at a till and staff clean away dirty crockery and glasses from tables.

Make a copy of the following table listing three problems that may occur and need to be reported for each area of service: food, beverage and service equipment.

Problems relating to food	Problems relating to beverages	Problems relating to service equipment
1		
2		
3		

Appropriate types of service equipment

The equipment you use will depend on the food and beverages you are serving.

Service units

Service units are specially designed equipment for displaying food and beverages. They enable customers to see what is on offer and make a choice. Presentation is, therefore, important as unclean, messy and poorly stocked service units can put off customers. There are two types of service unit.

- **Heated service units** are ideal for hot buffets where a variety of foods need to be served or for a carvery where there are a number of meats and vegetable dishes on offer.
- **Refrigerated service units** display a variety of cold foods, for example, salads, sandwiches, cold starters, cakes and desserts. These can also be used to store and display a variety of beverages.

Examples of both heated units and refrigerated units can be found at motorway service stations, buffet-style restaurants, canteens, cafés, fast food providers and retail shops.

> **Remember**
>
> Food items that are served in heated service units need to be held at 63°C or above for a maximum of four hours. After this time the product must be destroyed as it will have exceeded the legal limit for hot-holding.
>
> Cold food items need to be kept between 0°C and 8°C to prevent bacterial growth.
>
> Go to Unit 3, Learning aim A for more information about procedures to maintain food safety.

A heated service unit

A refrigerated service unit

Trays

Trays should be made from suitable materials that are easy to clean, strong and hard-wearing. Chipped or cracked trays must be thrown away as bacteria could harbour in the chipped or cracked area. Table 7.1 lists different tray shapes and their uses.

Link

Go to Unit 3: Food Safety and Health and Safety in Hospitality for more information about bacterial growth.

Table 7.1 Different tray shapes and their uses

Tray shape	Uses for this shape of tray
Square/rectangular/oblong	• Usually used to clear away cutlery, crockery and glasses to washing-up areas. • Can be used to deliver food dishes/items from the kitchen to a service station. • For customers to use when working their way through a self-service set-up, e.g. a self-service café.
Round	• Usually used for serving beverages and carrying food dishes to the table.

Store trays on, or near, the service or bar areas so that they are available for customers and staff to use as and when required. It is also helpful to leave linen napkins or paper serviettes near to the trays so that if needed, spillages can be wiped up.

Crockery and cutlery

Different businesses will have their own style, shape and size of crockery and cutlery, and often their choice can be influenced by cost and the image they are trying to portray. For example, a busy café might choose plain, hard-wearing crockery and stainless steel cutlery, whereas a Michelin-starred restaurant might choose fine bone china and silver cutlery.

If a business buys cheaper crockery that is less hard-wearing it can prove to be a false economy; it is more likely to chip and crack and then it cannot be used due to the risk of bacterial growth.

For hygiene reasons, cutlery in commercial food service businesses must be dishwasher-proof so that it is free of germs and bacteria.

Cutlery should also be kept free from smears. It is good practice to polish cutlery before laying it on a table to remove any smears. The storage area should be regularly cleaned too, as dirt and dust in containers or drawers can transfer to the cutlery items, which come into contact with the customer's mouth.

When laying a table, make sure there are no chips or cracks in the crockery and that the correct cutlery for the menu is placed on the table.

Remember

- Do not stack crockery in piles that are too high or unsafe.
- Store heavier items on lower shelves.
- Use trolleys when moving a lot of crockery.

Glasses

Glasses are chosen for their shape, size, pattern and feel. The type of glass a business uses will depend on the style of the business and whether it is running a special occasion or event. For example, if you are catering for a wedding, you must supply enough champagne flutes and wine glasses for the number of guests. A bar in a nightclub would need to stock glasses for all kinds of beverages from cocktails, to pints, to soft drinks. A café would need several types of glass for hot drinks and bottled drinks.

Did you know?

All glasses should be:
- stored upside down to stop dust collecting inside them
- kept in or near the bar/service area on a clean surface, which is free from debris or spillages, and on top of racking, which secures the glasses during storage
- grouped together by size and style, e.g. all pint glasses together.

Glasses are fragile and can crack and chip easily, so you must take extra care to make sure that the glasses given to customers are safe and fit for use. Dirty glasses can spread bacteria and germs so you must also make sure that they are clean.

Table coverings

A business will choose the style of table covering that reflects its image.

- **Tablecloths** can be made from linen, polyester, cotton or polycotton and will need to be laundered (an additional cost that may be passed on to the customer through the price of the food and beverages).
- **Disposable cloths** vary in shape, size, colour and quality. Paper cloths can only be used once whereas more hard-wearing and high-quality cloths can be used a number of times.
- **Place mats** or **table mats** can be used instead of a tablecloth or as a way to add colour on top of a tablecloth. They are available in a wide range of styles. They can even be personalised with printed designs of the business or its logo and so act as a form of advertising. Placemats can be permanent or disposable. Typical materials they can be made from include slate, glass, paper and plastic.

Menus

A menu is a list showing customers what is available to eat and drink and how much it costs. The type of menu usually depends on the style of service, the type of food being served and the atmosphere a business wants to create. Some businesses will provide simple printed paper or card menus. Others will write menus on blackboards, which are displayed around the business, and some will print elaborate booklet menus with leather covers.

Menus are laid out in the order in which dishes are served. So, starters are listed first, followed by main courses and then desserts. Beverages are usually found at the end of a menu. Menus which offer dishes that are individually priced are called à la carte menus, whereas set menus (where a number of dishes are charged at one set price) are known as table d'hôte menus. Both styles of menu can be offered to give the customer more choice.

Service utensils

Service utensils are used to serve food and must always be spotlessly clean. Examples include serving spoons, slotted spoons, fish/dessert slices and tongs. They should be kept in the service station in the cutlery drawer.

Condiments

Condiments improve the flavour of a dish or beverage. Condiments for beverages include sugars and sweeteners. Condiments for foods include sauces and dressings, and cruets (salt and pepper). You should be aware of which sauces/dressings complement the different menu options. A wide range of condiments should be available for a customer to choose from.

How condiments are served depends on the style of the business.

- They can be offered as individual pre-wrapped sachets. These sachets are convenient and hygienic, and are often used in fast food businesses.
- The bottles and containers the condiments are bought in are placed on tables. This is often done in cafés and pubs. You should make sure that bottles and containers are clean.

> **Remember**
> - Handle tablecloths as little as possible to prevent them creasing.
> - Choose a cloth that will cover the whole table and hang down each side by at least 30 cm.
> - Store table cloths in a dry area to prevent them from becoming damp and discoloured.

> **Did you know?**
> In the UK, a menu must be displayed, by law, either outside or near to the front of the business so that customers can see what is available and what the prices are before they go in.

• Sauces can be offered and served to customers by food service staff who bring them to the table in small bowls and place a small amount of the sauce on the customer's plate using a teaspoon. It is important not to put back in the original bottle or container any sauce that is not used.

Assessment activity 7.1

Imagine you are working in a restaurant as a food and beverage service assistant. Your manager, James, has asked you to prepare training materials for new members of staff to help them prepare the food and beverage service area.

In order to complete this successfully you need to:

1 investigate professional, safe and hygienic practices when preparing the food and beverage service area

2 produce a training handbook or other training materials that the new staff can use to learn about how to prepare the food and beverage service area.

The new members of staff are visiting the restaurant for a meeting. Your manager has asked you to demonstrate to the new staff how to set up a food and beverage service area in the restaurant where light refreshments will be served midway through the meeting. You will need to gather evidence to show and support your ability to demonstrate appropriate independent professional, safe and hygienic practices when preparing the area. At the end of the meeting you need to review how well you prepared the service area. You should reflect on, and evaluate, your own strengths and weaknesses when demonstrating professional, safe and hygienic practices.

Tips

• Speak to staff in hospitality businesses to learn about professional, safe and hygienic practices in the food and beverage service area.

• Observe staff in hospitality businesses preparing the food and beverage service area to help you put together your training handbook – if there is a staff handbook, ask to see it.

▶ Providing food and beverage service

Introduction

In this section you will explore the different styles of food and beverage service used by hospitality businesses.

Think about five local hospitality businesses and write down the different service styles that they use. Which styles seem the most professional to you? Do you think some types of service are safer/more hygienic than others? How did the service style affect the presentation of the food on the plate?

▶ Styles of food and beverage service

There are several styles that can be used to serve food and beverages to customers. The style used depends on various factors, including the type of business, the type of food and beverages and the cost of the menu.

Staff need to be skilled in the service style of the business for which they work so that food and beverages are served safely, professionally and hygienically. Careless serving conveys an unprofessional appearance to customers and spoils the presentation of the food.

In restaurants, pubs and cafés, the most common type of service is table service. This is when customers are seated at a table and their food is brought to them by waiting staff. Types of table service include:

- **Plated service** – food items are placed on the customer's plate in the kitchen and delivered to them at their table. Food should be presented well.
- **Platter service** – food items are placed in service dishes in the kitchen and carried to the table by waiting staff. Staff then serve the food with a spoon and fork onto customers' plates. This style is also known as 'silver service'. It can be used to serve several customers who are eating the same meal, for example, at a wedding. Food can also be placed on large trays in the kitchen and served to customers. For example, it may be suitable to serve **canapés** in this way at a wedding reception.
- **Family-style service** – the main part of the dish, for example, a piece of meat or fish, is served plated to the customer and accompanying items such as vegetables and potatoes are served in a dish. This is put on the table for customers to help themselves.

Service concepts

Popular food and beverage service concepts include buffet, counter, cafeteria and self-service.

Buffets offer customers a wide selection of foods presented on a table or purpose-built counter. Customers either help themselves or are helped by staff from behind the buffet. Buffets can be hot or cold and are often used to serve breakfasts in hotels. Many restaurants today offer 'eat as much as you like buffets' to entice customers. Buffet service allows for a large number of people to be served in a short space of time. It is important that buffets are attractively presented, that food is filled up regularly and that the service area is kept clean. Staff and customers should not mix or **contaminate** the different types of food and individual service utensils should be used for each type of food.

Counter service can take many forms including:

- **self-service** – a customer walks along a series of counters choosing hot and cold food and beverages and then moves along to the cashier point (a popular style in many retail-based operations such as IKEA, and in motorway service stations and office or college canteens)
- **carvery style** – the customer is normally served a meat item of their choice by a chef from a heated service unit. The customer then moves along the service counter to choose their own accompaniments such as vegetables, potatoes and condiments.
- **single point service** – a customer will collect everything they need from one place. This is the case in many retail operations such as cafés, fish and chip shops, kebab houses and other fast food operations where food is cooked to order.

Throughout service periods in businesses that use counter service, staff must make sure that the counters and service areas are kept clear and free from debris. Used cutlery, crockery and glasses need to be cleared away efficiently as customers will come and go quickly. Staff also need to consider health and hygiene practices.

Key terms

Canapés – small pieces of bread or pastry with a savoury topping.

Contamination – in food, any substance that has the potential to cause the customer harm or illness.

Link

Go to Unit 3: Food Safety and Health and Safety in Hospitality for more information about health and hygiene practices.

▶ Food types

Most food and beverage businesses will specialise in a particular style of food and the choice they offer customers is shown in their menu. Figure 7.3 shows the wide range of food types available for businesses to choose from. Can you think of any more types?

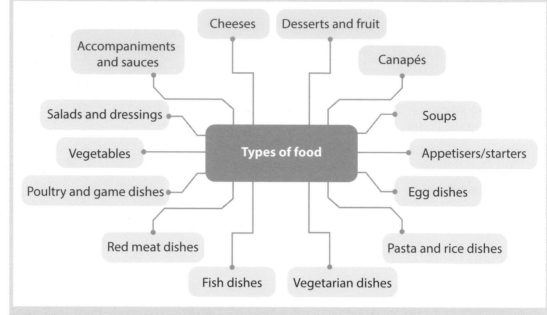

Figure 7.3   There is a huge choice of food types available.

The range and number of courses offered depends on the size and style of the business. Courses include: starters (also known as appetisers), main courses and desserts. Some businesses will also offer side dishes, soup courses and cheese courses. Table 7.2 lists the variety of food types that can be offered and when they might be served.

Activity 7.5   What goes with what?

There are lots of accompaniments and sauces listed in Table 7.2. Can you identify at least five more dishes and suggest what you could offer the customer as the accompaniment or sauce? The dishes can be either savoury or sweet, or a mixture of the two.

▶ Beverages

Many different types of beverages are offered within hospitality businesses, including:

- **hot beverages** – coffees, teas, hot chocolates, tisanes (herbal and fruit teas) and steamed milk beverages
- **cold beverages** – iced beverages, fresh juices, carbonated beverages, squashes, water and milk
- **alcoholic beverages** – wines and spirits, draught beers, lagers and ciders (bottled and canned options), liqueurs, mixers (drinks that are often served with spirits). The sale of alcoholic beverages is governed by licensing regulations and all staff must comply with, and understand, these regulations.

Table 7.2 Food types and when you might serve them

Food type	Example	When might this be served?
Canapé	• Mini vol-au-vents, pâté, blinis with cream cheese and salmon, etc.	• At a wedding, drinks reception, interval at a theatre event
Appetiser/starter	• Salads, soups, terrines, etc.	• At the start of a meal
Soup	• Minestrone, consommé, vegetable, tomato, etc.	• As a starter or as a soup course between the starter and main course
Egg dishes	• Eggs benedict, omelette	• As a starter or main course
Pasta and rice dishes	• Lasagne, paella, risotto, etc.	• As a starter, main course or side dish
Vegetarian dishes	• Meat-, fish- and poultry-free options	• Should be available for all courses and at all events
Fish	• Trout, sole, haddock, etc.	• As a fish course or main course, or as part of a starter
Meat	• Steak, burgers, pork, etc.	• As a starter or main course
Poultry and game	• Chicken, duck, pheasant, venison, etc.	• As a starter or main course
Vegetables	• Potatoes, carrots, peas, broccoli, leeks, etc.	• Usually as a side dish but can be a main dish, e.g. broccoli and cauliflower bake
Salads and dressings	• Green salad, chicken and bacon salad, etc.	• As a starter, side dish or main course
Accompaniments and sauces	• Parmesan cheese, horseradish sauce, apple sauce, tartare sauce, cheese biscuits, etc. • Custard, cream, ice cream, etc.	• With main dishes, e.g. spaghetti bolognaise, beef, pork, fish • With desserts, e.g. sticky toffee pudding, fruit pie
Cheese	• Cheddar, stilton, brie, etc.	• As a cheese course after dessert or instead of a dessert
Desserts and fruit	• Jam roly poly, cheesecake, mousse, fruit compote, fruit salad, etc.	• After the main course

You will need to know about the different types of drinks in order to work behind a bar or to be able to take orders and serve drinks in a restaurant effectively.

Beverages can be served in many ways and often this is dictated by the business in which you are working. For example, you would not expect to receive your afternoon tea in a disposable cup if you were dining at the Ritz. Equally, if you were at a stadium watching a football match you would not want your tea to be served in a cup and saucer!

Therefore, the type of business will specify:

• the type of service – whether at a bar or counter, or served at a table

• the type of cup or glassware to be used – for example, a flute for champagne or sparkling wine, half pint or pint glass for beer, cider or lager, and mugs and cups for teas and coffees.

Key terms

Draught – draught beverages are served at the bar by placing a glass under a tap and opening the tap to pull the beverage through a pipe from the barrel (usually kept in a cellar) to the glass.

Optic – a piece of bar equipment that is placed on to the mouth of a bottled beverage, for example, a wine or spirit. When pressed, it issues one measure of the beverage.

The type of business will also dictate whether alcoholic beverages such as beer and lager are served **draught** or whether they are served in bottles or cans. Non-alcoholic beverages such as carbonated fizzy drinks can also be served using a fountain or by giving customers bottles. Many alcoholic beverages, including wine and spirits, must be measured so that the correct amount is served. This is a legal requirement. When using a measure, you must fill it to the top and then pour the liquid into a glass. Make sure that you do not spill any of the liquid. Some bottled wines and spirits are connected to **optics**. This is a measure fitted on to the opening of the bottle. The bottle is then stored upside down, fitted onto the wall behind a bar. When you press the optic, it pours one measure of the beverage into a glass that you hold underneath the opening of the bottle.

At the beginning and end of service it is important to check equipment that will be, or has been, used. All equipment should be clean and hygienic, and there should be no cracks or chips as these can harbour germs and bacteria, which can be passed on to customers.

Activity 7.6   What are you drinking?

Visit two different hospitality businesses and find out about the different beverages that they offer and how they are served.

Link

For more on customer service and professional practices, see Learning aim A, Topic A.1 in this unit.

▶ Greeting customers and taking orders

It is important for staff to greet customers when they enter a hospitality business. We have already discussed the importance of good customer service. When customers enter a business, it is an opportunity to create a good first impression. It is important to greet them in a professional manner and make them feel welcome. A greeting as simple as 'Hello' or 'Good morning/afternoon/evening' will put customers at ease.

Identifying customers' requirements

You will then need to find out and understand what the customer wants. This can be done by asking 'Can I help you?' or 'Do you have a reservation?'. Many customers will arrive without booking. These people are referred to as 'walk ins'. Other customers will have pre-booked and will, therefore, have a reservation. You should ask for the name under which the booking was made and check the table plan to see where they have been seated. You should then take the customer to their allocated table and check that they are happy with it. Customers who have not reserved a table may need to be given a waiting time for a table if one is not available, or if possible, they can be shown straight to a table.

Some customers may have special requests relating to their table, and ideally these should have been made when they booked. You would need to make sure that they have been catered for. For example, a customer may request a table near the window while another may need a highchair.

Providing information and taking orders

Customers need to be given information about what is available to eat and drink. You should give customers a menu and inform them of any special dishes that may be on the menu that day. This is also the time to tell them about special offers to increase the order.

Communication skills are key to the role of food service staff because they are not only customer-facing but also in the position to sell the products/services to the customer. An excellent understanding of the menu items will make sure you can deal effectively with customer requirements.

Customers often know what they want, in which case you simply need to record their order. Some customers, however, may need advising and may want you to talk through the menu. If you are unsure about any of the items, always check with the chef or your supervisor – but the more knowledge you have, the more professional a service you can provide. Staff who explain menu items confidently are more likely to sell an item than those who hide behind a lack of understanding. Some key pointers for food service staff to know are:

- the menu items – the name of the dish
- the ingredients
- the cooking method
- the ingredients used in sauces/accompaniments
- the particular ingredients, especially those that might trigger an allergy, e.g. nuts, flour and garlic.

When taking orders either for food or beverages it is essential that food service staff are able to record any information about a customer's needs so that it can be passed on. How orders are taken down depends on the procedures of the business. Orders might be written on a pad by hand or a hand-held electronic keypad might be used.

Use the following tips for taking a food order.

- Make sure you take an order pad and pen, or electronic keypad to the table.
- Ask the customer if they are ready to order.
- Smile and look at the customer when they are ordering – positive body language is important.
- Answer any questions the customer may have – if you do not know the answer, ask your supervisor or the chef.
- Repeat the order back to the customer to make sure you have understood it correctly.
- Thank the customer for their order.

Activity 7.7　　Customer service

You and your family book a table at a local restaurant. On arrival it takes almost 15 minutes for someone to acknowledge you at the entrance and find your reservation. After being shown to your table and told who your waiter will be, you wait a further 20 minutes before you have to ask a passing waiter for a menu. When you ask for the menu, the waiter continues walking and ignores you. You know he heard you as he briefly turned his head when you spoke.

- How would you feel as the customer?
- Would you stay at the restaurant?
- Would you complain?
- What level of customer service would you have expected?

Activity 7.8   Customer service in action

In a small group carry out a role-play activity. Take it in turns to carry out the following three roles:

- a customer
- a member of the waiting staff
- an observer/manager.

Role play the following three scenarios that take place at a local restaurant. The member of waiting staff should greet the customer, seat the customer and take an order. The observer/manager should feed back to the group on how effective the customer interaction was.

Scenarios

- The customer has just walked in off the street to the restaurant and needs a table for six people, one of whom is in a wheelchair.
- The customer is on holiday in your local area and has been to the restaurant twice in the previous week. The customer walks into the restaurant with his family without a booking.
- The customer has pre-booked at the restaurant, bringing a party of people with him, including a vegetarian and someone with a nut allergy.

Discussion

Have you visited a business where the food service staff tried to boost sales?

- What did they offer you?
- What did they say to you?
- Do you think it was a successful technique?

Waiting staff can boost sales by offering the customer extras after the food order has been taken. For example, you could offer paid-for 'sides and sauces' to accompany a main course.

Passing and receiving orders

Orders need to be passed on to the kitchen and there is usually a formal procedure for doing so. Clear and efficient communication with colleagues is vital at this point in the process.

Written orders are taken to the kitchen or you might key in the order to an electronic system, which automatically sends the order to the kitchen. Either way, the order must be clear so that service is not delayed. If you have poor written communication, overcome this by using simple abbreviations that have already been agreed. For example, 'W/D' could be used for an order of steak to tell the kitchen that the customer would like it cooked well done. Getting the order right avoids delay and complaints from customers.

Activity 7.9   Abbreviate your order

Find a menu from a local restaurant and, in small groups, come up with abbreviations that you could use if you were taking customers' orders to simplify their orders and reduce the amount of writing you have to do. Discuss your ideas with others and note down any problematic areas.

It is good practice to make sure the kitchen has received the order and that it has been understood. When taking a new order to the kitchen it is normal to shout 'check on' to alert the team. You can also pass on to the kitchen key details about the customer, such as allergies, dietary requirements, religious requirements or other requests. For example, a customer might only be able to eat gluten-free products, may dislike a certain item, or families dining as a large party may want the children's meals to be served at the same time as the adults' starters.

It is important to adopt a team approach when passing on orders.

▶ Serving customers' orders

Customers must be served within a reasonable amount of time and you should tell them how long it is likely to take to prepare and serve their meals. Be friendly and helpful as this shows good communication and professionalism, and helps to keep the customer informed.

Here are some more useful tips to remember when you are serving customers' orders.

✓ Serve beverages as soon as possible – use the correct glasses and service.

✓ When enough time has passed for the food to be cooked, go to the kitchen to find out if the food is ready for the table number.

✓ Check that the order is complete and correct.

✓ Have the right service equipment ready – serve the order using the service style adopted by the business.

✓ Make sure you have appropriate condiments to hand and offer them to the customer.

✓ Do not leave crockery, cutlery and equipment on show for customers to see – work areas should be kept clean and hygienic.

✓ Restock service equipment throughout service, for example cutlery, glasses and crockery – do so quietly so you do not disturb customers.

✓ Be aware of stock levels of each menu and drink item.

✓ Ask customers if everything is okay and check they are happy with the food.

✓ Comply with food safety legislation (for example, the Food Safety Act 1990).

Ensuring customer payment

It is equally important that the customer is still looked after once the meals or beverages are finished and the table has been cleared. You will need the right training to deal with payments so that the customer's departure is not delayed. It is just as important to offer to help with coats, call taxis if needed and say thank you and good bye, as it is to greet the customer when they arrive.

Remember

An important part of the role of serving customers is being aware of time and how long customers have had to wait, for example, to be seated, to be given a menu and for their order to be taken.

Link

We covered service concepts and styles earlier in Topic B.1 of this unit. Revisit this information to recap on how food and beverages can be served.

Did you know?

In some businesses, chefs will let waiting staff know that food is ready for service by ringing a bell.

WorkSpace

▶ Hayley Williams

Restaurant supervisor

I joined a chain of restaurants straight from college in a waiting position. I worked my way up to supervisory level and now I supervise a restaurant that has a capacity of 120 covers and employs up to 10 waiting staff per shift. At lunchtime, the restaurant offers a buffet-style service whereas during the evening we offer a table d'hôte menu.

Although I start my working day later than the average person, I am used to working unsociable hours – I sometimes work into the early hours of the morning!

Restaurant work can be hard with long days spent on my feet and customers can sometimes prove difficult! Although I can find this a challenge, I do enjoy being in a customer-facing role.

It is important that my team of waiting staff give a good impression to customers at all stages of the service period. One member of my team is responsible for welcoming customers to the restaurant and finding out if they have a booking with us. This member of staff will seat customers and let them know who will be serving them.

Before the start of a service session I will create a table plan and allocate members of my team to different seating areas on the plan. They are usually responsible for looking after three or four tables. Allocating tables in this way makes sure that each customer receives a dedicated service and that every table is waited on.

One of the most important parts of our job is to keep the service area clean, safe, hygienic and tidy. There is nothing worse for customers than seeing piles of dirty crockery and glasses. All of my staff have received health and safety training so they understand the importance of a hygienic and safe workplace.

Think about it

1 Do you think you would enjoy Hayley's job?

2 What do you think Hayley could mean by 'difficult' customers?

3 How do you think the service requirements vary between the lunch and evening service?

Reviewing the effectiveness of food and beverage service provision

Introduction

There are many ways to review food and beverage service. This is essential if businesses are to meet the needs of customers and provide products and services that are of a quality that meets customer needs and provides value for money.

Investigate how at least three different businesses review their food and beverage provision. You could do this by visiting three different places or by looking at their websites on the internet.

Hospitality businesses need to review how well they are doing on a regular basis and they should regularly ask for customer feedback.

Feedback is needed to find out whether the business:

- meets the customers' expectations and needs
- provides good-quality products and services
- offers value for money.

It often reveals any needs that are not being met, recommends improvements that can be made, identifies new products or services that can be offered and highlights staff who have given exceptional service.

Review techniques

We know that customer service, whether it is poor or good, can significantly affect a customer's opinion of a business and the products and services it offers. Likewise, customer service can have a direct effect on the success of a business. If customers are happy with the service they receive, they will want to return and that in turn leads to the growth of the business. So, how can you gauge customer satisfaction?

Information should be sought from both staff and customers using the following methods.

- **Comment cards** – these are usually left at the table, in reception or at the bar area for customers to fill in. They sometimes ask for customer details such as their name and address, and many offer an incentive such as a prize draw entry. Cards are often small and contain a range of questions that need tick box responses. There is sometimes a small space for customers to add their own comments.

- **Questionnaires** – these will ask for more detail than a comment card and, therefore, will take longer to complete. Questions are often more in-depth and ask for customers to offer their own comments.

- **Staff meetings** – these meetings are normally held with a manager or supervisor. They give staff the opportunity to discuss the customer feedback they have received and to give their own opinions about the service provided. A disadvantage is that some staff

Take it further

Carry out research on the internet into other methods hospitality and catering businesses can use to gather customer feedback. For example, this might be by mystery diners, website blogs, online or printed reviews and letters of complaint.

may not want to discuss things in front of other staff members and so the full picture may not be given. If possible, ask staff for their views on a one-to-one basis.

- **Websites and apps** – Websites and apps owned by hospitality businesses often contain opportunities for customers to give ratings and leave feedback. Customers may also visit business websites to sign up for offers and promotions or to enter prize draws in return for giving feedback. Collaborative websites, such as TripAdvisor, are also places where customers can leave feedback. Businesses sometimes have the opportunity to reply to feedback, which is a good way of them engaging in conversation with their customers. If feedback is positive, businesses can thank the customer and encourage them to return. If feedback is negative, they can reassure customers that improvements are being made.

- **Social media** – this is a very popular method of gauging customer satisfaction. Many businesses have a Facebook page where they will post special offers in return for customer 'likes' and feedback. Twitter feeds are another way of gaining an insight into customers' opinions, wants and needs.

Activity 7.10   Customer feedback

Collect comment cards or questionnaires that have been left out for customers in at least two food and beverage businesses.

Compare:

- the language used
- the questions asked
- how much space is given for customers to respond
- any incentives given to encourage the customer to answer the questions
- the type of customer details requested by the business.

When you have done this, think about what makes a good comment card or questionnaire.

▶ Reviewing effectiveness

We review effectiveness to make sure that the business is providing the customer with what they want and need. Therefore, the questions that we ask the customer and our colleagues need to focus on:

- whether the service was provided in a timely manner
- the appropriateness of the service style
- the quality and appearance of the food and beverages served
- working methods
- the service skills of staff
- the attitude and behaviour of staff
- if the food and beverages were value for money
- whether the customer has any recommendations for improvement.

Figure 7.4 shows an example of some of the questions that might be asked by a hospitality business. In this example, the business is a staff restaurant.

Further questions might ask about the variety of foods on offer, whether customers are interested in 'healthy' options and if they would like to receive more information about the ingredients used.

Did you know?

Any customer details you collect must be stored securely and protected in line with the Data Protection Act 1998. Find out more about this Act by going to the gov.uk website. You can access this website by going to www.pearsonhotlinks.co.uk and searching for this title.

Discussion

Are there any other benefits of collecting the opinions of customers?

It is always good to include a mixture of open and closed questions as this encourage respondents to complete the questionnaire. If the questionnaire only requires 'yes' or 'no' type answers, the business might not find out enough information. It is also good to ask customers to supply a bit of information about themselves, for example, their age and gender. This allows a business to form a general idea about who their customers are.

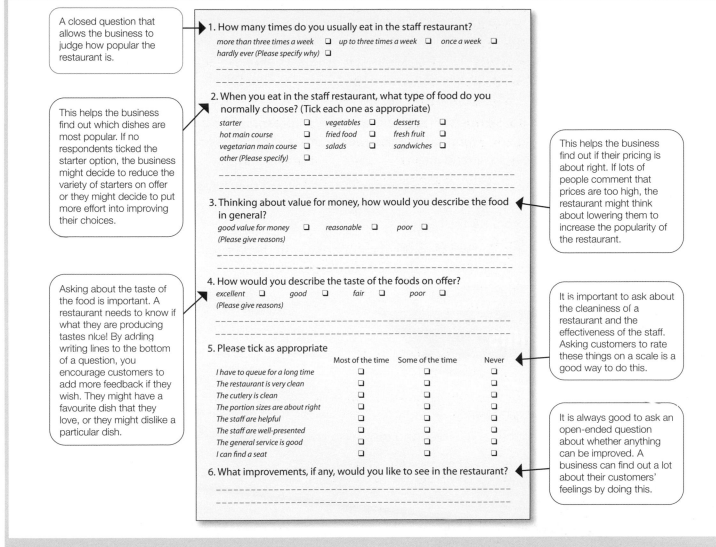

A closed question that allows the business to judge how popular the restaurant is.

1. How many times do you usually eat in the staff restaurant?
   more than three times a week ☐   up to three times a week ☐   once a week ☐
   hardly ever (Please specify why) ☐

This helps the business find out which dishes are most popular. If no respondents ticked the starter option, the business might decide to reduce the variety of starters on offer or they might decide to put more effort into improving their choices.

2. When you eat in the staff restaurant, what type of food do you normally choose? (Tick each one as appropriate)
   starter ☐   vegetables ☐   desserts ☐
   hot main course ☐   fried food ☐   fresh fruit ☐
   vegetarian main course ☐   salads ☐   sandwiches ☐
   other (Please specify) ☐

   ----

3. Thinking about value for money, how would you describe the food in general?
   good value for money ☐   reasonable ☐   poor ☐
   (Please give reasons)

This helps the business find out if their pricing is about right. If lots of people comment that prices are too high, the restaurant might think about lowering them to increase the popularity of the restaurant.

Asking about the taste of the food is important. A restaurant needs to know if what they are producing tastes nice! By adding writing lines to the bottom of a question, you encourage customers to add more feedback if they wish. They might have a favourite dish that they love, or they might dislike a particular dish.

4. How would you describe the taste of the foods on offer?
   excellent ☐   good ☐   fair ☐   poor ☐
   (Please give reasons)

   ----

5. Please tick as appropriate

	Most of the time	Some of the time	Never
I have to queue for a long time	☐	☐	☐
The restaurant is very clean	☐	☐	☐
The cutlery is clean	☐	☐	☐
The portion sizes are about right	☐	☐	☐
The staff are helpful	☐	☐	☐
The staff are well-presented	☐	☐	☐
The general service is good	☐	☐	☐
I can find a seat	☐	☐	☐

It is important to ask about the cleaniness of a restaurant and the effectiveness of the staff. Asking customers to rate these things on a scale is a good way to do this.

6. What improvements, if any, would you like to see in the restaurant?

It is always good to ask an open-ended question about whether anything can be improved. A business can find out a lot about their customers' feelings by doing this.

Figure 7.4 A sample customer questionnaire for a staff restaurant

Assessment activity 7.2 *English*   2B.P3 | 2B.P4 | 2B.M2 | 2B.M3 | 2B.D2 | 2B.D3

During a meeting with the new staff who are about to start work at the restaurant, your manager, James, would like you to demonstrate the two different food service styles that the restaurant uses to provide food and beverage service to customers. The restaurant uses plate service and family-style service to serve food. Beverages are brought to tables.

He would also like you to role play taking a customer order that contains a special requirement.

You will need to gather feedback from the new staff on your service style and use it to make recommendations for improvements to your own food and beverage service skills.

You should show how you gathered the feedback, how you have used the feedback and then analysed and made recommendations based on it.

Tip
● To gain a better understanding of how hospitality businesses gather feedback, you could speak to staff working in different restaurants. Ask to see examples of the tools they use, for example, comment cards.

Introduction

The front office is where a lot of activity takes place within a hospitality business. Front office is often referred to as 'reception', but it involves a much wider range of activities. It is the responsibility of front office staff to deal with the different stages of a customer's stay – before arrival, on arrival, during their stay and on departure. This includes taking bookings, checking guests in and out, administering bills and payments, and dealing with queries.

It is essential that front office staff create a good first impression with a customer, whether it is on the phone, face to face or in writing. They also need to make customers feel valued, so they want to come back to the business again and again.

Front office staff need to have good communication skills, as they have to deal with a wide range of people. They also need to know about the services their business offers, so that they can explain these to customers and promote the business.

This is a practical unit. You will be given the opportunity to demonstrate your front office skills and deal with different types of customer at all stages of the guest cycle.

Assessment: You will be assessed by a series of assignments set by your teacher/tutor.

Learning aims

In this unit you will:

A understand the purpose of front office services within the hospitality industry

B understand front office job roles and responsibilities

C demonstrate front office skills.

> During my BTEC Hospitality course I have learned about different types of customers, the problems they may have and how to deal with them. Hospitality can be vibrant and fast-paced. My work experience in a hotel reception gave me the confidence to deal with different types of customers and know who to go to for help. No two days were the same. I met some great people – some of them were on holiday and some on business. I made a difference to the experience some of our guests had. Sometimes it was hard work but it was a lot of fun!
>
> Chris, *BTEC Level 2 First in Hospitality student*

Front Office Services in the Hospitality Industry

8

BTEC Assessment Zone

This table shows what you must do in order to achieve a **Pass**, **Merit** or **Distinction** grade, and where you can find activities to help you.

Assessment criteria			
Level 1	**Level 2 Pass**	**Level 2 Merit**	**Level 2 Distinction**
Learning aim A: Understand the purpose of front office services within the hospitality industry			
1A.1 Identify front office areas in hospitality businesses.	**2A.P1** Describe, using examples, front office services provided in two contrasting hospitality businesses. **See Assessment activity 8.1, page 239**	**2A.M1** Explain the purpose of front office services provided in two contrasting hospitality businesses. **See Assessment activity 8.1, page 239**	**2A.D1** Analyse differences in front office services provided in two contrasting hospitality businesses. **See Assessment activity 8.1, page 239**
Learning aim B: Understand front office job roles and responsibilities			
1B.2 Identify the roles and responsibilities of front office staff in two hospitality businesses.	**2B.P2** Describe the responsibilities that apply to the stages of the guest cycle within front office services in two contrasting hospitality businesses. **See Assessment activity 8.2, page 255**	**2B.M2** Compare job roles and responsibilities in front office of two contrasting hospitality businesses. **See Assessment activity 8.2, page 255**	**2B.D2** Evaluate how front office staff can enhance the customer experience and contribute to business success when managing the guest cycle in a selected hospitality business. **See Assessment activity 8.2, page 255**
1B.3 Outline how front office staff manage the guest cycle in two hospitality businesses.	**2B.P3** Explain how front office staff manage the guest cycle in two contrasting hospitality businesses. **See Assessment activity 8.2, page 255**		
Learning aim C: Demonstrate front office skills			
1C.4 Maths English Use front office skills when dealing with customers at all stages of the guest cycle.	**2C.P4** Maths English Demonstrate effective front office skills when dealing with customers at all stages of the guest cycle in two different hospitality situations. **See Assessment activity 8.3, page 260**	**2C.M3** Maths English Demonstrate effective front office skills when dealing with customers at all stages of the guest cycle in two different hospitality situations, dealing with a special request that arises. **See Assessment activity 8.3, page 260**	**2C.D3** Maths English Demonstrate effective and confident front office skills when dealing with customers at all stages of the guest cycle in two different hospitality situations, dealing with a special request that arises. **See Assessment activity 8.3, page 260**

Maths / Opportunity to practise mathematical skills

English / Opportunity to practise English skills

How you will be assessed

This unit will be assessed by a series of internally assessed tasks. These tasks will be set by your teacher/tutor. You will be expected to show an understanding of the skills needed to work in front office within the hospitality industry and the importance to businesses of meeting customer needs. You will need to research two different hospitality businesses that require front office skills.

You will need to demonstrate front office skills in different hospitality business situations. Your teacher/tutor will observe you dealing with customers at all stages of the guest cycle in two types of hospitality situations.

You will review the effectiveness of your front office skills and make recommendations for improvement.

Your assessment could be in the form of:

- records of research to show that you understand the purpose of front office services
- log sheets to show that you understand front office job roles and responsibilities
- teacher/tutor observation records of your practical work
- feedback and self-evaluation about your front office knowledge and skills.

▶ Front office areas and services in hospitality businesses

Introduction

The front office plays an essential role in customer service and comprises the reception, guest services and porters. It is the focal point of the hospitality business for customers.

In small groups, list the hospitality businesses where someone might stay when they are away from home. Discuss the difference in services offered at these places. Consider the encounters guests may have with front office staff before and during their stay.

▶ Front office areas and their purposes

Knowing the different areas of front office and their purposes will help you to understand how the front office area operates and its importance in the **guest cycle**. Front office staff have a great deal of guest contact and they play a key role in providing the level of service that guests expect before and during their stay. The functions of front office may be split between the front and back office.

The purpose of front office is to:

- encourage people to make a booking when they make an initial enquiry
- provide guests with a positive first impression
- communicate the needs of guests to other business areas and staff
- play a vital role in making sure guests are happy during their stay
- encourage guests to spend their money in other areas such as the restaurant.

Reception

The duties of the receptionist may vary from business to business. The reception area represents the image of the business, so it is essential to create a good impression. Staff must be organised and able to deal competently with enquiries and guests. They must also be able to deal with any problems they come across. The purpose of this area is to:

- create a positive impression of the business at all times
- provide customer care and guest services.

Bell service

The purpose of the bell service is to assist guests with activities such as carrying, transporting and storing their luggage, taking guests to their rooms and explaining the features of their room.

Mail and information

In some businesses there may be a separate mail area where staff deal with incoming and outgoing post, and also internal mail. In other businesses, these tasks may be undertaken by the receptionist. There may be an information desk instead of a concierge service where guests can obtain literature about the local area or information about places of interest.

Concierge

A concierge interacts with guests and visitors. He or she will play a key role in the daily customer service operations. A concierge needs to be friendly and approachable and to have an in-depth knowledge of the local area in order to give guests the information and services they need.

Cashier's night audit

A night auditor provides a summary of the financial transactions of the day and prepares for operations the following day.

▶ Services

Front office staff provide a range of services to meet the needs of their guests.

Registration

When guests arrive at a hospitality business, they must check in and register. This is a legal requirement. Figure 8.1 outlines the duties of a receptionist.

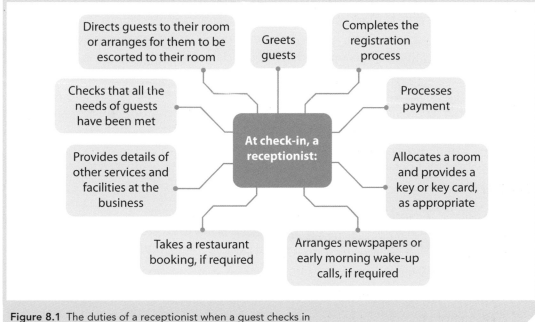

Figure 8.1 The duties of a receptionist when a guest checks in

The registration forms are usually prepared in advance to speed up the **check-in** process. Guests must complete and sign the registration form and keycard when they check in. The room keys or keycards act as a form of identification for the guest.

Reservation

Businesses that provide a reservation service need to make sure that staff sell rooms. The reservation service may be the responsibility of different staff members, depending on the type and structure of the business. When dealing with reservations, it is important that staff know the type and amount of rooms available and the price at which they can sell each room. Reservation staff must confirm the number of guests needing a room and any special requirements, as well as payment and cancellation arrangements.

Key term

Check-in – the procedures to follow on a guest's arrival.

Did you know?

It is a legal requirement to register the full name and nationality of all guests over the age of 16 who take accommodation at a hospitality business. Go to Topic B.2 in this unit for more details on this.

Key terms

Posting – putting charges on a guest's account during their stay.

VIP – very important person.

Accounting procedures

Charges for the cost of the room and money spent during their stay must be **posted** to guests' accounts. Charges may include beverages ordered in the bar, meals taken in the restaurant, telephone calls and room service. The receptionist or night porter usually undertakes this function. It is essential that all charges are correctly posted to the correct guest account before the final bill is presented to the guest on departure.

Electronic systems of accounting are typical in larger businesses. Smaller businesses may still use a manual system of recording expenses. Where credit is offered to guests, the receptionist must make sure that the guest does not exceed their credit limit.

Activity 8.1	Hotel services

Think about a hotel in your local area. What services does the hotel offer? How might these services contribute to the success of the business?

▮▶ Hospitality industry business types and situations

Hotels are not the only businesses that provide guest accommodation. This service is also provided by cruise liners, holiday centres, hostels, residential care and nursing homes, together with other accommodation providers such as universities, camping and caravan parks, hospitals, conference venues and bed and breakfast businesses. They may not all offer the full range of services provided by some hotels but guests still expect staff to provide good customer service and accommodation that is clean, comfortable and safe.

There may be other occasions where front office and reception services are required. Examples include:

- bars – staff welcome customers
- nightclubs – staff welcome customers, deal with entry fees, store customer belongings, liaise with security and external people, receive **VIP** guests and deal with lost property
- restaurants – staff welcome customers, take bookings and arrange seating
- small and large music venues (halls, theatres, arenas and festivals) – staff check tickets, undertake security checks and control crowds
- theatre – customers can book and collect tickets
- membership clubs – customers can register and pay membership fees
- other venues where weddings, meetings, conferences and events may be held.

Where catering facilities are not available on site, a contract food service provider can cater the event. Companies offering this service provide food ranging from small buffets to seven-course meals. They can also provide a managed catering service on site (such as in a college refectory).

These businesses may not provide residential accommodation but staff must deliver excellent front office customer service.

There are many businesses that provide accommodation – not just hotels.

Assessment activity 8.1

The local academy is hosting a careers open day to introduce learners to different types of industry and the principal would like you to help prepare for it.

The principal would like the learners to know about a range of hospitality businesses and services. There will be an opportunity for them to attend a short presentation and to participate in some practical activities to gain a full understanding of the industry and to help inform their career choices.

In particular, the principal is keen to see evidence of the opportunities for learners in front office roles, so you will need to research the range of hospitality businesses and the front office services they provide. He would like you to put together a PowerPoint® presentation of your research.

1 Do some initial research about local businesses that offer front office services. Visit two contrasting hospitality businesses and explore the full range of front office areas and services they provide.

2 In your presentation, describe the front office services available at the two contrasting businesses and explain the purpose of each service. Then, go on to analyse the differences in front office services provided in the two businesses.

Tips

- To gain a better understanding of front office areas and the services offered, you could speak to staff working in different front office roles.
- Make sure you prepare a list of questions to ask before you go on your visits and take detailed notes when you are talking to people in each business. Note: You will be required to visit two businesses in learning aim B so make sure you look at Assessment activity 8.2 at the end of Topic B.4 before you go.

- Use brochures from the two businesses, details provided on the businesses' websites, business charts and information in staff handbooks to find out about the areas and services offered.
- Prepare a table to record your findings to help inform the contents of your PowerPoint® presentation.

Learning aim B **TOPIC** **B.1**

▶ Front office job roles and responsibilities

Introduction

The function of the front office varies from one hospitality business to another. In smaller businesses, staff may undertake more than one job role, particularly during the evening and night. In smaller businesses such as bed and breakfasts, the owner or manager may be responsible for all front office services. In larger businesses, staff will be expected to work shift patterns and job roles will be more defined.

Using the internet, find some job adverts for staff needed for front office roles. For each role, note the qualities and skills that are required.

▶ Job roles and responsibilities

Staff working in hospitality businesses must create a positive impression of themselves and their business at all times. They need an eye for detail, must enjoy working with people and provide services to a consistently high standard.

Table 8.1 (on the next page) explains some of the typical job roles for front office services.

Table 8.1 Front office job roles and responsibilities

Job role	Responsibilities
Concierge	A concierge is based in the reception area and is in charge of the hall porters and door staff. It is the responsibility of the concierge to: • provide information and directions to guests • organise restaurant reservations • arrange car hire • organise tickets to the theatre, shows and tours • arrange tickets for airlines and trains.
Shift leader	In larger businesses, there will be a leader or supervisor on duty for every shift. These staff are responsible for: • supervising the daily operations of front office • staff training • assisting the manager to make sure operations and services are delivered and standards are met • taking the lead in emergency situations.
Hall porter	A hall porter is based in the reception area or porter's desk and is responsible for the bell services. There may be several hall porters on duty at any one time. They: • carry guest luggage • answer queries • take messages for guests • sort the mail • take charge of lost property • call taxis for guests.
Reservations	This role plays a vital part in making sure the business sells as many rooms as possible at the best possible price. These staff: • check that rooms are available • provide accurate details of room rates and what is included in the rate • explain the cancellation policy • provide details of the location of the business and its services • take accurate details of the booking • confirm payment details including deposit or full payment arrangements as required.
Telephonist	A telephone is usually based in the back office. There may be more than one telephonist in a large business. These staff: • operate the switchboard • answer enquiries • help callers to know who they need to speak to • take messages • can page a staff member.
Manager	The front office manager (or front of house manager) is responsible for staff, services and operations. They are responsible for: • meeting the budget and making decisions • running the front office function efficiently to the required standard • staff welfare, discipline, training and development • ensuring maintenance requirements are dealt with • key control • approving, issuing and controlling **floats**.

continued

Table 8.1 *(continued)*

Job role	Responsibilities
Receptionist	A receptionist is based in the entrance lobby of a business. Responsibilities include: • answering the telephone and taking reservations over the counter • dealing with booking amendments and cancellations • checking in and registering guests • providing customer care and guest services • posting charges to guest accounts • completing guest **check-out** • taking payments and issuing receipts.
Night audit	The person undertaking this role works through the night and must be good with numbers. Responsibilities include: • checking all cash, cheque and credit transactions of the day • calculating room occupancy and revenue • posting further room charges to guests' accounts and preparing customer bills.

Activity 8.2 — Interviewing front office staff

Visit two different types of business that offer accommodation. Choose the same two job roles in each business. Create two tables (one for each job role) with the following headings: Venue 1 and Venue 2.

Interview front office staff in each role about their responsibilities and make bullet points from their responses. How do the roles compare?

Key terms

Float – the amount of money in the cash till at the start of the day or the shift. This can be used to give change to customers.

Check-out – the procedures to follow on a guest's departure.

TOPIC B.2

Systems and procedures of front office

Introduction

In this section, we will look in more detail at the systems and procedures you need to be familiar with when working in a front office role.

Pay a visit to a local hotel to find out what kind of special requests are made by guests. Find out about the communication systems and documentation used by the hotel. What standards do they have and how do they comply with legislation? Prepare a checklist that you can complete with the information you find out.

Legal aspects

All hospitality businesses must comply with current legislation and regulations, and make sure that policies and procedures are in place to help staff know how to stay within the limits of the law.

Figure 8.2 outlines current legislation and regulations that affect front of office services.

Figure 8.2 Legislation and regulations that affect front office services

Take it further

For more information about data protection, visit the website for the Information Commissioner's Office. You can access this website by going to www.pearsonhotlinks.co.uk and searching for this title.

Key terms

Hazard – something that could be dangerous.

Risk assessment – a proactive review of what can cause harm and what can be done to control or prevent hazards.

Risk – the likelihood of a hazard causing harm.

Discussion

Discuss the possible causes of fire in a hospitality business. What prevention methods could be put in place in a small bed and breakfast?

Data protection

The holding and use of personal information about individuals is regulated by the Data Protection Act 1998. Staff must know how to handle personal information correctly and how to securely store data relating to guests. The front office must be a secure area. Only authorised people can access information about guests and other sensitive information such as debit/credit card details.

Health and safety

Hazards can arise in a front office area. Staff may have to take in deliveries, help guests take their luggage to their rooms or store luggage safely until a guest leaves the hotel. Main areas accessible by the public should be kept free from hazards as much as possible. Under the Health and Safety at Work etc. Act 1974 (HASAWA), employers and employees have responsibilities to ensure a safe environment.

Unfortunately, accidents and illness among guests will happen from time to time and front office staff may be the first point of contact. It is vital that front office staff know the correct procedure to follow to make sure customers get help and treatment as soon as possible. An accurate account of any accident should be recorded in an accident book, so that further action can be taken if necessary. This can also help to avoid similar incidents in the future.

Front office staff also need to look after their own health. Manual handling training should be given to any staff member who may be required to push, pull, carry or put down objects that are heavy or an awkward shape.

Fire safety

Hospitality employees must be able to locate, read and understand health and safety signs at work. In the event of a fire, delayed action could endanger lives. Staff must be trained in raising the alarm and also in evacuation procedures.

A fire safety **risk assessment** of the business's premises must be carried out under the Regulatory Reform (Fire Safety) Order 2005 to make sure that appropriate fire prevention measures are in place to reduce the **risks** from fire.

Consumer protection

Legislation exists to protect **consumers** from problems that can arise when buying goods and services. Front office staff should know their rights and those of the customers.

When providing information about goods and services, front office staff must do this accurately to comply with the Trade Descriptions Act 1968.

Customers may not be happy with the services or goods provided by the hospitality business and they have a right to complain under the Supply of Goods and Services Act 1982. For example, if a guest books an overnight stay with a spa treatment, and the treatment is not available or has been substituted for something else, they have the right to complain. It is important that front office staff know how to deal with customers in these circumstances.

Guest registration

It is a legal requirement to register details of all guests over the age of 16 in serviced and self-catering accommodation premises. Guests must complete a registration form providing at least their name and nationality. Guests who are not British, Irish or from the Commonwealth will need to add their passport details (passport number and place of issue) or provide alternative documentation that shows their identity and nationality. These guests also need to provide details of their next destination including the address, if known.

Equality legislation

When working with other staff, visitors and guests, it is important to treat them respectfully and to abide by the Equality Act 2010. Standards of expected behaviour and responsibilities will be outlined in a business's equality policy, together with the procedures for dealing with complaints relating to equality.

Hospitality businesses are responsible for making reasonable adjustments to accommodate visitors and guests with limited mobility and who have special access needs. Adjustments may include providing ramps for wheelchair users and lifts to help people access different floors and areas of the building. Guests may also need help from staff to carry luggage or escort them to their rooms or to other departments.

Front office staff should communicate with the housekeeping department to make sure that rooms are adequately prepared for guests with special needs.

▶ Meeting customer needs

There are many ways in which front office staff can meet the needs of customers and guests.

Rooms and price

Most businesses offering accommodation have different types of rooms available (see Table 8.2 on the next page). Front office staff need to be able to explain the different types of accommodation on offer and price bands.

Key term

Consumer – someone who buys goods or services (e.g. customers booking a room, guests eating in a restaurant or purchasing a treatment in the spa).

Discussion

Complying with legislation
What could be the consequences if you do not comply with legislation when working in front office? Think about and research consequences relating to:

• data protection
• health and safety
• consumer protection
• equality.

Table 8.2 Types of hotel rooms

Room type	Description
En-suite rooms	Any type of room with a private bathroom or shower room
Single	Contains a single bed for one guest only
Double	One double bed for two guests
Twin	Two separate single beds for two guests
Family	Rooms with a range of sleeping arrangements for up to five guests including bunk beds, sofa beds and cots. Interconnecting rooms may also be available for families in some hotels.
Deluxe, executive and superior rooms	These rooms provide a more luxurious environment than the standard rooms above. There is usually more space, a sitting area and desk to provide extra comfort.
Suites and mini suites	Suites provide a substantial form of accommodation with separate living and sleeping areas. There may also be a kitchen area.

Families may request a small bed be placed in their room for a young child.

Discussion

In pairs, think about two customers with different special requests you heard about during a previous visit to a hospitality business. How did the business accommodate their needs? Were their requests recorded in the guest history?

Link

Go to Topics C.1 and C.2 in this unit to look at customer service skills in more depth.

Packages

In addition to offering accommodation, hotels often offer special rates to regular customers and for those making longer stays. Hospitality businesses also offer a range of packages to give their guests a memorable experience. They may work with partner businesses to provide packages that include discounted prices for theatre or concert tickets, spa treatments and spa breaks, themed dining, sporting events and wedding bundles.

Special requests

Customers may make special requests before or during their stay. For example, a guest might want non-allergenic pillows, adjoining rooms, bed/cots for children, wheelchair access or have special dietary requirements.

Make a note of the special request(s) so it can be followed up and saved in the guest history for future reference. Promptly communicate requests to the correct person or department if this is not done through an automated system. Businesses should try to fulfil reasonable requests made by guests to make sure their stay is as comfortable as possible.

Guest history

Many businesses keep a profile record of their customers so that when they return, front office will already have their details. This improves customer service. Records may contain information relating to previous special requests and requirements. They may show if there have been problems in the past such as non-payment of a bill or damage to a room. The guest history may also be used to compile a mailing list to inform customers of promotional offers and marketing information with their consent.

Customer service skills

Providing excellent customer service is vital to the success of a hospitality business and to encourage repeat business. The front office team have a big responsibility to make sure guests are made to feel welcome, relaxed and valued.

▶ Communication

Having excellent verbal and written skills is essential for the various responsibilities of front office staff.

Reservation systems

The systems and records needed to manage guest reservations vary between hospitality businesses. Most hotels now operate an electronic system to manage the guest stay but a smaller bed and breakfast may use a manual system. In all businesses, front office staff must make sure these systems contain the correct information. Computerised systems include features such as room availability and tracking systems. They can generate reservation forms when required.

Electronic systems are also available to manage online bookings and update instantly on availability, rates, descriptions and special offers. They speed up the booking process considerably.

Reports

Front office staff may be required to produce verbal, written or computerised reports of activity (such as a departure list). Reports may be needed to help improve efficiency (occupancy levels). Staff need to make sure the reports are in the requested format and contain the relevant information.

Liaison with other departments

Other staff and departments in a hospitality business rely on front office staff to communicate information about guests checking in.

The housekeeping department will want to know about guests' specific requirements, so rooms can be prepared and ready on their arrival. The kitchen and restaurant department will want to know about specific dietary requirements and when tables have been booked, so they can prepare ingredients and meals at the requested times.

Communicating with the guest

Each time a guest interacts with staff, they form an impression of that individual and of the business. Remember to be polite and courteous at all times and listen to what the guest has to say. As the hub of the communication centre, front office staff must be able to provide guests with the information they need, or refer them to someone else who can help.

Hotels welcome guests from all over the world, so it is very useful for front office staff to understand different cultures and subtleties in social etiquette to avoid offending guests unintentionally.

Answering queries

Front office staff need a good knowledge of the business and its services in order to deal effectively with customers' queries. If the business does not employ a concierge team, this may include knowledge of the local area. Staff need to be confident in their role and know who to pass queries on to if they are unable to deal with them personally. Queries should be recorded using the internal system so authorised staff can access this information. This allows staff to check on the progress of queries, particularly when other people or departments are involved.

Activity 8.3

Getting it right

Watch an episode of *Fawlty Towers*. What do the characters do rightly and wrongly?

Thinking about front office staff, how could you avoid upsetting customers during the guest cycle? What should you do and not do?

? **Did you know?**

In many countries it is acceptable to point at things when giving directions. However, in many Asian countries, such as China, pointing with the forefinger in public is considered quite rude. An alternative is to indicate towards the point of interest with an open palm that faces upwards.

How might problems occur when front office staff communicate or leave messages for other staff members? How might communication problems affect guests? Discuss these questions in pairs. Come up with a checklist of things to remember when communicating with staff internally.

Dealing with complaints

You will have to deal with complaints from time to time and to do this effectively you need to know what the procedures are for dealing with them. Table 8.3 explains one approach you could take when talking to a guest. It is called the LAST approach: **L**isten, **A**pologise, **S**olve, **T**hank.

Table 8.3 The LAST approach

Listen	<ul><li>Concentrate on what the customer is complaining about.</li><li>Use open body language to show the customer you are listening.</li><li>Ask relevant questions and politely ask the customer to repeat any information you have missed.</li><li>Write down the key points of the complaint.</li><li>Summarise the complaint to check you have understood it correctly.</li></ul>
Apologise	<ul><li>Remain calm, polite and professional.</li><li>Use appropriate language, tone and body language.</li><li>Do not make excuses or put the blame on people.</li><li>Keep in control of the situation.</li></ul>
Solve	<ul><li>Solve the problem yourself or pass it on to someone who can deal with the issue.</li><li>Deal with the situation immediately.</li><li>Let the customer know what you are going to do and by when.</li><li>If you pass the complaint to someone else to deal with, follow it up and keep the customer informed.</li></ul>
Thank	<ul><li>Always thank the customer for bringing the problem to your attention.</li><li>Be sincere in your tone – sound like you mean it.</li></ul>

It is important that front office staff know the correct procedure to follow when dealing with customer complaints.

Selling products and services

Front office staff should be aware of what the business has to offer and what makes it special. For example, if:

- it has any special awards (for example, for **sustainability**, design or customer service)
- the restaurant has a Michelin star
- there is a spa
- it is close to a visitor attraction.

Some of the products will be freely available to guests but others will need to be purchased. Staff must know about the products and services in order to sell them. A person's sales technique develops over time but, generally, staff should explain the benefits of staying in the hotel to help the customer visualise the products and services and try to promote them whenever possible.

Giving information

Any information given to customers must be accurate. Typical requests for information may relate to the check-out time, opening hours of the restaurant and information about other services such as the equipment available in the conference rooms. By talking to your customers, you will be able to find out their exact requirements.

Products and services may change constantly and it may not be possible to remember everything you are being asked about. You should, however, be able to answer queries by using reference material. Keep resources such as street maps, brochures and taxi numbers to hand, so you can give correct and up-to-date information.

▶ Property management systems (PMS)

Many businesses use electronic systems to record information. These systems play a very important part in communicating information between front office staff and other departments, for example, the finance team, housekeeping, the restaurant and bar. A property management system (PMS) allows information to be updated immediately.

Typical management systems allow businesses to manage:

- bookings (provisional and actual)
- debit/credit card storage
- guest history and profiles
- occupancy
- availability of rooms for hire for conferences and events
- daily, weekly and monthly reports
- accounts
- maintenance and repairs, so staff know which rooms to allocate to guests
- mailshots.

▶ Documentation

There are many types of documentation used in the hospitality industry. These may be computerised or paper-based. Let's take a close look at documentation used in the front office.

Arrival and departure lists

An arrivals list includes all the guests that are expected each day, their time of arrival, how long they are staying and any special requirements they may have. The departures list gives details of guests expected to leave each day. It also includes a note of those who have requested a late departure time to prevent housekeeping disturbing them.

Room status report

This document is usually produced by front office but used by housekeeping staff. It is produced on a daily basis and provides information to help the housekeeping team know which rooms they need to clean each day. The report confirms the status of each room: occupied; available; departure; unavailable.

Registration forms

When guests arrive they must, by law, check in and complete a registration form which states their full name and nationality and requires a signature. It may also ask for other information such as home address and car registration number.

All guests are required to fill in a registration form.

Special requirements

When a guest makes a request, a note should be made so it can be followed up. Examples include a request for a cot, a room with a view or a room on the ground floor.

Guest list

This document is a list of all guests and their room numbers. It may be needed in the event of an evacuation.

Keycards

When guests are allocated their room, they are either given a key or a keycard. This is usually a plastic card with a magnetic strip to access the room. They can also be used to purchase other goods and services within the business.

Guest bills

This document is presented to the guest and confirms how much they need to pay the business. A guest bill may be presented at the bar, in the restaurant or other areas of the hotel. It is always given to the guest at the end of their stay and outlines the purchase history.

Payment documentation

When a guest settles their account, they are issued with a receipt to confirm that they have paid.

▶ Organisational standards

Organisational standards are essential to a business for continued success and to maintain industry quality standards, such as the five-star rating system, Rosette scheme and Gold, Silver and Breakfast awards agreed by the AA and VisitBritain.

At the start or end of every shift, staff may have a checklist to complete to confirm that routine jobs to maintain standards have been carried out. The front office should be kept clean and clear, staff should appear smart and in uniform and they should maintain a high level of personal presentation.

▶ Statistics

Statistics are important to any business to find out how well it is doing.

Room occupancy

Room occupancy is the most common statistic used in accommodation businesses. It shows the number of rooms sold as a percentage of the total number of guest rooms available. For example, if the Sands Guest House has 20 rooms and sells 16 of them, the room occupancy is calculated as follows.

Worked example: Calculating room occupancy

(Rooms sold ÷ total number of rooms) × 100

(16 ÷ 20) × 100 = 80 per cent occupancy

Take it further

Visit some providers of accommodation in your local area. Interview some of the staff to find out:

- if the venue has a star rating
- if the business must maintain quality standards
- how standards are maintained
- the dress code or uniform of front office staff
- how guests are welcomed to the business
- if they have checklists to complete during their shift.

Average room rates

This is the average price that rooms have been sold for. Some rooms cost more than others and prices may vary according to season and special offers/discounts. To work out the average room rate, you add all of the room prices together and then divide by the total number of rooms. For example, if the room **revenue** at the Sands Guest House is £720 and it has sold 16 rooms, the average room rate is calculated as follows.

Worked example: Calculating an average room rate

Room revenue ÷ number of room sold

720 ÷ 16 = £45.00

Forecasting

It is important for businesses to forecast revenue as this can be used to plan resources and inform staffing rotas in various departments, such as housekeeping, leisure services, the kitchen and restaurant. Forecasts can be produced by:

- looking back at the occupancy for the same period last year
- checking advance bookings
- considering changes in the market such as if there are local events taking place, new visitor attractions or promotions in the local area.

▶ Maximising revenue

There are many ways in which hospitality businesses can maximise their revenue (bring more money in) at the front office.

Up-selling

Front office staff need to know how they can sell products and services to different customers.

When **up-selling** to a customer:

- explain the advantages, benefits or differences between products and services
- read the customer's body language carefully
- know the limitations of up-selling (particularly for room rates)
- be aware of the company policy for room upgrades or discounts
- describe rooms and upgrades by using words such as 'exclusive', 'superb', 'luxurious', 'unique' and 'elegant', and make reference to the views from the rooms, if this is of interest to the customer.

Guaranteed versus provisional bookings

Some customers will make provisional bookings when they enquire about products and services. Where possible, you should try to guarantee a booking. A guaranteed booking may also be known as a confirmed booking. To do this you might need to take a deposit or payment from a customer. When taking a part payment, it is important to take the necessary card details from the customer to secure full payment at a later date. Some bookings are non-returnable, particularly if it is a late booking or a limited special offer.

When customers make provisional bookings, they may not turn into actual bookings. Some customers may cancel their booking in line with the cancellation policy. In these cases, rooms can be released. The business will have procedures for this, with which front office staff need to be familiar.

Overbooking

Occasionally, staff may have to deal with a situation when more rooms have been sold than are actually available, or if there is more than one booking for a certain room. This can happen when the business uses third parties to sell their rooms.

In these situations, the most common solutions are to offer customers a different room, an upgrade where available or alternative dates (rather than offering a refund straightaway).

Getting the best rate possible

Providers of accommodation advertise their rooms in a variety of ways. For example, this could be via leaflets or on the internet. Some businesses use online travel and leisure retailers to sell their rooms, for example, Lastminute.com, LateRooms.com, TravelRepublic.co.uk and Expedia.co.uk.

▐▶ Security

It is essential that systems are in place to make sure staff and guests feel safe and secure.

Safe deposit

Guests often travel with valuable items such as jewellery, passports and important documents. Many businesses provide safes in the bedrooms for valuables. These often have security combinations that guests can set themselves. Some businesses offer to keep guests' valuables in safety deposit boxes at reception, or even in the hotel safe.

Lost property

When an item is found by staff, it is usually reported to the front office and kept in a central location. A list of lost property will be kept at reception, as this is usually the point of contact if a guest has lost something.

Data protection

Front office staff hold a lot of information about guests, including their personal information. They may also have access to staff details for contact purposes. Care must be taken not to disclose information inadvertently. Do not leave the desk unmanned without closing computer screens or locking away documents or information relating to staff or guests. There should be strict levels of access to computerised systems.

Control of keys

Front office staff should be aware of the systems for issuing room keys, collecting them from departing guests and reporting lost room keys.

LateRooms.com sell hotel rooms on behalf of the accommodation provider. Can you think of the advantages for the provider of doing this?

Some hotels provide safes in guests' rooms.

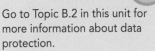

Link

Go to Topic B.2 in this unit for more information about data protection.

They may also be in charge of monitoring a master key (which opens all doors) and a sub-master key (which may open a selection of doors, such as rooms on a whole floor). There should be records to outline which keys have been given out and to whom. These records should be kept secure.

Use of computer passwords

There are many different uses for computers in hospitality businesses at the front desk and in other areas. The computers may be part of a property management system, which links the different departments and points of sale. Managers and administrative staff may use other software to send emails and produce documents, presentations and reports.

It is important to keep passwords secure and to change them on a regular basis to prevent unauthorised use. Never give out your computer password to anyone.

Dealing with suspicious individuals

Hospitality businesses are predominantly public places. They may be targeted by thieves looking for cash or goods to steal. They may also be a target for terrorism. Some hospitality businesses employ security staff or have closed-circuit television cameras installed.

Make sure you know what to do and how to report suspicious behaviour. Staff should think about their own safety as well as that of guests.

Following security policies and procedures

Hospitality businesses should have a security policy to protect the business from threats that could potentially disrupt it.

The policy should consider confidentiality and legislative and regulatory requirements, and should require a **business continuity plan** to be produced, maintained and tested. The policy also ensures that staff receive sufficient training in security measures that are appropriate to their role.

Having a security policy and appropriate procedures in place should improve the guest experience. Staff should comply with the rules of the business and know what to do to maintain the security of information and the building. Staff should never leave keys in locks or leave secure areas unlocked and unattended.

Reporting unusual and non-routine incidents

Hospitality staff should always be vigilant at work. It is vital that anything out of the ordinary is reported. It may turn out to be important at a later date. These incidents may be observed in a number of areas and reporting helps to build up an overall picture. Reporting also helps to prevent similar occurrences, or accidents, from happening in the future. Staff should know how to report any unusual or non-routine incident.

Emergency evacuation procedures

In the event of an emergency, it is essential that staff know what to do and follow the correct procedures, as outlined in an employee handbook or on posters around the building. Make sure you practise the evacuation routine so you know how to exit the building quickly and safely and assemble in the designated area.

Activity 8.6

Describing skills

Consider your descriptive skills. In pairs, look at a busy scene for one minute. You could look out of the window or look at an image in a book. Afterwards, write as much detail as you can remember and compare notes. Choose one person in the scene and provide a description of them as if the details were to be recorded on an incident report.

Signs like this help signpost to guests how to leave the building in an emergency.

Managing the guest cycle

Introduction

The guest cycle describes the activities a guest goes through when staying in a business that provides accommodation, as well as the contact he or she has with the business.

In small groups, think about a time when you have stayed away from home. Make a list of the contact you had with the business and the processes you went through, from making an initial enquiry to leaving the business.

Stages of the guest cycle

There are four stages of the guest cycle which describe the flow of business during a guest's stay. These four stages are shown in Figure 8.3.

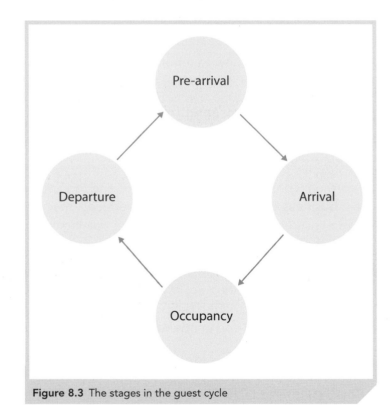

Figure 8.3 The stages in the guest cycle

1 Pre-arrival

A manual or electronic booking system should be in operation to take a guest's booking. In some businesses, customers can also make reservations online. Some larger chains have a central reservations office where staff can take bookings for all the venues in that chain.

Information about the booking should be communicated to other departments. Registration documentation relating to the guest should be prepared in advance and available when the guest arrives.

2 Arrival

This is known as check-in. This process includes guest registration and room allocation. Front office staff must check that relevant information about the guest has been communicated to other departments and that the guest has everything they need.

3 Occupancy

Throughout a guest's stay, the front office will remain the focal point of their contact with the business. Once guests have checked in, charges can be applied to their accounts, for example, when they buy beverages in the bar, meals in the restaurant or treatments in the spa.

4 Departure

The final stage of a guest's stay is the departure or check-out process. As part of this process the guest will settle their account (pay their bill), if they have not already paid it on arrival. Front office staff must handle guests well at this stage. A bad experience could spoil a pleasant stay and discourage a repeat visit.

Creating a good first impression at check-in is vital.

TOPIC   B.4

▶ The importance of front office

Introduction

As you have already learned, it is important to create and maintain a positive guest experience. This section looks in more detail at how this can be achieved in front office.

In small groups, think about times when you stayed away from home. Did anything make a positive difference to your stay? Compare your first impressions, experiences during your stay and the attitude of the staff.

▶ Customer experience

First impression

Creating the right first impression is essential. Customers want to feel important, valued and well looked after. A lot of this responsibility for customer care sits with front office staff.

Table 8.4 (on the next page) explains the importance of creating a good first impression and gives examples of how front office staff can do this.

As well as taking payment, do not forget to ask the customer if they have enjoyed their stay. Listen carefully to what they say – they could give you valuable feedback.

Guests may have forgotten about some of their expenditure such as beverages in the bar area before a meal, using the minibar or having a bottle of wine with a meal. Staff will need to be confident in the system and politely remind guests where or when these expenses have been incurred. Know the limits of your role and seek help if necessary.

In some instances, bills are not paid by the guest directly but are put on an account which will be settled by another business. For example, an employer often pays the bill of its employees who are travelling on business. The company may place a limit on the amount the traveller is allowed to spend on their business account. Front office staff need to confirm if certain expenses will be paid by the guest (for example, beverages at the bar or spa treatments) or by the employer (for example, breakfast) and be able to explain this sensitively to customers on check-out.

Assessment activity 8.3   *English, Maths*   2C.P4 | 2C.M3 | 2C.D3

The principal is expecting the learners to take part in practical activities during the careers open day at the local Academy. The aim of these is to help the learners appreciate the skills involved in different types of front office job roles.

The principal has given you a set of role-play scenarios to deal with customers at all stages of the guest cycle in two contrasting hospitality businesses.

She would like you to demonstrate a role play for two hospitality situations: one will take place in a pub that has accommodation and the other will take place in a hotel.

You will need to demonstrate effective and confident front office skills in taking reservations, meeting and greeting guests, dealing with special requests and dealing with their departure.

Tips

- To gain a better understanding of how to deal with different situations and special requests, you could speak to staff working in different roles and businesses.

- Make sure you prepare a list of questions to ask before you go on your visits and take detailed notes about the skills required at each stage of the guest cycle when you are talking to people in each business.

- Use brochures from tourist information offices, local magazines and company websites to find out about the amenities and special events in your area in order to prepare for dealing with special requests.

.WorkSpace

▶ Neela Gupta

Hotel receptionist (Apprentice)

I have been a receptionist at the local three-star hotel for over a year. I have responsibility for meeting and greeting the guests, allocating rooms and dealing with their final bills.

Following the research I did at the hotel for my Level 2 Hospitality course, I was invited to become an apprentice here. I was nervous at first but, over time, my confidence has developed.

The qualification provided me with a valuable insight into the work of front office. I used the knowledge and skills I learned on the Hospitality course to develop my practical skills further.

The hotel is busy all year round. We have 60 rooms in total, including two suites, over three floors. I deal with a lot of people in my role who come from different walks of life, and from different countries. I think of myself as quite a sociable person, but this role has given me a more professional approach to dealing with people. I have developed basic phrases in French, Spanish and Polish and I'm starting night classes to learn more Spanish soon. It helps to welcome the guests and put them at ease.

I particularly enjoy problem solving. We have guests who have special requests and requirements. Some are easy to arrange, others take a little more time. We work as a team to make sure the guest is entirely satisfied. Some guests come back time and again – this is reward in itself!

All the teams in the hotel work together to keep up standards and build our reputation. We have a number of important functions and special events coming up. Our computer system has all the details. I use this on a daily basis to generate guest lists and bills, and to produce all of the documents in the guest cycle I need to use.

I hope to continue in this role and complete my Apprenticeship. There is a definite career progression opportunity. The path isn't always easy as it involves shift work. The reward, however, is the opportunity to make a difference to our guests who stay with us for business and for pleasure.

Think about it

1 When working in front office, why are confidence and organisational skills so important?

2 What legislation and regulations do front office staff have to comply with during the course of their work?

3 Can you identify the different roles in front office? What are the career opportunities? Why are these roles so important to the business as a whole?

Introduction

This unit introduces you to the meaning of healthy living and the role a balanced diet plays in a healthy lifestyle. You will discover the nutritional values of foods and the reasons why it is important to eat a wide variety of foods. When looking at a healthy lifestyle we will also consider alcohol consumption, its effects on individuals and the guidelines set by the government to make sure that alcohol is consumed within safe limits. In addition, you will learn about the importance of exercise, as well as rest and relaxation, as part of a healthy lifestyle.

Today, people are becoming increasingly aware of what makes a healthy lifestyle and you may have seen many healthy living campaigns in the media. The hospitality industry must tailor their products and services to respond to the changes that are happening in the public arena.

In this unit, you will learn how the importance of a healthy lifestyle affects the hospitality industry and the products and services that it must provide. These effects can be both positive and negative. In part, this links to customer service and how customer expectations can be met.

Assessment: You will be assessed using a paper-based exam lasting 1 hour and 15 minutes.

Learning aims

In this unit you will:

A know what makes a healthy lifestyle

B understand what the hospitality industry does to support and promote healthy lifestyles.

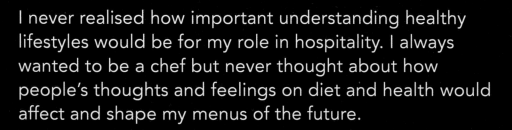

I never realised how important understanding healthy lifestyles would be for my role in hospitality. I always wanted to be a chef but never thought about how people's thoughts and feelings on diet and health would affect and shape my menus of the future.

Emma, *21-year-old trainee chef*

How the Hospitality Industry Contributes to Healthy Lifestyles

9

▶▶ What is a healthy lifestyle?

Introduction

We are all encouraged to lead healthy lifestyles and in this topic we will look at what that means: from watching what we eat to taking exercise, and why it is so important that we take care of ourselves, inside and out.

In pairs, discuss what you think the phrase 'healthy lifestyle' means. Write a short description explaining your conclusions. Create a list of the areas that you believe contribute to a healthy lifestyle.

▶ The concept and importance of a healthy lifestyle

It is important to understand what is meant by 'a healthy lifestyle'. It does not just mean losing weight or eating more fruit and vegetables. Rather, it means adopting a healthy attitude to all aspects of your life, including eating a balanced diet, drinking alcohol within safe limits, taking regular exercise and making sure you make time to rest and relax properly. By not adopting a healthy lifestyle, that is, eating a poor diet, smoking, drinking too much alcohol, not taking exercise and not getting enough good-quality sleep, you run the risk of developing many health problems, both physical and mental. By contrast, people who adopt healthy lifestyles are less likely to suffer from poor health.

Compared to 20 years ago, people are living longer. However, there has also been a rise in the number of **clinically obese** people. Although more people are aware of healthy lifestyles, certain diseases linked with poor diet, lack of exercise, smoking and alcohol misuse are also on the rise, for example, heart disease and diabetes.

There are lots of reasons why a healthy lifestyle is important:

- to give us a better diet
- to improve our health
- to increase our lifespan
- to improve our sense of emotional wellbeing.

▶ The influence of diet on health

One of the most important influences on a healthy lifestyle is a balanced diet. Diet is all that we eat and drink. We have a balanced diet when we eat a variety of foods, which give us the necessary **nutrients** in the correct proportions to maintain our health. Eating too much of any one food is not good for us.

Our bodies need to have an intake of a certain amount of nutrients and these fall into five different categories or food groups. They are:

1 carbohydrates, for example bread, potatoes, pasta and rice
2 proteins, for example meat, poultry, fish and pulses
3 fats, for example dairy foods including butter and cream
4 vitamins, for example vitamins B, C and K found in fruit and vegetables
5 minerals, for example iron in green, leafy vegetables and potassium in bananas.

Key terms

Clinically obese – when being overweight causes medical complications.

Nutrient – a substance which provides nourishment that is essential for good health and growth.

Calorie – a unit of energy in food.

Discussion

How many brands of health food can you think of? Do you think there has been an increase in the number of health foods and health-related products on the market? Would you say this is a good area of the food business to be in?

Eating too much of any one of these nutrients is not healthy. You can find out the amount of nutrients in foods by looking at nutritional labels on food packaging. These labels usually include information on the number of **calories** in the food item and the amount of protein, carbohydrate and fat. They might also show the amount of saturated fat, sugars, sodium, salt and fibre.

The Department of Health in association with the Welsh, Scottish and Northern Ireland governments has created an eatwell plate, which shows how much of what we eat should come from each food group. This includes everything we eat in a day, including snacks. Figure 9.1 shows this eatwell plate.

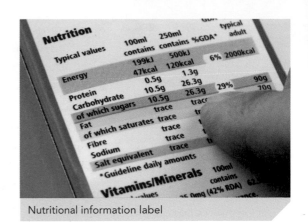

Nutritional information label

Use the eatwell plate to help you get the balance right. It shows how much of what you eat should come from each food group.

Fruit and vegetables

Bread, rice, potatoes, pasta and other starchy foods

Meat, fish, eggs, beans and other non-dairy sources of protein

Foods and drinks high in fat and/or sugar

Milk and dairy foods

Department of Health in association with the Welsh Government, the Scottish Government and the Food Standards Agency in Northern Ireland.

Figure 9.1 The eatwell plate

Source: © Crown copyright. Department of Health in association with the Welsh Assembly Government, the Scottish Government and the Food Standards Agency in Northern Ireland.

The eatwell plate groups different foods together and shows the proportions we should eat of each food group to have a balanced diet. It shows that we should eat:

- plenty of fruit and vegetables
- plenty of bread, rice, potatoes, pasta and other starchy foods – you should choose wholegrain varieties whenever you can as these are better for you
- some milk and dairy foods – you should choose lower fat alternatives whenever possible or eat higher fat versions infrequently or in smaller amounts

Link

For more information on calories, look at Topic A.3 in this unit.

Did you know?

One portion is considered to be about 80 g. The fruit and vegetables that you eat do not have to be fresh to count as a portion, nor do they have to be eaten on their own – you can eat them as part of a meal. For example, you could add a handful of raisins or berries to your breakfast or add carrots to your spaghetti bolognese.

Take it further

Although the government-backed '5 A DAY' campaign urges us all to eat a balanced diet that includes at least five portions of fruit and vegetables each day, other countries offer different advice.

Carry out some research into the fruit and vegetable guidelines suggested by other countries. You may be surprised by what you find!

- some meat, fish, eggs, beans and other non-dairy sources of protein – you should choose lower fat alternatives whenever possible or eat higher fat versions infrequently or in smaller amounts
- just a small amount of foods and drinks high in fat and/or sugar.

How often we eat and the portion sizes we consume per day will vary depending on our age, gender and occupation. The government recommends that we eat at least five portions of a variety of fruit and vegetables a day and at least two portions of fish a week, including a portion of oily fish.

Healthy eating patterns also play a major role in maintaining a balanced diet and healthy lifestyle. Figure 9.2 gives you some pointers on how to keep up healthy eating habits.

Healthy eating habits

✓ Eat three healthy and balanced meals a day – do not skip breakfast!

✓ Avoid too much snacking, especially on unhealthy items of food.

✓ Eat at regular times.

✓ Do not eat late at night.

✓ Avoid a heavy evening meal.

✓ Use guidance available to help plan your eating, e.g. the eatwell plate and '5 A DAY' guidelines. You can access these guidelines as well as useful information about eating healthily on the NHS website. You can access this website by going to www.pearsonhotlinks.co.uk and searching for this title.

Figure 9.2 Tips for healthy eating habits

Assessment practice 9.1

1 **State two benefits of maintaining a healthy lifestyle. [2]**

2 **State three nutrients that are needed in a healthy, balanced diet and for each one give an example of a food that contains it. [6]**

Other factors that influence health

A healthy lifestyle is not just about the food we eat. There are other influencing factors that need to be taken into account.

Exercise and fitness

Some people enjoy exercise, whereas some simply exercise because they know it is good for their health. Others exercise to try to lose weight, to maintain a healthy weight or to prevent weight gain. People's lives are increasingly busy and it is the norm to eat out or get takeaways. However, the importance of exercise should not be underestimated.

Did you know?

Exercise can help to reduce a range of diseases, e.g. coronary heart disease, stroke and type 2 diabetes.

Adults should take part in exercise activities that add up to at least 150 minutes each week. One way to approach this is to exercise five times a week for 30 minutes. The exercise should be of moderate intensity. There are different guidelines about the exercise times and frequency for children and older adults. Table 9.1 sets out these guidelines.

Table 9.1 Physical activity guidelines for children and adults

Age	How much exercise?
Under 5s – infants who are not yet walking	Floor-based play and water-based activities and as little time spent sitting or lying still as possible (except when sleeping)
Under 5s – children who are walking	Physically active for at least 3 hours each day (spread throughout the day)
5–18 years	Moderate to vigorous physical activity for at least 60 minutes and up to several hours each day
19–64 years	• Over a week, activity adds up to at least 2½ hours of moderate activity, e.g. 30 minutes on at least 5 days per week • Or 75 minutes of more strenuous activity spread over a week
65+ years	• Over a week, activity adds up to at least 2½ hours of moderate activity, e.g. 30 minutes on at least 5 days per week • Or 75 minutes of more strenuous activity spread over a week • Plus activity to improve muscle strength and balance/coordination 2 days per week

Source: © Crown Copyright 2011. Department of Health, Physical activity guidelines: Fact sheets 1–5.

? Did you know?

• The Department of Health states that for a person weighing just over 9 stone (57 kg), 30 minutes of running at 6 miles per hour will burn 300 calories and 30 minutes of cycling at 10 to 12 miles per hour will burn 240 calories.

Remember that this will vary slightly depending on the individual, their height and their weight.

Source: Department of Health (2004), 'At least five a week: Evidence of the impact of physical activity and its relationship to health, A report from the Chief Medical Officer.' © Crown copyright (2004).

Exercise should be both **load bearing** and **aerobic**.

🔑 Key terms

Load bearing – where the weight is on the limbs, includes jogging and dancing

Aerobic – moderately intense aerobic exercise includes running, swimming and cycling.

Case study: Diet, weight and self-esteem

Gina has just moved to your local area with her daughters, Emma (15) and Amy (19). Both of them were bullied throughout school due to their weight. For their school lunch, Gina gave them each a lunchbox filled with chocolate, sweets, crisps, cheese and biscuits. As a family, two of their weekly meals came from their local fish and chip shop and they regularly had a Chinese takeaway at the weekends. Gina had put on five stone in the past three years and used the car to drive to the local shop, which was about a two-minute walk away from their house.

Gina and her daughters have decided to change their lifestyle and start a healthy eating regime to help them lose weight and improve their emotional wellbeing.

1 Looking at the items in Emma's lunchbox, what changes could you suggest she makes to improve and balance her diet?

2 Suggest what else the family could do to aid their weight loss.

3 Amy and Gina have decided to get fit. Can you recommend a local gym and find out what classes they can offer them?

4 In addition to the gym, Gina is afraid that unless she goes to a group and monitors her weight on a weekly basis, she will not be able to motivate herself to continue with the diet and changes to her lifestyle. Therefore, Gina needs a group that meets on a weekly basis that will support her on a diet programme and monitor her weight. Can you research what would be available to her and make recommendations about where she could go?

Food and nutrition in relation to health

Introduction

In this topic you will learn about different food types and what makes a balanced diet in more detail. You will also learn about the different nutrients and their food sources.

Link

Go to Topic A.1 in this unit to recap on what makes a balanced diet.

A balanced diet

A balanced diet is one of the most important ways of contributing to a healthy lifestyle. We know we have a balanced diet when we eat a variety of foods to give us the necessary nutrients in the correct proportions. When we do this our body is able to function correctly. It can grow and develop, and repair and heal itself.

It is important to remember that what makes a balanced diet varies between individuals, depending on a number of factors, including their gender, age, height, weight and the amount of exercise they undertake. Table 9.2 provides some information about the nutritional needs of people at different ages.

Table 9.2 The nutritional needs of different groups of people

Group	Nutritional needs
Babies and young children	Babies and young children need high-energy foods and vitamins and minerals for growth and development.
Teenagers	Boys need more energy than girls. During puberty, girls should have a higher intake of iron.
Pregnant women/ nursing mothers	Women in this group should eat high-energy foods that contain vitamins and minerals for growth and development to pass on to the baby.
People who are very physically active	These people require high-energy foods.
Elderly people	The elderly need lower-energy foods, and vitamins and minerals to maintain good health.
People who are ill	Individuals in this group may need special diets due to medical issues.

Macronutrients

Macronutrients are nutrients that the body uses and needs in relatively large amounts to provide a lot of energy. These are carbohydrates, proteins and fats. A nutritionally balanced meal for an active person might include a good-sized portion of potatoes or pasta (the carbohydrate element of the meal). Although not usually considered macronutrients, water is also needed in large quantities and fibre (carbohydrate compounds), which has positive effects on our health. Table 9.3 explains why the body needs these things.

Table 9.3 Types of nutrient, food sources and purpose

Macronutrient	Type of food	Why it is needed
Carbohydrates (**complex** and **simple**)	• Simple carbohydrates: sugars and sweet foods – easily digested and an instant source of energy • Complex carbohydrates: starchy foods such as potatoes, bread, rice, pasta – take longer to digest so provide a slow release of energy	• To provide energy • To help digestion and prevent constipation

continued

Key terms

Macronutrient – a nutrient required in relatively large amounts by the body.

Complex carbohydrates – found in starchy foods such as vegetables, breads, pasta and cereals; they help you to feel full for longer as they are broken down more slowly by the body.

Simple carbohydrates – often found in foods such as fruit, milk and milk products; are broken down quickly by the body to be used as energy. They are also found in refined and processed products such as white sugar, cakes, sweets and soft drinks.

Key terms

Pulses – beans, peas, lentils and chickpeas, known as pulses, all have a high amount of fibre and are a good source of protein. They also provide important vitamins and minerals.

Micronutrient – a nutrient required by the body in relatively small (trace) amounts, e.g. calcium and iron, are particularly important for growth and health.

Link

For more information on saturated and unsaturated fats, go to Topic A.3 in this unit.

Did you know?

Without water a human can only survive for a few days.

Take it further

The body needs 13 vitamins and 18 minerals. Research what these are and the reasons why the body needs them.

Table 9.3 (*continued*)

Macronutrient	Type of food	Why it is needed
Fibre (soluble and insoluble)	• Soluble: fruit, vegetables and **pulses** • Insoluble: whole grain cereals and pulses	• To help reduce the amount of cholesterol in the blood (soluble). • To prevent constipation (insoluble).
Fats (saturated and unsaturated)	• Saturated: butter, lard, hard cheese, fatty meats, biscuits, pastries, cakes • Unsaturated: oily fish, nuts, seeds, olive oil	• To provide energy • To help the body absorb certain nutrients • To help absorb some vitamins • To support brain development and the immune system
Protein	• Meat, fish, eggs, cheese, lentils, peas, beans, nuts	• Essential for the growth and repair of body tissue • Excess is used to provide energy
Water	• Taken into the body from solid foods and drinks • The Department of Health recommends that we drink 1.2 litres of fluid a day (6 to 8 glasses)	• Aids digestion and helps get rid of waste • Needed for most other body processes • Essential for the body to function and to help maintain mental awareness

▶ Micronutrients

Micronutrients are nutrients that the body needs in small amounts. They are vitamins and minerals. Table 9.4 lists different types of micronutrients, their food sources and explains why the body needs them.

Table 9.4 Types of nutrient, food sources and purpose

Micronutrient	Food source	Purpose
Vitamins – water soluble, such as vitamins B and C and fat soluble, such as vitamins A and D	Fruit, vegetables, meat, fish, poultry, dairy products, cereals, nuts and seeds	• To fight infections • To contribute to the maintenance of the skin • To form new cells • To maintain muscle tone • To form red blood cells • To promote healthy teeth and bones
Minerals – iron, calcium, potassium, zinc, sodium, iodine		• To help regulate body fluids • To help the blood clot • Essential for tissue growth • To help the formation of strong bones and teeth

Activity 9.2　　Food poster

Create a poster to provide information on the different nutrients, food sources and their nutritional purposes.

Assessment practice 9.3

1　State three macronutrients and then state why each is needed. [6]

2　What is a micronutrient? Write a definition and give two examples. [3]

▶ Food in relation to nutrition

Introduction

It is also important to look at how we group foods in general and understand the quantity in which each food group should be consumed. Not all foods are good for us if we eat too much of them and, therefore, hospitality businesses need to know what makes a healthy meal.

Discuss which foods you think we need to eat in smaller quantities and why we should eat less of them.

▶ Food groups

Earlier in the unit we looked at the eatwell plate and at how the government breaks down food into different food groups.

Table 9.5 shows these key food groups and the main nutrients they provide us with.

Table 9.5 Key food groups and their micronutrients and macronutrients

Food groups	Food sources	Micronutrients	Macronutrients
Cereals	Bread, cereals, rice, couscous, pasta, flour and associated products, porridge and breakfast cereals	• Vitamins B, E • Minerals: magnesium, selenium	• Carbohydrates • Protein • Fibre
Pulses and potatoes	Pulses, lentils, potatoes	• Vitamin B • Minerals: magnesium, zinc	• Fibre • Protein • Carbohydrate
Fruit and vegetables	Fruits, vegetables, fruit juice, vegetable juice, pulses (peas, beans and lentils)	• Vitamins A, B, C, D, E, K • Minerals: iron, calcium, magnesium, potassium	• Carbohydrate • Fibre • Protein

continued

Table 9.5 *(continued)*

Food groups	Food sources	Micronutrients	Macronutrients
Dairy foods	Milk, cheese, yoghurt, cream, eggs, butter	• Vitamins A, D • Minerals: calcium	• Carbohydrate • Fat • Protein
Protein foods	Meat, fish, lentils, nuts, eggs	• Vitamin A • Minerals: iron, zinc	• Protein • Fat • Carbohydrate
Fats and foods high in sugar	• Foods with fats: suet, dripping, lard, oils, vegetable suet, processed foods and convenience produce • Foods high in sugar: chocolate, sweets, biscuits, cakes, pastries, jams, sweetened/carbonated drinks	• Vitamins A, D, E	• Fat • Carbohydrate

Activity 9.3   What are you eating?

List the different items of food you ate yesterday and then identify the food groups in which the items belong.

• What is your diet lacking?

• What are you eating too much of?

• How might your current diet affect your health and lifestyle?

• How might your current diet affect you in the future?

Link

Look back at Topic A.1 in this unit and the eatwell plate for a reminder of the different food groups and the guideline daily amount for each one.

Assessment practice 9.4

Baked beans on wholemeal toast is a healthy and balanced snack, especially if you drink a glass of fresh orange juice with it. Complete the table below by:

1 **identifying one other vitamin and one other mineral that can be found in this meal**

2 **describing how each one contributes to good health. [4]**

An example has been given to help you.

Vitamin or mineral	How it contributes to good health
E.g. Vitamin: vitamin C in orange juice	*Helps the body to absorb the iron in the baked beans/helps the body to heal and fight infections*
Vitamin:	
Mineral:	

Calories/kilojoules

All food items have a value in calories and kilojoules. A calorie is the amount of energy that is contained in food or beverages. The NHS recommends that an average man needs around 2,500 calories a day and an average woman needs around 2,000 calories a day. These amounts will vary depending on the individual's age, height, weight, and the level of physical activity they undertake. The more active a person is, the more calories they will use up. To keep to a healthy weight, you need to balance the amount of calories you get from food and beverages with the amount of calories you burn through physical activity. To have a healthy diet, the calories should be from a variety of products and in the right proportions.

Figure 9.4 gives an example of a nutritional information label that can be found on the side or back of pre-packaged food items. Many food manufacturers also display nutritional information on the front of pre-packed food. This label is useful if you want to glance quickly at how many calories are in an item and to compare the nutritional information in different products. The label shows the number of calories and grams of sugars, fat, saturated fat and salt per portion of the food. It also shows these things as a percentage of your recommended daily amount.

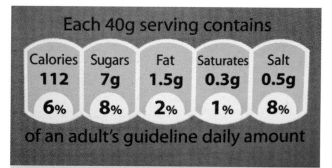

Each 40g serving contains

Calories	Sugars	Fat	Saturates	Salt
112	7g	1.5g	0.3g	0.5g
6%	8%	2%	1%	8%

of an adult's guideline daily amount

Figure 9.4 A nutritional information label on the front of a pre-packaged food item showing the number of calories in the food item

---

Activity 9.4 Calorie content

Visit a fast food restaurant and pick out three popular menu items. Research the calorie content and nutritional value for each item. In a group, discuss the items you researched.

- Were you surprised at how many calories were in each item?
- Did you think there would be fewer calories in the items?

Take it further

You can find out more about the recommended daily amount for calorie intake by visiting the NHS website. You can access this website by going to www.pearsonhotlinks.co.uk and searching for this title.

Healthier alternatives

In developing menus and preparing dishes, hospitality businesses and caterers should produce balanced meals using healthy ingredients. Menus should contain healthier choices for health-conscious individuals. These dishes are usually highlighted on menus by using a special symbol so that customers can quickly spot them.

Wholefoods

Wholefoods, often referred to as unrefined foods, are foods that have not been stripped of mineral content and laced with artificial additives and sugars. **Refined foods** are proven to be harmful for perfect health. In order to put unrefined or wholefoods back into diets and menus we need to:

- avoid using white flour and eating white bread – replace them with wholemeal bread, flour, oatcakes, rice cakes and pumpernickel
- avoid eating white rice – instead use brown rice

Key terms

Wholefood – food that is in its natural state, e.g. brown sugar, brown rice and wholemeal flour.

Refined foods – foods that have been processed or altered in such a way that they are no longer in their natural state. Nutrients such as vitamins, minerals and fibre may have been removed, reducing the food's nutritional value.

- avoid sugar, sweets, cakes and biscuits – replace them with fruit (fresh or dried)
- avoid eating processed meals, for example, frozen ready meals, which may be high in fats, sugar and salt – instead, use fresh natural ingredients to make a meal.

Fresh foods

Fresh foods are a good source of fibre, vitamins and minerals, and, therefore, it is a good idea to choose fresh ingredients when making a meal. Examples of fresh foods include fruit, vegetables, bread, potatoes.

Healthier cooking methods

Some dishes can be easily adapted during the cooking process to make them healthier. Examples of healthier cooking methods are:

- **Steaming** – cook food such as vegetables in steam so that nutrients are not boiled away.
- **Baking** – bake food in the oven without adding fat.
- **Stir frying** – stir fry vegetables, meat and fish using a small amount of oil.
- **Roasting** – roast food in the oven with only a small amount of fat.
- **Grilling** – grilling food allows fat to drain away.
- **Poaching** – poach fish, fruit and eggs in liquid without adding extra fat.
- **Boiling** – boil food such as potatoes in water.

Many hospitality businesses are taking steps to offer more healthy alternatives on their menus.

Retaining nutritional value

The nutritional value of an item can be reduced through cooking and preservation methods. For example, vitamin C is destroyed by heat; this means that canned fruit will have less vitamin C than fresh fruit.

Use cooking methods that preserve nutritional value. For example, steamed vegetables are likely to retain more nutritional value than boiled vegetables as nutrients can be destroyed during the boiling process. Grill foods, for example, sausages, rather than fry them. When foods are fried they absorb a lot of fat, whereas the fat will drip off when grilling. Fried vegetables lose some of their vitamin content whereas grilled vegetables cook more quickly and retain more nutritional value.

Key term

Trans-fat – a type of unsaturated fatty acid, commonly found in margarine and some processed foods, which has been shown to be bad for human health and which can lead to heart disease.

Activity 9.5   Cooking methods

Research different cooking methods and state which cooking methods are healthier and why. Then identify those that are better at retaining nutritional value and the reasons why.

▶ Foods to avoid

Foods that are high in calories or foods with low nutritional value should be eaten in small amounts or, ideally, avoided. These include:

- processed foods, e.g. processed meats, sugary breakfast cereals and canned foods with large amounts of salt or fat
- convenience foods, for example, ready meals where the calorie content, amount of sugar and fat might be high (it is a good idea to look at the labels on convenience foods and think about the contents before buying them)
- foods high in sugar, salt and fats
- foods that need the addition of fat, for example, for frying.

Assessment practice 9.5

1 State three food groups and give an example of a food source for each one. [6]

2 What is the recommended daily allowance of calorie intake for an average man? [1]

3 Give an example of a wholefood and an example of a refined food. Which is better for you, and why? [4]

? Did you know?

A report by the British Hospitality Association in May 2011 shows the achievements of the hospitality industry towards healthier eating:

- 80 per cent of respondents offer lighter meals and low calorie alternatives
- 62.5 per cent have cut out all artificial **trans-fats** from their menus
- 50 per cent have reduced salt levels by 10–15 per cent.

Source: 'Health Works: a look inside eating-out: A Report by the British Hospitality Association.'

You can access the full report by going to www.pearsonhotlinks.co.uk and searching for this title.

TOPIC   A.4

▶ Specific diets and concepts linked to a healthy lifestyle

Introduction

It is essential that you have an understanding of specific dietary requirements when working in the hospitality industry – ignoring special diets and dietary requests by customers can have serious consequences.

Choose one of the following dietary requirements and prepare a short presentation to inform others about what people with the requirement can and cannot eat.

- Gluten-free diets
- Low-salt diet
- Low-sugar diet
- An allergy to nut products

People have special dietary needs for different reasons; these may be medical, cultural or from choice. It is important that you understand what these needs are in order to carry out your responsibilities properly.

▶ Dietary requirements linked to health

People may have a special diet due to a medical condition.

- **A low-salt diet** – people who need a diet with low levels of salt may have kidney problems or high blood pressure. Reducing their salt intake may reduce the severity of these problems.

- **A low-sugar diet** – those with a low sugar diet may have diabetes, problems with tooth decay or weight problems linked to obesity.

- **Diabetes** – this is a medical condition where a person has too much sugar in their blood. The blood sugar level, therefore, has to be balanced, either by diet or medication, depending on the type of diabetes and how serious the condition is.

- **A gluten-free diet** – people who need a gluten-free diet avoid products made with wheat or rye and barley. The more serious form of gluten intolerance is called **coeliac disease**.

▶ Specific dietary requests

When you are working in the hospitality industry you also need to be able to cater for a range of special diets.

Vegetarianism/Veganism

A vegetarian avoids all products that involve an animal being killed to produce them. Vegetarians will not eat meat, poultry or fish but may drink milk or eat milk products, butter and **free range** eggs. Some vegetarians eat any cheese but others will only eat vegetarian cheese produced without the use of animal **rennet**. People may be vegetarian because they are against suffering to animals, for religious reasons or they may not like meat.

A vegan will not eat animal-based products of any kind. Often, vegans are also particular about what they wear, for example, they will not wear leather and will not use toiletries or cosmetics that may contain animal products.

Branded and fad diets

There are many branded and fad diets in circulation today. Fad diets claim that they can help you lose a lot of weight and often in a very short time. They 'work' by starving the body in order to speed up weight loss.

This type of diet is never recommended as it is difficult to sustain the weight loss in the long term. As soon as you start to eat healthily again, the weight goes on. The diet aims to starve the body so the body's natural reaction is to shut down and protect itself, so it begins to starve. People who follow these types of diet will often have nutritional problems as the diet excludes some of the body's essential nutrients.

Key terms

Coeliac disease – hypersensitivity to wheat gluten, which leads to a failure to digest food.

Free range – a term used to describe the type of farming where animals can roam freely rather than being caged or enclosed.

Rennet – produced in a calf's stomach and used in the process of hardening cheese.

Cultural diets

People's cultural and religious beliefs can shape their lifestyle. Their beliefs are vital to their way of life and must be respected. Examples of cultural and religious diets include:

- a kosher diet – this diet follows Jewish food laws: meat and poultry must be ritually slaughtered; they will not eat blood products or pork; fish must have fins and scales intact, dairy and meat must be stored, prepared and eaten separately
- a halal diet – this diet follows the Muslim food laws: meat must be prepared according to Muslim law, that is, ritually slaughtered and after a prayer has been offered to Allah; they will not eat blood products or pork.

? Did you know?

When an animal is ritually slaughtered its throat is cut very quickly and the blood is completely drained from the carcass.

Activity 9.6	Culture, religion and food

Choose one culture or religion that we have not covered and find out how the religion and its beliefs affect what a person can and cannot eat.

▶ Foods that may trigger allergies

Some people's bodies react badly to certain foods, which can make them very unwell. More serious health problems may be created by **allergies** to certain foods, which include:

- nuts
- peanuts
- wheat
- artificial flavourings and colourings
- dairy products
- shellfish
- chemical preservatives.

We all have our own genetic make-up so it is possible that an individual could be allergic or **intolerant** to any particular food item.

People who have an allergy can become ill even from a tiny amount of the food that causes the allergy. This can lead to the person going into **anaphylactic shock** and needing immediate medical attention. People who have an allergy can be prescribed medicines by their doctor. These medicines can reduce/eliminate the symptoms of an allergic reaction if a particular food is eaten. Different people will require different amounts of medication. They are likely to carry their medication at all times and may wear an identification necklace or bracelet so that others are aware of their allergy.

🔑 Key terms

Allergy – when a person has an allergic reaction to a food item. The reaction can sometimes be life-threatening.

Intolerance – when a person's body reacts badly to certain foods, causing them to become unwell.

Anaphylactic shock – a life-threatening reaction to an allergy.

Activity 9.7	Allergies and intolerances

Record what you have eaten over the past three days. Using the information you have learned in this unit, circle all of the items that you might not have been able to eat if you had any allergy or food intolerance.

Having circled the items, suggest how not being able to eat a particular food item would affect your lifestyle.

Key terms

Organic – foods produced using organic farming methods, e.g. they are free from pesticides and chemical fertilisers.

Sustainability – that is, using natural resources in a responsible and managed way so that stocks do not run out and an ecological balance is maintained.

Pesticides – substances which prevent or destroy insects harmful to plants.

Carbon footprint – the amount of carbon dioxide generated by an action, e.g. producing or transporting food. By choosing to use local products, which have not been transported hundreds or even thousands of miles by road or air, you are helping to reduce their carbon footprint.

▶ Concepts connected to healthy lifestyles

The concepts of **organic**, locally sourced and free range foodstuffs are linked with a healthy lifestyle. We will explore these in a little more detail in this section.

Organic and locally sourced foods

With raised media awareness of 'green' issues such as **sustainability**, the hospitality industry should aim to source and support local farmers and growers.

Using organic, local foods allows you to check that the foods have been produced in a healthy and humane manner. Organic means that the food must have been produced in a natural way without chemicals such as **pesticides**.

Some advantages of using locally grown food are listed here.

- The premises can be visited to check the method of production.
- The premises can be checked for their cleanliness.
- A good relationship can be developed between the business and the food producer.
- Local products reduce the **carbon footprint** of food supplies as they do not have far to go to be delivered.

Free range

There is more awareness today about the conditions in which poultry and other animals are kept. As a result, more people are buying free range products. In general the term 'free range' relates to how the animal has been kept and the facilities and space that the animal has to move around in. Free range animals can roam freely for food, rather than being confined in an enclosure. People who know about the differences between a free range hen and a battery hen are more likely to buy free range eggs. However, free range produce is often more expensive to buy, so cost can be a barrier.

Assessment practice 9.6

1 State three foods that might trigger allergies. [3]

2 James owns a vegetarian restaurant but a rival restaurant has recently opened nearby. James is worried that he might lose customers so he has decided to make his menu more appealing by using local and organic food supplies as much as he can. What two claims can he make when he lets customers know he only uses fresh, local and organic ingredients? [2]

WorkSpace

▷ Gareth Williams

A cook at a residential care home

I have been working in the same care home since I left college two years ago. I started working there after I completed a stint of work experience and then worked part-time as a general kitchen assistant. When I qualified with a BTEC Level 1/Level 2 First Diploma in Hospitality and an NVQ Level 2 in Kitchen and Larder, I fell straight into the assistant cook's role. I am now on target to take over as head cook later this year when the cook retires.

The care home has 50 residents, many of whom have special dietary requirements. I have to cater for needs such as diabetes, a lack of nutrients, low/high cholesterol and many other medical conditions relating to diet. In addition, I have to remember that not all of the residents can chew foods and some may need foods that are liquidised or soft enough for them to eat.

As I am partly responsible, under the supervision of the head cook, for preparing and cooking all of the residents' meals and snacks, we have to make sure that we are providing everyone with a healthy, nutritional and balanced diet. Occasionally, other staff plan trips out for the residents and I need to prepare food for some, if not all, the residents to eat while they are out and about. However, some residents may use this as a chance to treat themselves and eat out.

I have faced a few challenges in my role including:

- coping with the change of being my own manager
- training a new assistant cook
- making sure the menu I provide covers a balanced diet
- presenting dishes in an appealing way
- catering for different dietary needs.

I am looking forward to the challenge of my new role later on in the year and I am very excited about running my own kitchen and making sure I meet the residents' needs.

Think about it

1 What information does Gareth need to know about each of the 50 residents in order to cook for them?

2 Give three recommendations that would make the food at the care home appealing.

3 Design a menu that Gareth could use for one day covering breakfast, lunch and dinner, which would show a balance of different foods and nutrients for the residents.

▶ Links between lifestyle and problems with health

Introduction

Media coverage increasingly tells us about how our lifestyles and eating habits relate to health problems. The hospitality industry has a role to play in making sure that healthier alternatives are offered to customers. Therefore, to try to prevent health problems as a result of diet or poor lifestyle choices, it is important that we are well informed about what causes them.

Obesity is a term we hear on an almost daily basis. Why do you think this is?

Key terms

Obesity – when someone is very overweight with a high degree of body fat.

Malnutrition – when someone does not have proper nutrition due to not having enough food to eat or not eating enough of the right things.

Sedentary – describes a person who is inactive and takes little exercise.

It is important that we understand which lifestyle factors can lead to health problems so that we can make informed decisions about how we live our lives.

▶ Eating the wrong types of food

Eating more than the recommended daily calorie intake or GDA of particular nutrients can result in:

- increased weight gain (which can lead to being overweight)
- obesity
- **malnutrition**
- an imbalance of chemicals in our bodies, for example, too much salt.

Table 9.6 highlights some of the consequences of eating too much of certain food types.

Table 9.6 Consequences of eating too much of the wrong types of food

Food type	Consequences of eating too much of this type of food
Foods high in salt, e.g. crisps, processed foods	• High blood pressure • Increased risk of stroke • Increased risk of heart disease
Foods high in sugar, e.g. sweets, biscuits, cakes and sugary drinks	• Increased weight gain • Becoming overweight • Obesity • Tooth decay • Vitamin deprivation
Foods high in saturated fats, e.g. dairy products, meat and meat products	• Increased risk of heart disease • High cholesterol • Increased weight gain • Becoming overweight • Obesity

Excess consumption of alcohol

Drinking too much alcohol can become a health problem. It can lead to weight gain, inappropriate behaviour and illness, and can make people more at risk of accidents. This is because the misuse of alcohol can lead to a lack of self-control and people's reactions to danger can be a lot slower.

Those who consume alcohol regularly can become dependent on it and face an increased risk of long-term health effects, for example, liver and kidney failure.

Link

Refer back to Topic A.1 in this unit for more information on alcohol.

Activity 9.8   The dangers of alcohol

In pairs, investigate the long-term effects of excessive alcohol consumption.

Assessment practice 9.7

1 Which **two** of these problems are linked to a diet high in sugar, salt and fat? [2]

   A Obesity ☐   C Hair loss ☐   E Irritability ☐

   B Poor memory ☐   D Weight gain ☐

---

2 State three problems associated with drinking too much alcohol on a regular basis. [3]

Sedentary lifestyles

People who have a **sedentary** lifestyle have no regular activity. They may be inactive and spend much of their time seated. If you lead a sedentary life you run the risk of:

- becoming overweight
- obesity
- laziness
- poor self-esteem and body image
- depression
- high blood pressure (related to a lack of exercise)
- heart disease (related to a lack of exercise).

Figure 9.5 Do you think these people might be storing up health problems for themselves in the future?

? Did you know?

The Department of Health states that 61.3 per cent of adults, 23.1 per cent of 4–5 year olds and 33.3 per cent of 10–11 year olds are overweight or obese. They also state that health problems associated with being overweight or obese cost the NHS more than £5 billion every year. They have a policy that aims to reduce the number of overweight or obese adults and children by 2020. They are doing this by helping people and businesses to make healthier choices.

Source: Department of Health (2011) 'Healthy Lives, Healthy People: A Call to Action on Obesity in England'. © Crown copyright 2011.

You can find out more information about the government's policy to reduce obesity and improve diet by going to www.pearsonhotlinks.co.uk and searching for this title.

▶▶ Not getting enough rest and relaxation

If you do not get enough rest and relaxation you are more likely to be at risk of:

- problems with your immune system
- an increase in stress levels
- high blood pressure
- heart disease.

People with high-pressured jobs and busy work schedules are often more likely to be at risk of these problems because, even when they have time off, their mind is still focused on work. They fail to shut off, which means they are not truly able to rest or relax.

Take it further

Produce a list of activities that people could try to help them rest and relax. You could visit the NHS website to get some ideas. You can access this website by going to www.pearsonhotlinks.co.uk and searching for this title.

Activity 9.9   Rest and relaxation – it is not a luxury!

Carry out some research to identify the top five most stressful jobs where people may fail to get the rest and relaxation needed for a healthy lifestyle.

Assessment practice 9.8

1 State three risks of eating too many sugary foods. [3]

2 What three risks might you run if you lead a sedentary life? [3]

▶ Trends and development relating to healthy lifestyles

Introduction

The demands of customers wanting to live their lives in a healthy way have naturally changed the types of products and services offered by the hospitality industry.

Visit a local restaurant and find out:

- how the menu has changed in the past three to five years
- whether healthy eating has had an effect on the drinks offered
- how they deal with a customer who has a specific dietary requirement.

The trend for improving our lifestyles can be seen throughout the hospitality industry, from the food we consume to the products that are offered, marketed and promoted.

▶ Restaurants

As professionals in the hospitality industry it is important that we focus on healthy eating. We have a responsibility to make sure the food that we prepare and provide for our customers is healthy and nutritious. This means ensuring that there are healthy alternatives on our menus including dishes that are lower in calories, fat, sugar and salt.

Availability of ingredients

Today, there are many more foodstuffs available and so it is possible to develop and change existing menus. We live in a global economy where imports and exports are daily events. It is, therefore, easy for businesses to get hold of more and more products that can influence the foods we eat. In your local supermarket there are now aisles containing foodstuffs from around the world, as well as locally sourced organic ingredients.

New providers

You may also be aware that people who eat out have much more choice than ever before in the type of restaurant they go to. New providers such as vegetarian restaurants, wholefood restaurants and health food restaurants have opened up the market, attracting health-conscious customers. Many more oriental restaurants have also opened up, offering world dishes that are seen as healthier options.

Market expansion

By listening to customers' specific or special dietary needs, restaurants can expand their **market share**. For example, many restaurants now offer gluten-free products to appeal to people who may not have been able to dine with them previously. Restaurants that focus on world cuisines have in the past been seen as **niche markets** but they are becoming more mainstream as people see the contribution they make to healthy eating.

Not all customers want a main meal – often people only have time for a light bite or snack. People who are following a diet may be calorie counting. This gives hospitality businesses an opportunity to offer lighter alternatives and smaller portions which still satisfy customer needs and increase business.

▶ Pubs, bars, nightclubs and membership clubs

Products

Over the past decade, the range of products offered in pubs and clubs has expanded massively. Not only is there a wider range of alcoholic beverages available but also non-alcoholic ones too.

Due to the increased media coverage on a healthy, balanced diet, there are increased ranges of low-calorie drinks and healthier snacks such as low-fat crisps available together with healthier items on the main menu. A change in cooking methods, that is, moving away from fried foods towards grilling and roasting food items, shows that pubs and clubs are considering their products and the effects they have on lifestyle and diet.

🔑 Key terms

Market share – the amount of trade a company has in comparison to the entire trade that is available to trade in.

Niche market – a product that targets a very specific area of the market, e.g. restaurants that only serve halal meat.

↗ Take it further

Choose a traditional pub menu item and identify ways in which the dish could be made healthier. Then carry out some research into low-calorie drinks and non-alcoholic cocktails. Known as 'mocktails', they are growing in popularity.

The smoking ban

Smoking is a danger not only to the health of smokers but also to anyone who breathes in the smoke. The smoking ban, which took effect between 2006 and 2008, means that people cannot smoke in an enclosed public place. This is good news for hospitality staff and customers alike who are no longer at risk of passive smoking. Now that smoking is not allowed, premises are easier to keep clean and are free of the grime caused by nicotine and smog. Many more families are happy to visit a pub now for a meal, as children are not subjected to passive smoking and food can be consumed in a more pleasant 'smoke free' environment.

Sports clubs' memberships

Health-conscious individuals are increasingly joining sport clubs to improve their health. It is likely that within your local area there will be a large health club, council-led leisure centres and sports clubs or a small independent gym. These facilities offer gyms, exercise classes, swimming pools, restaurants and bars. The trend for people to seek enjoyment by doing exercise has encouraged sports clubs to expand the range of classes on offer. You may attend some of the following yourself or know people who do: bikram yoga, zumba, hula hooping and spin classes.

> ### Activity 9.10   Drinks and diet
>
> Visit a local pub and record the number of drinks they offer. Categorise what is offered into alcoholic and non-alcoholic options. Circle those that would be better for people following a balanced diet.

Link

For more information on these service areas, go to Unit 1: Introducing the Hospitality Industry.

▶ Contract food service providers

When people are at home they can cater for themselves and follow a healthy diet if they choose to. However, this is not the case for everyone, particularly those who have their meals prepared for them, for example:

- in hospitals
- in care/residential homes
- in schools
- at events.

Some organisations run their own in-house catering operations but in others the catering services are managed by a contract catering company. People who work in the catering sections of these settings and who work for the contract caterer have to make sure that the food they provide helps towards a balanced diet. We will look at a few of these providers in more detail.

Schools

Jamie Oliver has played a large role in lobbying for healthier school meals and for cooking and life skills to be a compulsory part of education for all children and young adults. The government also provides a set of standards that must be met for school food. These include making it compulsory for schools to provide meals containing starchy foods, fruit and vegetables, meat, fish and non-dairy sources of protein, and dairy foods. Those providing food in schools should also think about providing healthy snacks for break times and offering a salad bar and lunchtimes.

Schools no longer just offer a school lunch: most schools now offer a breakfast club, lunch and after school club. Many schools only accept payment for food on lunch cards. The data collected on these cards might prove invaluable when assessing how healthy and balanced a child's diet is. The provision of healthy options should go hand in hand with education about healthy diets.

Care homes

Caterers in care homes also have a responsibility to offer residents foods that help them to maintain a healthy diet. Meals should be full of nutrition. The elderly may need vitamin D to help prevent bone loss, especially if they do not go outside much. Vitamin D is made by the effect of the sun on the body. Meals should also include zinc. Some residents may require or may prefer softer food that is easier to chew and swallow. The managers of care homes also have a responsibility to offer a regular activity plan for residents, which includes elements of social and physical activities, for example, outings and visits.

Does your school or college offer plenty of healthy eating options on a daily basis?

Hospitals

The food offered in hospitals has to cater for all the patients' needs. This can make menu planning difficult as some requirements will not be known until the day the meal is to be served. This means that kitchen staff need to plan in advance to cater for a variety of special and medical diets.

Due to the size of hospitals, and the numbers of people who are catered for, much of the food produced needs **regeneration**. Staff must use **Hazard Analysis and Critical Control Points (HACCP)** procedures to make sure the food is safe to eat and that the quality of dishes is high. Hospital caterers must include foods from around the world, in order to appeal to people from all backgrounds and cultures. However, it is equally important to avoid too many spicy foods, as this may cause stomach upsets, particularly among those who are already ill.

For patients recovering from operations and those who have been ill for a long period of time, hospital staff need to consider a fitness plan to get patients back to good health. This could be offered by a physiotherapist who might give patients exercises to perform. On some wards, communal sitting rooms are also offered to provide a source of rest and relaxation for patients.

Events

There has been an increase in events linked directly to healthy lifestyles, including:

- farmers' markets
- healthy eating fairs
- local and national festivals
- seminars and conferences on health issues and healthy lifestyles
- exhibitions.

These are aimed at people who are trying to adopt a healthy lifestyle or who are in the business and need menu and supplier ideas.

Take it further

The Hospital Caterers Association runs a 'Better Hospital Food Programme' to make sure the quality of food in hospitals is high. Visit their website to find more information about best practice to support the delivery of food in hospitals. You can access this website by going to www.pearsonhotlinks.co.uk and searching for this title.

Link

Go to Unit 3: Food Safety and Health and Safety in Hospitality for more information on HACCP.

Food markets are a good place to sample local, healthy and home-made produce.

Assessment practice 9.9

1 State three benefits of the smoking ban for the hospitality and catering industry. [3]

2 Janice is the head cook at Heyport Comprehensive and caters for pupils aged 11 to 18. She has decided she would like to encourage the pupils to eat a healthy diet. Explain two ways in which she and her staff could do this. [4]

▷ Hotels and residential accommodation

Hotels and residential accommodation providers have made major changes to respond to the trend and impact of healthy eating and lifestyles. Many hotels have updated or included facilities for customers who wish to follow a healthy lifestyle such as:

• increased availability and access to leisure and recreational facilities with the use of: a gym; sports facilities; swimming pools and spa facilities

• an alternative to restaurant and bar facilities, giving customers access to: vending machines; mini bars; room service; water/ice dispensers; complimentary products such as shampoo/conditioner/toothpaste (places abroad may even provide suntan lotions); food and beverage services – some hotels offer breakfast to take away or your preferred choice of newspaper with breakfast.

In recent years, business travel has increased due to businesses going global and improved travel routes by the sea and airways. This means that many customers or hotel guests may spend more nights in a hotel during the week than at home. Therefore, the hotel must cater for a balanced diet and offer the business customer leisure and relaxation facilities, so that they can exercise and unwind – important elements of a healthy lifestyle.

Activity 9.11   Hotels and business clients

Research a local hotel and identify how it would meet the health and lifestyle needs of business clients.

Take it further

Choose one area in the UK where people regularly go to experience the outdoors. Identify the different types of activities that are available in the area and then research the types of accommodation in which people could stay.

Many TV programmes reflect the beauty of the great outdoors and show what people can do in, and expect from, different areas of the United Kingdom (UK). Many people are now more inclined to spend time outdoors as they recognise how it can improve their lifestyles. This trend has resulted in an increase in the number of camping facilities and youth hostels.

TOPIC   B.2

Impact of lifestyle choices on products, services and operations

Introduction

Any change to the way a product or service is offered will have an effect on the way a business operates. In order to maintain market share, hospitality businesses need to adapt to, and cater for, current trends in people's lifestyle choices. However, being adaptable and keeping up with customer requirements can be costly.

Discuss how the importance of healthy eating and lifestyle might affect the staff working in a hospitality business. How could this impact on the business as a whole?

Staffing

If you are an employer in the hospitality industry, making changes to your products and services can have an impact on the working conditions of your staff and the training you provide for them.

Working conditions

Jobs in the hospitality industry are often seen as low paid and with long, unsociable hours. Although staff sign up to working hours and are, by law, allowed breaks, it is not always possible to stick to them. For example, a function could start later than planned so waiting staff will have to work longer in order to meet the customers' needs. It is also not easy for staff working in the kitchen preparing meals to take a break. Therefore, they may need to take their break either before or after the lunch period. This may be at a time when they are not really hungry or it may be late in the evening. It follows then, that staff can become used to poor eating habits, for example, by not eating regularly or not eating enough.

Training

Training staff in the benefits of a healthy diet and lifestyle can have a big impact on what a customer eats.

Staff can be trained to:

- be aware of diet and how it contributes to a healthy lifestyle
- advise on the nutritional content of foods
- be familiar with, and able to give advice on, health warnings
- serve the correct portion size
- monitor waste and see what food is left on plates, that is what is not eaten
- contribute to the appearance of food
- prepare and cook food in a way that preserves nutritional content.

Once staff have received training they will be able to use and demonstrate their increased skills. This may encourage them to produce new dishes which reflect healthier food options.

Case study: A stressful job

Danusha worked as a waitress in a large, busy hotel. She was paid the minimum wage and often had to work split shifts. This meant working at lunchtime from 10 a.m. until 2.30 p.m. and then coming back at 5 p.m. to set up for the evening service, and then serving customers. Sometimes, evening events meant that she had to work extra hours and she often stayed late to clear up. She often ate her lunch in the afternoon and her evening meal, if it was more than a hurried snack, might be eaten very late at night, just before she fell into bed. Danusha's normal days of work included weekends. She had missed a couple of family events, including her cousin's wedding, because she could not take time off. She also missed socialising with her friends on Friday and Saturday nights. Danusha often felt very tired and stressed. She was also starting to feel rather low and isolated. It seemed that all she ever did was work and when she did have a couple of hours off during an afternoon she found it impossible to relax because she knew she would soon be back at work.

1 List the negative effects of a job like Danusha's in the hospitality industry.
2 What could Danusha's employers do to help her find a better life/work balance?

Adapting products and services to provide healthy living

Products and services can be adapted to encourage healthy living for customers and staff. We have already looked at many of the ways in which this can be done.

Meeting customer needs

If businesses do not offer dishes to meet special diets, not only do they lose out on market share but they also fail to offer products that contribute to a healthy lifestyle. Most chefs will have an awareness of the different dietary requirements but those who are not certain should update their training.

Wherever possible, businesses should use healthy cooking methods and should not add extra fat or cook foods in a way that causes a loss of nutritional value. Businesses should also try to restrict the use of additives, such as food colourings, flavourings and chemical preservatives. Additives not only decrease the nutritional value of the food item but they can also cause allergic reactions. Any additives that are allowed within food items should be clearly described on the food label, so that customers can make an informed decision about whether to purchase the item.

Presentation at point of sale

Good presentation of food is an important part of the meal, eating experience or food purchasing decision. If food looks unattractive, customers will be less likely to enjoy a meal or may not buy an item at all if the food item is poorly packaged.

Take it further

Take a look at an article about the food posting craze on the British Hospitality Association website. You can access this article by going to www.pearsonhotlinks.co.uk and searching for this title.

Well-presented meals make a big difference to the opinion of many people about the hospitality business.

The way food is described on a menu or on packaging can also attract customers to choose or buy it. Descriptions should be clear, enticing and accurate so as not to fool customers into buying an item.

A good way to encourage sales of packaged food is to show a level of care and commitment to the environment by using sustainably sourced packaging materials.

Healthy dishes should be priced as average on a menu and should not be more expensive than less healthy options. You may have seen a number of restaurants offering smaller portions of a main meal, for example, a pasta or pizza dish and adding a side salad to encourage people to take up healthy options.

Menu design

A healthy menu is an important factor in a healthy lifestyle. Staff who are responsible for menu design have a big influence of people's lifestyles. In order for customers to make an informed choice about a dish, it is helpful if the menu includes the nutritional value of the dish.

Labelling and menu terminology

Food labelling is covered under the Food Labelling 1996 Regulations. Food labels today include a lot of nutritional information. However, not all businesses use the same type of food labelling and this can lead to customer confusion.

The law states that a food label must show: the name of food and processing method; the weight or volume; a list of ingredients – in order of weight from largest to smallest; a use-by or best-before date; guidance on how to store the item; instructions for preparation; the name and address of manufacturer; a production lot number.

Some companies also choose to add: nutritional information (in relation to recommended daily intake); cooking and serving suggestions; data reflecting how the product contributes to recommended daily intake of calories; organic food labelling; additive-free information; labelling to show that a product is suitable for vegetarians.

This information is not required by law but it is good practice to give a customer as much information as possible before they decide to buy a product.

Activity 9.12   Food label poster

Collect different food labels and record the information that you find on each one on a poster. Identify any differences between the three labels. Which type of label do you think is the most useful for health-conscious people?

Take it further

Visit the Food Standards Agency website to find out about the 'balance of good health' programme. You can access this website by going to www.pearsonhotlinks.co.uk and searching for this title.

Complying with government guidelines

The government and catering industry experts regularly investigate issues about the health of the population. Current advice from these investigations includes the following.

- Eat at least five portions of fruit or vegetables a day.
- Eat two portions of fish per week, including one portion that is oily.
- Increase the amount of fibre in your diet.
- Reduce the amount of salt in your diet.
- Reduce the amount of sugar in your diet.
- Reduce the amount of saturated fat in your diet.

Developing new product and service packages

The hospitality industry has to look at key, current trends and incorporate them when they are developing new products or services. For example, a five-star hotel could offer a special mid-week stay for two, which includes a fruit platter in your room on arrival, a treatment in the hotel's spa in the afternoon, an evening meal and breakfast for £139. They would be offering a new product with a service focusing on rest and relaxation and a healthy fruit platter on arrival.

Link

For more information on how to handle and store food supplies safely and hygienically, go to Unit 3: Food Safety and Health and Safety in Hospitality.

▶ Supplies

With new menu options you may need to find suppliers that offer a different product range. For example, if you have been used to buying processed, packaged, frozen items you may need to source an alternative supplier for fresh ingredients. As we have already learned, there is an increasing need to source local suppliers of fresh (and sometimes organic) food.

▶ Promotion and sales

Healthy dishes should be priced fairly; when they are priced higher than other dishes customers are not encouraged to purchase them or to eat healthily.

When promoting foods, caterers can focus on the healthy eating aspect and balanced nutritional value of a dish to create unique selling points (USPs). Promotions could be used to give customers information about the importance of healthy eating and why the dish is healthy. Supermarkets could learn from this by replacing the chocolate and sweets at the point of sale (the till) with healthy alternatives, for example, muesli bars and fruit, to encourage customers to choose a healthier option.

All promotions should contain accurate and relevant information and must not be misleading. Customers should know what they are going to receive and the benefits of choosing that product.

Promotional offers can include meal deals, for example, buy one meal, get one free and happy hours. How many other promotional activities can you think of which hospitality businesses could offer?

Marketing campaigns

Marketing campaigns can have both benefits and drawbacks. These are shown in Table 9.7.

Table 9.7 The benefits and drawbacks of marketing campaigns

Benefits	Drawbacks
• Increased business • Raised awareness • Increased market share	• Costs are incurred, e.g. for promotion, materials and new ingredients. • Not all campaigns are a success. • The business may need to take on more staff. • There may be a need for staff training, which increases the cost of the campaign. • It would be seen as irresponsible to promote foods that were not contributing to a healthy lifestyle.

Assessment practice 9.10

1 **Which two of these items must be included on a food label by law? [2]**

   A Food colour ☐

   B Weight or volume ☐

   C Nutritional information ☐

   D Cooking instructions ☐

   E Use-by date ☐

2 **Explain one reason why staff should be well trained to know about the products or services they are selling. [2]**

Key term

Constraint – a limitation or restriction on something.

Link

For more information on pricing and profit margins, go to Unit 4: Costing and Controlling Finances in the Hospitality Industry.

▶ Finance

The main **constraints** that hospitality businesses face when contributing to healthy lifestyles are financial. Pricing and profit margins must be taken into account when offering healthy alternatives. When there is a limited budget to buy ingredients, cheaper suppliers may have to be chosen. Budget constraints may make a business less likely to make a positive contribution to healthy lifestyles. They may affect how many dishes can be included on a healthy menu, the complexity of dishes on offer and may not allow for staff training. The budget available will depend of the type of business – a large chain hotel will have more to spend on catering than a small bed and breakfast.

▶ Constraints within the hospitality industry

Introduction

As you learned in Topic B.2, hospitality businesses need to adapt to trends in the market to hold their market share and advantage over competitors. However, change can be difficult to put in place and has both staffing and financial constraints.

Link

- For more information on government guidelines for safe levels of alcohol intake, go to Learning aim A, Topic A.1 in this unit and to the website for Drinkaware, a business that aims to change and improve the UK's drinking habits. You can access this website by going to www.pearsonhotlinks.co.uk and searching for this title.

- For more information on HASAWA (1974) and health and safety guidelines that affect hospitality businesses go to Unit 3: Learning aim B, Topic B.1.

▶ Compliance with guidelines and legislation

Hospitality businesses must consider and comply with government guidelines and legislation, which can restrict what they, as a business, are allowed to do. Legislation and guidelines that may affect hospitality businesses include:

- licensing laws – the Licensing Act 2003 states that alcohol may only be sold by businesses that have been granted a special licence by the local authority. It is illegal to sell or provide alcohol to anyone under 18 in most circumstances. You must ask for proof of age if you are working in a hospitality business and you think a customer who asks for alcohol is underage. Alcohol must also only be sold within permitted hours

- the smoking ban – a law banning smoking in pubs, bars and restaurants and all enclosed work and public places came into force in England in July 2007 (as a result of the Health Act 2006)

- guidelines for safe alcohol consumption – the government provides information about the maximum number of units of alcohol people should consume per day

- the Health and Safety at Work etc. Act 1974 (HASAWA).

Financial limitations

Financial constraints may be a much bigger factor for smaller businesses than larger ones, because a larger business is likely to have more money to spend and invest.

Costs

When businesses decide to promote healthier diets and lifestyles through the products they offer, it can lead to increased costs. This is because the products can be more expensive to produce. People may believe that healthy foods cost more and so they may not buy them. The healthy additions may cost extra money to promote and market them.

Budget

Budget is always a major constraint. If only a small budget is available then a business may have to source cheaper ingredients. Areas within the hospitality industry more likely to suffer financial constraints are:

- hospitals
- schools
- care/residential homes
- prisons
- contract catering.

Figure 9.6 shows how a tight budget can affect a business.

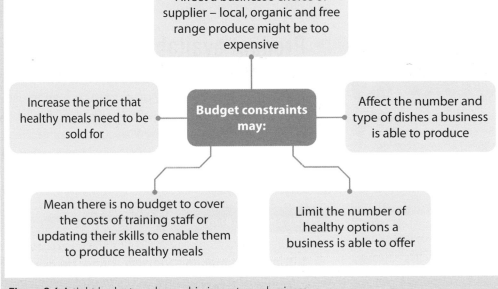

Figure 9.6 A tight budget can have a big impact on a business.

Pricing

When adding healthier alternatives to a menu it is important for businesses to think about the price that can be charged for them. If healthy dishes or healthy food products are much higher in price than other items, then a customer is not encouraged to adopt a healthier lifestyle – and they may not be able to afford to do so. People on low incomes may choose to spend less on fresh food and instead may use convenience foods. They are more likely to buy the cheapest brands, which may have lower nutritional values. People on low incomes may also have less money to spend on exercise and fitness activities. The leisure industry should therefore think about pricing their membership packages so that people are encouraged to exercise. This could be done by offering promotions.

Activity 9.13	Affordable healthy eating?

Visit two similar catering businesses and research the healthy eating options on their menus. Record the prices of the healthy options.

Review the healthy eating offerings and identify any similarities and differences between the dishes offered and the prices charged. Would you improve/change either dish?

Staffing limitations

It can be difficult to introduce new dishes to a menu and new product offerings within a hotel. One of the main reasons for this is the availability of staff and the cost of updating their skills. You may:

- need staff to work at different times when they are not usually available
- not have money in the budget to update the skills of staff to enable them to complete the tasks required.

When making the type of changes we have covered in this unit, staff need to be trained to be aware of things such as special dietary needs, be able to advise customers on the nutritional content of foods and be aware of the role diet plays in a healthy lifestyle. New health products and services, such as the introduction of new exercise classes require staff to be trained effectively.

Product availability

When introducing healthier options to a menu and using fresh foods, it is important to consider the availability of the products you wish to use. If you intend to use locally grown products then you have to look at what is available and when (seasonal availability). Therefore, you may need to think about changing the menu to fit the season. For example, asparagus is in season in May and June, strawberries are at their best from June to August and courgettes between June and September. It is also well known that in-season food tastes better, is often cheaper and better value, and is better for the environment.

Assessment practice 9.11

1 Kim has a mobile sandwich round. He drives around in a small van selling sandwiches, soup and cakes to employees of local offices and businesses. He has many regular customers, some of whom are asking if he can offer more healthy options. Explain how each of the following constraints might impact on his business?

- Budget [2]
- Government guidelines and legislation [2]

Responsibilities of hospitality industry employers towards employees

Introduction

Under the Health and Safety at Work etc. Act 1974 (HASAWA) employers have a responsibility to provide their employees with a safe and healthy workplace.

With the above statement in mind, list five points that you feel are the responsibility of an employer to their staff in terms of healthy eating and lifestyles.

▶ An employer's responsibility towards staff

As already mentioned, all employers have a legal responsibility to make sure their workplace is a safe and healthy place for their staff. Figure 9.7 shows some of the measures employers can take to achieve this and to encourage their staff to adopt a healthy diet and lifestyle.

Figure 9.7 A responsible employer will help staff to adopt a healthy diet and lifestyle.

▶ Benefits of upholding responsibilities

Showing that you care about your staff and upholding your responsibilities to them is more likely to result in:

- staff efficiency
- better trained staff with improved skills
- happier staff
- more motivated staff
- reduced sickness and absence
- staff loyalty and commitment
- the possibility of recognition of the business and staff in local and national awards.

Remember

Happy staff are more likely to create happy customers!

Assessment practice 9.12

1 Which Act states that employers have a responsibility to provide staff with a safe and healthy workplace? [1]

2 Explain three measures employers can take to encourage their staff to adopt a safe and healthy lifestyle. [6]

BTEC
Assessment Zone

This section has been written to help you to do your best when you take the onscreen test. Read through it carefully and ask your teacher/tutor if there is anything you are still not sure about.

How you will be assessed

For this unit you will be assessed through an examination that lasts 1 hour and 15 minutes. The examination paper will have a maximum of 50 marks. The number of marks available for each question will be shown in brackets, e.g. [2], with the total for each question being shown at the end of the question.

Disclaimer: These practice questions and sample answers are not actual exam questions and have been provided as a practice aid only. They should be used as practice material only and should not be assumed to reflect the format or coverage of the real external test.

A **Questions where the answers are available and you have to choose the correct answer(s) that fit.** *Tip. Always make sure that you read the instructions carefully. Sometimes you may need to identify more than one correct answer.*

Examples:

Identify from the list two food items that a person who is intolerant to gluten can not eat. [2]

A	Nuts
B	Wheat
C	Sugar
D	Caffeine
E	Barley

Answers: B and E

Identify from the list one nutrient that helps the body to digest and absorb food. [1]

A	Carbohydrate
B	Fat
C	Fibre
D	Protein

Answer: C

B **Questions where you are asked to give a short answer worth 1 or 2 marks.** *Tip. Look carefully at how the question is set out to see how many points need to be included in your answer.*

Example:

Explain the importance of having a balanced diet. [2]

Answer: A balanced diet helps us to maintain a healthy lifestyle so that our bodies are able to function correctly and are able to grow, develop, repair and heal.

State two different food sources that you could add into a person's diet if they needed to increase their intake of dairy products. [2]

Answer: To increase a person's dairy intake you would need to add in items such as cheese, milk, cream, butter and yoghurt to their diet.

C **Questions where you are asked to give a longer answer – these can be worth up to 8 marks.** *Tips: make sure that you read the question in full, and answer all of the parts of the question that you are asked. It is a good idea to plan your answer so that you do not forget anything and remember to check your answer once you have finished.*

Example:

Discuss how you could amend a typical, traditional pub dish such as a lasagne, chips and peas to offer a healthier alternative to the customer. [8]

Answer:

Replace the pasta with whole grain pasta, make sure the mince used is lean mince and you could replace the beef mince with turkey mince (as this is lower in fat) or Quorn mince.

You could add more vegetables into the lasagne mix to increase the number of vegetables within the dish. By adding vegetables this increases the contribution towards the customers' intake of five portions of fruit and vegetables a day. The peas could be left as they are but you could also add a substantial side salad and the chips could be replaced with potato wedges or a jacket potato.

In order to make the chips healthier, you could roast or bake them. This is healthier than frying them. By keeping the skin on the chips, the nutritional value is also increased.

The customer could also be informed that salt has not been added during cooking. They could also be encouraged not to add any salt or condiments to their meal (e.g. tomato ketchup, mayonnaise) by the introduction of healthy eating literature on all tables.

Hints and tips

- **Use the time before the test.** Make sure that you have got everything you will need. Check that your pen works properly and make sure you have read the instructions on the front of your examination. Try to make yourself comfortable and relaxed.

- **Keep an eye on the time.** The examination will last 1 hour and 15 minutes, and you should be able to see the clock in the examination room so that you will know how long you have got left to complete the paper. As a rough guide, allow one minute for every mark on the paper. This means that a question work five marks should take you around five minutes to complete.

- **Read the questions fully.** Make sure you read the question through enough times to be sure that you understand what you are being asked to do. It is easy to misread a question and then write an answer that is wrong. Check you are doing what you are being asked to do. This is where many learners lose marks.

- **Plan your answers.** For longer questions, it is worth spending a minute or two writing down the key points that you want to include in your answer. If you are being asked to evaluate, you will need to think about positive and negative points. Using a plan will allow you to make sure you include both in your answer.

- **Read through longer answers.** Read through your longer answers to make sure your answer makes sense, and you have answered the question fully.

- **Check your answers.** Once you have answered all of the questions on the paper, you will probably have a few minutes to spare. Use this time to check your answers and maybe fill in any parts that you have left blank. You should try to answer every question on the paper.

- **Make sure you have completed the front of the paper.** Once the examination has ended, check that you have written your name and candidate number on the front of the paper. This is important so that you will gain the marks for your work.

How to improve your answer

Read the two student answers below, together with the feedback. Try to use what you learn here to improve your answers in your examination.

Question

Identify two different food types that should be avoided to maintain a healthy lifestyle and a balanced diet, and state a reason why each should be avoided. [4]

Student 1's answer

Foods that we should not eat are those that are high in sugar, fat and salt. We should not eat too many fried foods and foods that are bought from shops and takeaways.

Feedback:
The learner has identified two different types of food that should be avoided – foods high in fat, sugar and salt and foods that are fried. The learner's answer does not give reasons for why these foods should be avoided. The learner would only receive two marks for this.

Student 2's answer

Foods that should be avoided are:

- foods that are high in sugar, salt and fat
- convenience and processed foods
- foods that require the addition of fat, e.g. fried foods.

All of these should be avoided as they are high in calories and often low in nutritional value.

Foods high in sugar, salt and fat can lead to poor health and heart problems. Convenience and processed foods have high levels of sugar, salt and fat. It is important to look at nutritional value labels when buying such items to make sure we understand what it is that we are eating. Foods that are fried often increase the amount of fat intake a person has and, therefore, fried foods should be avoided.

Feedback:

The learner has understood the question and would receive full marks for this answer. Two marks are awarded for identifying at least two different food types that should be avoided and a further two marks are awarded for the giving reasons why they should be avoided.

Assess yourself

Question 1

A vegetarian would not eat which one of the following foods? [1]

A Poultry

B Artichokes

C Pasta

D Rice

Question 2

State the specific dietary requirements of a person who has an allergy to nuts and nut products. [1]

Question 3

Donna needs to limit her sugar intake because she has diabetes. Explain two other different dietary requirements linked to health. [4]

Question 4

Hotels can support and promote healthy lifestyles by increasing the availability of leisure facilities as this encourages customers to exercise. Explain two other ways in which hotels can promote healthy lifestyles. [4]

Answers can be found on page 310.

Glossary

A

Accident – an unplanned event that may include injury or property damage.

Accessibility – the extent to which a customer or user can obtain a product or service at the time it is needed.

Aerobic – moderately intense aerobic exercise includes running, swimming and cycling.

Allergy – when a person has an allergic reaction to a food item. The reaction can sometimes be life-threatening.

Ambient – relates to the immediate surroundings. Ambient temperature is the temperature in a room or surrounding an object.

Anaphylactic shock – a life-threatening reaction to an allergy.

B

Bacterial growth – growth of germs. Some bacteria are harmful and can cause food poisoning. Bacteria need food, time, temperature (between 5–63°C) and moisture to grow.

Barista – someone who serves in a coffee bar.

Bias – people often have strong opinions about certain topics. This is called 'bias'. Newspaper or magazine articles, or information found on the internet, may be biased to present a specific point of view.

Breakeven – when enough revenue has been made to cover the costs involved. A business that has reached break-even point has made zero profit but also zero loss.

Brewery – a place where beer is made on a commercial scale so that it can be sold to pubs, bars and restaurants.

Business continuity plan – a document that sets out how a business will respond to accidents, emergencies, disasters and threats with minimal disruption to its main operations.

C

Calorie – a unit of energy in food.

Canapés – small pieces of bread or pastry with a savoury topping.

Carbohydrates – food containing carbon, hydrogen and oxygen, which supplies energy (calories) to the body in the form of starch and sugar.

Carbon footprint – the amount of carbon dioxide generated by an action, e.g. producing or transporting food. By choosing to use local products, which have not been transported hundreds or even thousands of miles by road or air, you are helping to reduce their carbon footprint.

Check-in – the procedures to follow on a guest's arrival.

Check-out – the procedures to follow on a guest's departure.

Clinically obese – when being overweight causes medical complications.

Coeliac disease – hypersensitivity to wheat gluten, which leads to a failure to digest food.

Competitive intelligence – the action of defining, gathering, analysing and distributing intelligence about products, customers and competitors.

Complex carbohydrates – found in starchy foods such as vegetables, breads, pasta and cereals; they help you to feel full for longer as they are broken down more slowly by the body.

Compliance – acting in a way that follows a set of rules, policies or standards.

Constraint – a limitation or restriction on something.

Condiment – used to add flavour to food, e.g. sauce, relish, pickle.

Consumer – someone who buys goods or services (e.g. customers booking a room, guests eating in a restaurant or purchasing a treatment in the spa).

Contamination – in food, any substance that has the potential to cause the customer harm or illness.

Core temperature – the temperature at the centre or thickest part of food. When probing, be careful not to spear through the food and touch the pan or pot with the probe as this will give a false reading.

Cost of sales – the cost of producing a product.

Courteous – polite and respectful.

Cover – a place setting at a table in a restaurant.

Crockery – the china that you use to serve dishes to customers at their table, e.g. plates and bowls.

Credit – the money that is owed to the supplier for items/goods that have already been delivered.

Cruet – salt and pepper pots.

Cross-contamination – can occur when bacteria that may cause disease are transferred to food, for example, from hands, kitchen equipment or from other foodstuffs (e.g. blood dripping from raw meat onto a trifle that has been stored below it in the refrigerator).

Cutlery – the tools or equipment that we use to eat with.

D

Danger zone – the temperature at which bacteria are able to grow in food items (between 8°C and 63°C).

Demographics – studies of a population based on factors such as age, race, sex, economic status, level of education, income level and employment.

Disciplinary – when an employer raises concern about the conduct, work standards or absence record of an employee.

Disposable income – the money left over from someone's wages after they have paid their taxes and basic living costs.

Domesticated – animals bred for their meat, milk and eggs, e.g. cows, sheep, goats, pigs and hens.

Draught – draught beverages are served at the bar by placing a glass under a tap and opening the tap to pull the beverage through a pipe from the barrel (usually kept in a cellar) to the glass.

E

Economic boom – an increase in the level of economic activity, and of the goods and services available in the market place.

Economic recession – a general slowdown in economic activity over a period of time.

Eliminated – completely removed or destroyed.

Entrepreneur – a person who organises, operates and assumes the risk for a business venture.

Ethics – the moral principles that should underpin decision-making. Businesses can provide moral and ethical guidelines for how their business affairs are conducted.

Exempt – If a product is exempt from VAT, you do not have to pay VAT on it.

Expenditure – money that a business spends.

F

Fibre – a substance that travels through the body as waste to help food pass through the digestive system more easily.

FIFO – 'first in, first out'.

Float – the amount of money in the cash till at the start of the day or the shift. This can be used to give change to customers.

Food poisoning – a gastric illness caused by eating pathogens in food. Symptoms include vomiting, diarrhoea, severe stomach pains and a raised temperature.

Footfall – the number of people who go into a business in a particular period of time.

Free range – a term used to describe the type of farming where animals can roam freely rather than being caged or enclosed.

Freezer burn – occurs when frozen food has been damaged due to air reaching the food. On meat it shows as a greyish brown discolouration. It generally occurs when food is not wrapped in air-tight packaging. Although unsightly, freezer burn is not a food safety risk, but it does affect the food's quality and taste.

G

Gluten – a source of protein found in wheat, rye and barley.

Gluten intolerance – known as coeliac disease, causing inflammation and damage in the small intestine. People with gluten intolerance need to avoid foods containing wheat, rye and barley.

Grievance – when an employee formally raises a concern or problem or wants to complain about their employer.

Gross profit – the amount of money made from selling a product after the cost of producing that product has been deducted.

Guest cycle – the four stages of a guest's interaction with a hospitality business, including before arrival, on arrival, during their stay and on departure.

H

Hazard Analysis and Critical Control Point (HACCP) – a system used by food businesses to look at how they handle food, to help them put in place procedures to prevent food safety hazards and to make sure the food they produce is safe to eat.

Hazard – something that could be dangerous.

Hors d'oeuvres – small and savoury appetisers served hot or cold.

High-risk foods – include pre-prepared food items that can be eaten without further cooking, and which may easily become infected with bacteria.

I

Implement – to use or put something in place.

Income statement – this shows the money that has come into a business and the money that has gone out over a fixed period of time (usually a year). In this way, a business can see if it has made a profit or a loss. It is also known as a profit and loss account.

Infestation – the presence of pests in a food premises, particularly in large numbers, or when difficult to remove.

Inflation – the rise or fall in the general level of prices of goods and services in an economy over a period of time.

Intolerance – when a person's body reacts badly to certain foods, causing them to become unwell.

Invoice – a list of the items/goods that form the order being delivered. The invoice also lists the cost of the items/goods being delivered.

J

Jargon – words or expressions that are used by particular professions (e.g. chefs), which are not commonly used elsewhere and which may be difficult for others to understand.

L

Legislation – a set of laws.

Licensee – someone who holds a special licence to sell something, in this case alcoholic beverages.

Load bearing – where the weight is on the limbs; includes jogging and dancing

Loss – occurs when expenditure is more than income.

M

Macronutrient – a nutrient required in relatively large amounts by the body.

Malnutrition – when someone does not have proper nutrition due to not having enough food to eat or not eating enough of the right things.

Margin of safety – this is the difference between the number of units of planned or actual sales and the number of units of sales at break-even point.

Market intelligence – primarily external data collected and analysed by a business about markets that it anticipates participating in (used to make decisions).

Market research – research that gathers and analyses information about moving goods or services from producer to consumer.

Market share – the amount of trade a company has in comparison to the entire trade that is available to trade in.

Micronutrient – a nutrient required by the body in relatively small (trace) amounts, e.g. calcium and iron, are particularly important for growth and health.

Mise en place (pronounced miz on plas) – a French phrase meaning 'putting in place'. In a kitchen, this refers to having all your ingredients prepared and ready to start cooking.

Mission – a mission statement describes the purpose of a company, organisation or person – its reason for existing.

Mystery shopper – a person employed to visit businesses and report on their experiences of them. They may be employed by the business itself or by a third party.

N

Near accident – an event that could have caused harm but did not.

Net profit – the amount of money made from selling a product after all costs (expenditure) have been deducted from the gross profit.

Niche – a specialised but profitable segment of the market.

Niche market – a product that targets a very specific area of the market, e.g. restaurants that only serve halal meat.

Nominated supplier – a business's main or preferred supplier.

Non-compliance – where rules are in place but they are not followed.

Nutrient – a substance that provides nourishment which is essential for good health and growth.

O

Obesity – when someone is very overweight with a high degree of body fat.

Occupancy – the number of rooms being used.

Optic – a piece of bar equipment that is placed on to the mouth of a bottled beverage, for example, a wine or spirit. When pressed, it issues one measure of the beverage.

Organic – foods produced using organic farming methods, e.g. they are free from pesticides and chemical fertilisers.

Outsourced – when a business decides to ask a contract food service provider to meet their catering needs.

Overheads – the everyday running costs of the business, e.g. electricity, gas, water and telephone bills.

Owner-managed – when the owner of a business is the same person who runs it.

P

Pathogenic bacteria – microorganisms that can cause illness.

Perishable – food that can spoil or go off very easily.

Pesticides – substances which prevent or destroy insects harmful to plants.

Plagiarism – If you are including other people's views, comments or opinions, or copying a diagram or table from another publication, you must state the source by including the name of the author or publication, or the web address. Failure to do this (so you are really pretending other people's work is your own) is known as plagiarism. Check your school's policy on plagiarism and copying.

Policy – documents about how an organisation operates, particularly over complying with legislation and regulations. For example, all organisations should have in place a health and safety policy, as required by the Health and Safety at Work etc. Act 1974 (HASAWA).

Portion control – the amount of food that needs to be given to make sure that every customer receives the same amount.

Posting – putting charges on a guest's account during their stay.

Procedure – a series of actions carried out in a certain order; an official way of doing something.

Profit – the amount of money a business makes after taking all its costs into consideration – occurs when income is more than expenditure.

Prohibition – when someone is forbidden to do something. For example, a restaurant must not serve food to customers that is past its use-by date.

Protein – a source of energy necessary for the growth and repair of the body.

Protocols – a set of rules or procedures.

Pulses – beans, peas, lentils and chickpeas, known as pulses, all have a high amount of fibre and are a good source of protein. They also provide important vitamins and minerals.

Purchasing cycle – a system used to place, receive and pay for goods ordered from an outside supplier.

R

Rack rate – the standard price for a hotel room before any discounts or offers have been deducted. The rack rate can vary depending on factors such as the day of the week or the season.

Refined foods – foods that have been processed or altered in such a way that they are no longer in their natural state. Nutrients such as vitamins, minerals and fibre may have been removed, reducing the food's nutritional value.

Regeneration – the process whereby a food product has been cooked and cooled and is then later reheated to serve to a customer.

Regulation – a rule made by an authority.

Rennet – produced in a calf's stomach and used in the process of hardening cheese.

Repeat business – when a customer returns to a business.

Retailers – often known as the 'middle man', they buy goods in bulk from wholesalers and then sell them to the end users in smaller portions.

Revenue – the income of an organisation, especially a large amount.

Risk assessment – a proactive review of what can cause harm and what can be done to control or prevent hazards.

Risk – the likelihood of a hazard causing harm.

S

Sedentary – describes a person who is inactive and takes little exercise.

Seminar – a meeting where people can get together to discuss business or to receive training.

Simple carbohydrates – often found in foods such as fruit, milk and milk products; are broken down quickly by the body to be used as energy. They are also found in refined and processed products such as white sugar, cakes, sweets and soft drinks.

Sober – when someone is not affected by alcohol.

Spoilage – food that is no longer safe to eat. It will look, smell, feel and/or taste wrong.

Stakeholder – a person with an interest or concern in a business.

Stock rotation – a process of making sure that items of stock with the shortest expiry date are used before ones with a longer expiry date. Products that need to be used first are stored at the front of the storage area.

Sustainability – that is, using natural resources in a responsible and managed way so that stocks do not run out and an ecological balance is maintained.

Systematic – to do something methodically, according to a fixed plan or system.

T

Tendering – when a company is given the chance to win the contract to supply goods or services to another company.

Thaw – melt.

Trans-fat – a type of unsaturated fatty acid, commonly found in margarine and some processed foods, which has been shown to be bad for human health and which can lead to heart disease.

Turnover – the amount of money taken by a business in a specific period.

U

Unlimited liability – the owner of the business has a legal obligation to pay any debts/losses made by the business, even if this means selling their own possessions to do so.

Up-selling – a sales technique used to persuade a customer to purchase more expensive items or services (e.g. a higher grade of room).

V

VIP – very important person.

Vision – an imaginative description of what an organisation would like to achieve in the mid-term or long-term future.

W

Wholefood – food that is in its natural state, e.g. brown sugar, brown rice and wholemeal flour.

Wholesalers – these businesses buy goods in bulk directly from farmers/growers and manufacturers, and then sell them on in smaller quantities to retailers.

Index